Steven M. Cohen

Center for Modern Jewish Studies,
Brandeis University and Queens College, CUNY

American Modernity
and Jewish Identity

Foreword by Charles E. Silberman

TAVISTOCK PUBLICATIONS
New York and London

First published in 1983 by
Tavistock Publications
733 Third Avenue, New York,
NY 10017
and 11 New Fetter Lane,
London EC4P 4EE

Typeset in Great Britain by
Scarborough Typesetting Services
and printed in the
United States of America

*Library of Congress Cataloging in
Publication Data*

Cohen, Steven M.
American modernity and Jewish identity.
Bibliography: p.
Includes index.
1. Jews – United States – Social
conditions. 2. Jews – United States –
Cultural assimilation. 3. Judaism –
United States. 4. United States –
Ethnic relations. I. Title.
E184.J5C63 1983 305.8'924'073
83–4831

ISBN 0–422–77740–4
ISBN 0–422–77750–1 (pbk.)

*British Library Cataloguing in Publication
Data*

Cohen, Steven M.
American modernity and Jewish identity.
1. Jews – United States
I. Title
305.8'924'073 E184.J5

ISBN 0–422–77740–4
ISBN 0–422–77750–1 Pbk

Contents

This book is dedicated to my parents,
Max and Toby Cohen

Acknowledgements

Many people and institutions provided me with invaluable advice and assistance in the preparation of *American Modernity and Jewish Identity*. Several scholars (most of whom are social historians) helped me through the early drafts of the first two chapters, which draw heavily on Jewish historical research. These include Robert Chazan, Paula Hyman, Shulamith Magnus, Marsha Rozenblit, and Robert Seltzer. Three of my dearest friends and colleagues – Samuel C. Heilman, Harry Levine, and Paul Ritterband – not only read several chapters closely, but through our frequent interaction, also stimulated and encouraged me throughout the writing of the book. My close friend, Janet Leuchter, provided much needed psychic support, and offered highly detailed editorial comments and suggestions for rewriting the parts of the manuscript most in need of her deft editorial attention. My new colleagues at Brandeis University, Jay Y. Brodbar-Nemzer and Jonathan Woocher, offered several useful comments on the Epilogue for which I am grateful. Charles Liebman and Daniel Elazar, whose provocative analyses of American Jewry I have long admired, also offered encouragement, guidance, and useful advice.

I owe a very special debt of gratitude to two men who read virtually every draft of every chapter and gave freely of their astute advice. Charles Silberman, who is now completing a volume of his own on American Jewry, graciously shared the insights gleaned from his months of intensive field work in various American Jewish communities and settings. Most critically, Charles inspired me to rewrite nearly every chapter so that my book would be palatable, if not attractive, to lay as well as scholarly readers.

viii *Acknowledgements*

I also am deeply indebted to Calvin Goldscheider, sociologist-demographer at The Hebrew University, who also recently completed a monograph on American Jewry (he analyzed extensively the 1975 Boston Jewish community survey, data which I too analyze in this work). Calvin provided much sound and detailed methodological and interpretive advice; in so doing, he caused me often to reinterpret my data and to perform additional analyses. Most importantly, his relatively optimistic view for American Jewish continuity challenged my initial interpretations and provoked me to rethink them. It is no accident that the Epilogue, written upon completion of the rest of the work, is probably somewhat more hopeful for the future vitality of American Jewry than are my preceding chapters. I can safely say that I wrote this volume with two readers in mind – Charles Silberman and Calvin Goldscheider – both of whom are critics who demand lucid writing, clear thinking, sound documentation, and sophisticated empirical analysis.

I also wish to thank the people and institutions who provided essential clerical assistance. These include Rae Simmons, Norma Gayne, and the Word Processing Centers of Queens College, as well as Sarita Ledani and Jeff Sokoloff of the Brandeis University Center for Modern Jewish Studies.

The Combined Jewish Philanthropies of Greater Boston graciously shared their 1965 and 1975 population studies with me. Without such assistance, this study would have been impossible. The American Jewish Committee supported the collection of data in the 1981–82 National Survey of American Jews which forms the basis for the two chapters on political behaviour. Calculogic, Inc. of New York ably performed much of the more complicated programming and data analysis.

The City University of New York (CUNY) provided me not only with stimulating colleagues at Queens College, but with research support by way of several CUNY Research Foundation grants, and released time from teaching through the Center for Jewish Studies at the CUNY Graduate School and University Center. The Brandeis University Center for Modern Jewish Studies, under the direction of Marshall Sklare and supported in part by a grant from the Revson Foundation, provided the very attractive and stimulating setting where I completed the manuscript during the Fall and Winter of 1982–83.

My greatest debt of gratitude I owe to my family, particularly my parents, whom I have learned to appreciate more and more with each passing year: I dedicate this book to them.

Foreword

"We live in the description of a place and not in the place itself," Wallace Stevens wrote, in his poet's version of a familiar sociological axiom. But how do people live when the place itself is changing, and when those presumed to be adept at description cannot agree on where it is located, or whether it still exists at all?

The question is more than academic; it confronts American Jews, as well as Italian, Polish, and other hyphenated Americans, who think of themselves as inhabiting both a particular ethnic and a general American place. Over the last thirty years, ethnic Americans have been buffeted by wildly differing descriptions of the place they occupy in American society.

In *American Modernity and Jewish Identity*, Steven Martin Cohen has made a major contribution to our understanding of where and how American Jews live. Marshaling a mass of survey data, much of it untapped until now, he describes, in concrete detail, the various and complex ways in which continued exposure to American society is affecting the religious, communal, familial, economic, and political lives of American Jews from one generation to another. This is a scholarly book in the best sense of the term; but for all his abundant use of statistics, Cohen reports his findings in lucid English prose. The book is easily accessible, therefore, to the professional staff and lay leaders of Jewish organizations, as well as to sociologists, historians, and demographers. It should be read by any one concerned with the future of ethnic groups in general, and of American Jews in particular.

To understand the magnitude of Cohen's contribution and the nature of the void he has filled, the lay reader needs to know something of the scholarly debate over ethnicity to which his book is addressed. For thirty years or more, scholars have disagreed over the strength and durability of ethnic groups in America − over whether ethnic cultures can withstand the lures of the dominant culture, and whether American society is richer or poorer for their presence.

During the 1950s, for example, scholars announced the disappearance of ethnicity as a significant factor in American life. In his enormously influential book, *Protestant, Catholic, Jew*, published in 1956, Will Herberg argued that religion had replaced ethnicity as the *locus* of group identity. In Herberg's scheme of things, ethnicity was a brief and transitory stage through which immigrants and their descendants passed, on their way to becoming Americans of the Protestant, Catholic, or Jewish persuasion. In accordance with what has come to be called "straight-line theory," assimilation was seen as an inexorable historical trend that proceeds, generation by generation, until each ethnic group is fully absorbed into the larger society.

Herberg recognized that American Jews were something of a special case, i.e., that they were both a religious and an ethnic group; Judaism never has distinguished the religious from the ethnic, national, and cultural aspects of identity. But Herberg argued that the ethnic factor was receding − that like Italian and Polish Catholics, Jews were abandoning their distinctive ethnic ways and becoming a purely religious community.

Like the reports of Mark Twain's death, Herberg's obituary for ethnicity was premature; less than a decade later, Nathan Glazer and Daniel P. Moynihan surveyed the field and announced that ethnic groups were alive and well and flourishing in New York. "The point about the melting pot," they wrote, "is that it did not happen." The assimilating power of American society profoundly changed the cultures immigrants brought with them, to be sure; but the fact that ethnic cultures had been transformed into something other than what they had been in the old country did not make them any less distinctive or identifiable − or any less significant to those adhering to them. Glazer and Moynihan's *Beyond the Melting Pot* was followed by a rash of scholarly books and articles describing (and often celebrating) the new assertiveness on the part of previously discriminated-against ethnic groups.

Most sociologists, however, either deplored the "new ethnicity," as it came to be called, or denied its existence. Robert N. Bellah questioned "whether a 'return' to inherited ethnic and religious identities . . . would be particularly healthy," while Herbert Gans denied that such a return would, or even could, take place. "The raw materials for an ethnic cultural revival in America are unavailable," Gans wrote in 1974, "and despite the claim of some ethnic intellectuals, so is the interest for such a revival."

Five years later, Gans seemed less certain that ethnicity was on its way out; even after five generations in the United States, he conceded, German, Irish, and Scandinavian Americans retained a distinctive ethnic identity. "The changes that the immigrants and their descendants wrought in America now make it unnecessary for ethnics to surrender their ethnicity to gain upward mobility," he wrote in a 1979 article. At the same time, the larger society also seems to offer some benefits for being ethnic.

> Americans increasingly perceive themselves as undergoing cultural homogenization, and whether or not this perception is justified, they are constantly looking for new ways to establish their differences from each other.

Indeed, "now that it is respectable and no longer a major cause of conflict," ethnicity seems "to be ideally suited to serve as a distinguishing characteristic."

Even so, Gans continued to deny that any ethnic *revival* was taking place. Acculturation and assimilation were continuing to erode traditional ethnic cultures, he argued, in accordance with "straight-line theory;" far from returning to the ways of their grandparents or great-grandparents, younger ethnics were adopting what Gans called "symbolic ethnicity," i.e., ways of identifying with the group that did not affect the contents of their lives or interfere with full participation in American society. Members of the third and fourth generation were less interested in *being* ethnic, Gans suggested, than in *feeling* ethnic; the old concern with ethnic organization – with membership in the group – was being replaced by a new emphasis on identity.

Stripped of its polemics – whether contemporary ethnicity is "symbolic" or "real" is more a rhetorical than a substantive issue – Gans' new position substantially narrows the terms of the debate. No one denies that acculturation and assimilation are ongoing processes; but ethnic vitality does not require isolation, nor does contact with another culture necessarily mean disintegration or loss of *élan*. To the contrary, as historians such as Jacob Neusner of Brown and Gerson D. Cohen, Chancellor of the Jewish Theological Seminary of America, have demonstrated, the most creative periods in Jewish history have been those in which Jews have had close and prolonged contact with other cultures. The Babylonian Talmud, after all, was the product of a Diaspora analagous, in many respects, to the American one. Indeed, assimilation has been the key to Jewish survival, Gerson Cohen argues, rather than a threat: Jews have been able to maintain their identity because of their ability to adopt the mores of the societies in which they have lived without losing essential continuity with the past.

The issue, then, is not whether acculturation and assimilation are going on in the United States – of course they are – but how those processes are affecting Jews, Judaism (the religion of the Jews), and Jewishness (their ethnic culture), and what the significance of these changes may be for the future of Jewish life in America. These are the questions to which Steven Cohen's *American Modernity and Jewish Identity* is addressed – questions about which there has been a great deal of speculation, but, until now, remarkably little quantitative information.

Because the United States Census does not ask questions about religion, there are no governmental statistics about American Jews; and because Jews are such a small proportion of the American population, public opinion and market research surveys rarely include a large enough sample of Jews to permit reliable conclusions to be drawn. The only national data, therefore, come from the 1971 National Jewish Population Survey, whose results have not yet been fully reported, and whose sample design left something to be desired. (Because costs were running well ahead of projections, the size of the sample was cut in half midway through the survey; demographers disagree, therefore, over how reliable the findings are.) Except for a relative handful of papers and a Ph.D. dissertation analyzing some of the NJPS findings, demographic and other quantitative data on American Jews have come primarily from demographic surveys of individual communities. Until recently, however, most of these community surveys have been badly flawed: questionnaires were often poorly drawn, and the sample design did not give a reliable picture of the total Jewish population.*

---

* In the most frequently used technique, the "Jewish community" was defined simply as those people on the Jewish Federation's mailing list, thereby omitting all those outside the institutional network. Since no one knew what proportion of the Jewish population that group constituted or how its members differed from affiliated Jews – these were among the questions the surveys were supposed to answer – there was no way to estimate the size of the sampling error.

The situation has improved considerably in recent years; Jewish communities have become more serious, and a good bit more sophisticated, about the demographic surveys they commission, and they have been able to draw on a new generation of scholars trained in survey techniques and statistical and demographic analysis. As a result, recent surveys of communities such as Los Angeles, Denver, Cleveland, Boston, Kansas City, and New York have used carefully designed samples and elaborate questionnaires that permit detailed analysis. With one exception, however, these surveys have been one-shot affairs — snapshots of a community at a single moment in time. As a result, trends can only be inferred by comparing one age group with another.

Boston is the lone exception: using essentially the same questionnaire and sampling technique, social scientists commissioned by the Combined Jewish Philanthropies of Greater Boston conducted demographic surveys of the Jewish population of the Boston metropolitan area in both 1965 and 1975. Although separated by only ten years, the two surveys caught the Jews of Boston during an historic change: their transformation from a predominantly second-generation community to one in which the third generation emerged as the largest group.

The choice of years proved felicitous for other reasons as well: in 1965 (unlike the situation ten years later), Boston still contained enough first-generation Jews to permit comparisons between their Jewishness and that of members of the second and third generations; while in 1975 (unlike the situation ten years earlier), there were enough fourth-generation Jews to enable the comparisons to be extended to that generation as well.

All told, the two surveys provide an unprecedented amount of information about the generation-to-generation changes in Jewish life — changes in the amount of education Jews receive; the occupations at which they work; the incomes they earn; the rates at which they marry, divorce, and have children; the frequency with which they move from one neighborhood or geographic area to another; and the effects each of these changes has on each generation's religious and ethnic identity. This is the data base Steven M. Cohen has chosen to analyze in depth, supplemented, in some instances, by data from surveys of other cities, as well as by data from a national survey he directed for The American Jewish Committee in the late fall of 1981 and early winter of 1982.

The result is a major breakthrough in our understanding of the ways in which acculturation and assimilation affect the lives of American Jews. To be sure, Boston is not a typical American Jewish community; no community is. But there is no reason to believe that the process of generational change is fundamentally different in other parts of the United States.

In short, *American Modernity and Jewish Identity* is not a book about the Jews of Boston; it is a book about the Jews of the United States, using the Boston data as the primary, but not the only, source. More specifically, it is a book about the different ways in which succeeding generations of American Jews have sought – and, increasingly, have achieved – full participation in American life without surrendering their identity as members of a distinct (and distinctive) religious and ethnic group. Those reading it to find support for some preconceived position may be disappointed, for Cohen refuses to tailor his data to fit either an optimistic or a pessimistic prognosis for American Jewish life. Reality turns out to be far more complex than the views of either side generally allow.

Straight-line theory, for example, provides an inadequate guide to the effects of acculturation and assimilation; generation-by-generation changes in religious and ethnic behavior turn out to be non-linear and offsetting. For example:

– Second-generation American Jews observe fewer religious rituals and are a bit less likely to belong to a synagogue than members of the first generation, but they are considerably *more* likely to contribute to Jewish charities and to belong to other kinds of Jewish organizations. Both traditional religious observances and rates of synagogue affiliation decline from the second to the third generation, but there is evidence of stabilization, or even a slight increase, among fourth-generation Jews.

– Changes in religious behavior are not at all uniform. The generation-by-generation reduction in observance of some rituals, such as lighting Sabbath candles and keeping a kosher home, is accompanied by a generation-by-generation increase in observance of others – in particular, attending a Passover Seder and lighting Chanukah candles. A generation-by-generation reduction in the number of Orthodox Jews has been accompanied by a generation-by-generation increase in the proportion who observe the more stringent rituals. A generation-by-generation increase in the number of Reform Jews, on the other hand, has been accompanied by greater laxity in observance, e.g., the proportion of Reform Jews lighting Sabbath candles declined by 50 per cent between 1965 and 1975, and the proportion attending synagogue services dropped even more sharply.

– Although the university has often been called a "disaster area" for Jewish life and professionalization has been thought to be inimical to Jewish observance, Jewish professionals turn out to be *more* religiously observant than members of other occupations. When one compares one profession with another, moreover, college professors observe at, or above, the average for the professions as a whole.

– Despite widespread acceptance of John Wesley's view that "wherever riches have increased, the essence of religion has decreased in the same proportion," the relation between affluence and religious observance also turns out to be complex. Wealthy Jews are somewhat less likely than their less affluent peers to practice the least popular, i.e., least widely observed, rituals, such as kashrut, but they are more likely to practice the most popular ones (attending a Seder, lighting Chanukah candles), and every bit as likely to attend synagogue services or to fast on Yom Kippur.

– Cohen's findings controvert some widely-held views about the relation between religiosity and political behavior, while supporting others. As might be expected, Orthodox Jews are a good bit more conservative politically than Reform Jews, who, in turn, are more liberal than Conservative Jews. Contrary to popular impression, however, secular Jews are not the most liberal group within the Jewish community. To the contrary, they turn out to be almost as conservative politically as Orthodox Jews. On most issues, moreover, Jews continue to be the most liberal religious or ethnic group in the United States; Jews abandon traditional liberal views only on those matters on which group survival, rather than class interest, appears to be at stake.

And this summary gives only a tiny glimpse of the richness of Cohen's analysis and the significance of his findings. He provides a wealth of information on the demographic changes from one generation to another – the aging of the Jewish population; the fact that Jews stay single longer than they used to, or than do Protestants and Catholics, and have fewer children; the increase in divorce (Jews divorce more often than they used to, but less often than Protestants or Catholics); the growth in geographic mobility; the dramatic growth in educational attainment, and the equally dramatic occupational shifts – in particular, the rapid professionalization of the Jewish labor force and the equally rapid decline in business entrepreneurship.

Equally important, Cohen analyzes the impact that each of these demographic changes appears to exert on Jewish identity. He is scrupulous about pointing out the limitations of the data and of his analysis, and imaginative in the use of corroborative information. Because Cohen presents both the data and his analysis in such a lucid and comprehensive way, readers are free to draw their own conclusions about the significance of the various changes. Far from implying that he has answered all questions and settled all debates, Cohen freely acknowledges those issues that seem to him to be unresolved.

Years ago, when I earned my living as an economist, my colleagues and I used to distinguish two kinds of economic statisticians: those who were interested only in "the numbers," as they invariably called the data they collected, and those who understood that "the numbers" were simply one important clue to the complex, living reality that lay behind them. Much the same distinction applies to demographers and quantitative sociologists. Steven M. Cohen is a sociologist of the second sort, which is why *American Modernity and Jewish Identity* contributes so much to our understanding of the rich and complex and often infuriatingly contradictory realities of American Jewish life.

Charles E. Silberman

Introduction
The modernization perspective

Assessments of American Jewry's vitality and prospects for group survival must paint a very mixed picture.[1] According to some indicators, Jewish ethnic and religious life is quite healthy. American Jews are highly organized into synagogues, schools, philanthropic and social service agencies, fraternal organizations, political groups, and other national and local bodies.[2] They publish hundreds of periodicals reaching millions of readers. They are socially concentrated: more often than any other major white American ethnic groups, Jews marry, make friends with, and live near one another (Cohen, 1980b). Many of them observe traditional religious practices, including those which find little cultural support in a society which has been ambivalent and sometimes even antagonistic toward highly distinctive ethnic or religious behavior.[3]

Quantitative evidence alone does not tell the whole story of Jewish vitality. Recurrent hostilities surrounding the State of Israel have helped spark widespread interest in Jewish communal affairs. As a case in point, the United Jewish Appeal claims that its Young Leadership Cabinet enrolls two or three thousand new members annually. Most of these new recruits to philanthropic activity are young couples with apparently little familiarity with Jewish ritual practice or organizational life. Many of them eventually acquire significant knowledge in Judaica; they begin to observe more of the ritual practices and to increase dramatically their communal activity (Woocher, 1980, 1981a, 1981b, 1982). Concurrently, from five to ten thousand Jews have organized scores of *havurot* (religious fellowships) providing a new dimension to American Jewish religious life (Neusner, 1972; Reisman, 1977). Moreover, since the early 1970s, several hundred (the number is unknown) largely youthful and relatively assimilated Jews are thought to have entered sectarian, Cassidic communities (Glanz and Harrison, 1978).

There are, however, signs of weakening communal coherence and personal identification as well. The memberships of many Jewish organizations are aging and diminishing as few young people join to replace their elders;[4] Jews are dispersing across the geographic and social maps, thereby attenuating their ties to one another (Goldstein, 1981; 1982); today's younger, later-generation Jews practice fewer rituals and other culturally distinctive Jewish activities than did their elders (Fowler, 1977; Goldstein and Goldscheider, 1968); and, not least, intermarriage statistics continue to mount (Sherrow, 1971; Goldstein, 1981; Farber and Gordon, 1982; Schmelz and DellaPergola, 1983). Moreover, with Jewish birthrates estimated to fall below replacement levels, some have projected a dwindling Jewish population as we move into the twenty-first century (Lieberman and Weinfeld, 1978; Schmelz, 1981).

In light of this mixed evidence, one cannot easily generalize about the state of American Jewish life. Undoubtedly, American Jews are in a state of flux, moving in several directions simultaneously. Some are assimilating (dropping many aspects of social, cultural, and religious distinctiveness); some are traditionalizing (practicing ancient observances); others are transforming modalities of Jewish expression (establishing new rituals, liturgies, communities of worship, and organizations); and still others are moving in combinations of these directions simultaneously.

Coincident with ongoing changes in identification, American Jews have experienced significant social and demographic developments, the most important of which can be subsumed under four broad areas. They have become more *generationally distant* from the European, traditional heritage which has been a principal source of ethnic and religious vitality. They have experienced rapid *social mobility* in the form of educational attainment, professionalization, and increased affluence. They continue to move frequently to, and within, new neighborhoods, cities, and regions of Jewish settlement; and their *geographic mobility* inevitably encompasses repeated uprooting and residential dispersal. Fourth, Jews have been making different *family* decisions; they are marrying later (and less often within the group), divorcing more frequently, and having fewer children.

I would venture that seemingly diverse trends in Jews' group identity and their socio-demographic character are actually part of a package, albeit loosely constructed and ever-changing. Several empirical investigations, in fact, have documented modest connections among many of these changes. Research on generational differences, for example, reports that later-generation Jews exhibit lower levels of ritual observance, communal involvement, in-group marriage and friendship, residential concentration, and birthrates, as well as higher levels of educational attainment, professionalization, and income (Goldstein and Goldscheider, 1968; Fowler, 1977). Other research has linked religious observance with higher birthrates;[5] while, conversely, families with children are more likely to join synagogues and practice religious rituals (Goldscheider, 1973; Cohen, 1982a). All principal forms of Jewish activity − for example, synagogue attendance, ritual observance, organizational membership, and charitable giving − are empirically interrelated. That is, in general, those who observe, belong; those who give, pray; those who pray, observe; and so forth.

To further understand this as yet ill-defined package of group identity and socio-demography, we may take American Jewry and place it in either of two types of comparative perspectives. One would hold time and space constant, so as to compare American Jews with other twentieth-century American religious and ethnic groups.[6] This comparison would ask whether changes in generation, social class, residence, and family occur at the same pace for Protestants and Catholics − or for Irish and Hispanics − as they do for Jews, and whether they are as tightly interrelated. In this work, I eschew the cross-group perspective; for despite its many attractions, it has considerable difficulty in comprehending the most interesting changes in religious and ethnic identification. Social segregation measures (those relating to spouses, friends, neighbors, and co-workers) can indeed be applied to all groups; but culturally specific identificational behaviors (e.g., taking Communion, fasting on Yom Kippur) are, by definition, idiosyncratic to each group, making important comparisons across groups quite difficult.

A second way to understand how and why Jewish identification has changed over time is to place American Jews into a historical or developmental context, one which holds the group constant and varies time and space. This perspective perforce asks whether several social, demographic and identification trends in contemporary Jewry have had approximate and instructive parallels in other Jewries of earlier times.

The difference between a contemporary, cross-group perspective, and a historical, group-specific one is crucial in evaluating American Jewish group life. Many of today's observers who proclaim ethnic and religious vitality among American Jewry use other contemporary national origin or religious groups as a baseline for comparison. (Relative to Italo-Americans, say, American Jews are vibrant, well-organized, deeply committed to their group.) Those using historical yardsticks, though, have a different context in which to make such evaluations, and they tend to arrive at more sober analyses and prognostications.

If we examine the last two centuries of Jewish history, we do find several instructive parallels between American and European Jewries. Several recent studies of eighteenth- to twentieth-century Western Jewry rely upon the notion of a transition from tradition to modernity to understand diverse changes in Jewish community and identity (e.g. Meyer, 1967; Hertzberg, 1968; Katz, 1971; Heller, 1977; Endelman, 1979; Hyman, 1979). As an enormously broad-based and multi-faceted phenomenon, encompassing significant historical and regional variation, this transition (or "modernization") has eluded a single widely accepted definition or description. Yet, most social theorists share some common understandings of modernization. These shared understandings may be applied to the study of American Jews. In so doing, we would posit the transition from traditional to modern society – European/American Jews' modernization – as the key to understanding a wide diversity of social changes which have characterized American Jewry in recent decades.

If the modernization perspective is useful, then several pieces of evidence should emerge. First, we should be able to elucidate certain similarities in the rather varied experiences of nineteenth-century West European Jewries and contemporaneous American Jewry, both of which encountered and experienced "modernity." If these Jewries underwent essentially similar processes of social change, they should, in some manner, look the same. Second, we also should be able to show that the modern experience of American Jews has in fact constituted an empirical package, where their social and demographic trends – expressed in class, family, residential, and generational terms – should be associated with religious and ethnic transformation as well.

To address these tasks, the first chapter, below, outlines how Western Jewry initially shaped its community and identity in a traditional cultural and social matrix, and how the shift to modernity impelled changes in Jewishness, changes whose after-effects and momentum we still observe in today's American Jewry. The chapter's descriptions are cast in very general terms, intentionally downplaying important national, regional, and historical variations. It does so in order to establish a general model of the modern transformation, one which would apply reasonably well to the experience of most Ashkenazic (Western) Jewries. Chapter 2 then gives an overview of the variety of Jews' mass and elite responses to the transition from traditional to modern societies. This discussion in turn sets the stage for the subsequent empirical investigation (Chapters 3 through 8). That enquiry examines American Jews' changing social and demographic character (trends indicative of greater integration into America's modern society), and how these changes have been associated with simultaneous developments in Jewish identity and community.

1 The challenge of modernity

In the last two centuries or so, the transition from "tradition" to "modernity" in the West encompassed profound changes in the society at large; and, consistent with centuries of Jewish adjustment and transformation, it also significantly influenced various components of Jewish identity and community. Elements of contemporary Jewish rituals, myths, symbols, communal structures, and ideologies were, in somewhat different form, woven into the fabric of a traditional Jewish life developed in a very different social context. Thus, in order to understand how and why some historic aspects of Jewish identity have been abandoned or modified in recent years, even as some others have emerged in their stead, we would do well to briefly examine the broad contours of the West's transformation from tradition to modernity. In doing so, we can suggest how traditional Jewish identification reflected and comported with its social surroundings as well as suggest some factors which compelled Jews to adjust to a new social context, one broadly referred to as Western modernity.[1]

Traditional society, traditional consciousness

Classical sociological thinkers (Marx, Durkheim, and Weber in particular) sought to understand what distinguished traditional from modern societies, and thereby to characterize modernization, particularly in the European context. They focused on such developments as the rise of cities, bureaucracy, the nation-state, capitalism, the bourgeosie, and secularism, as well as the correlative decline of small-town life, local political autonomy, the agricultural economy, the nobility and landed aristocracy, feudalism, and religious authority. Recent scholarship has gone a long way in demonstrating how closely these analyses were bound to particular times and places (post-Renaissance Europe); however, we can still speak in very broad terms of the societies in which Ashkenazic Jews lived before 1750 or so, and how key aspects of those societies profoundly influenced what we can call "traditional" Jewish life.

The most fundamental feature of traditional societies that differentiated them from their modern successors was the predominance of small towns and rural villages, or what some have called "face-to-face communities." Many traditional people were born, grew up, married, and died in just a few localities or single area. Jews, though generally more migratory than their contemporaries, still experienced the essential qualities of life in face-to-face, intimate communities, in particular, the high personalization of what today would be impersonal interactions. For example, since long-time residents of a particular locale can call upon their intimate and extended association with one another, a simple purchase from a local merchant would often go beyond a straightforward economic encounter. It might simultaneously, even if briefly, activate historic family and community ties in such ways as gossip or in patterns of deference between merchant and shopper.

Just as what we now call "personal" often entered the economic sphere, so too did economic considerations penetrate what moderns view as the personal realm. Marriages, for example, were constructed so as to maximize the household's economic self-sufficiency or to forge instrumental links between extended families (Shorter, 1975). Small, stable communities could develop and maintain notions of "family honor" because members could learn and preserve knowledge about the position and achievement of several generations of family members (Berger, 1977).

Since people tended to associate with one another for years, if not a lifetime, one got to know a limited number of people rather well. One's friends and family were themselves interconnected (they too knew each other well). One's family life tended to be relatively visible to merchants and co-workers. Thus, what moderns would define as the public and private spheres were once unified in the traditional community, Jewish or otherwise.

In this context, we note the high value traditional societies of medieval times placed upon religious symbols and institutions. Religion was a ubiquitous mode of public identification often made visible by dress or language. Religious symbols and myths permeated the culture of both the public and the intelligentsia. Religion provided people with an ultimate meaning structure, with a sense of connectedness backwards and forwards through time, and with a sense of purpose, legitimation, and social location. It tried to guide people in a wide variety of behaviors embracing politics, economic life, community affairs, and family decisions. (The ancient Jewish legal code governing interpersonal relations and ritual life in intimate detail certainly obtained more legitimacy in this context than it does today.)

Religion in traditional European society differed from its modern descendant in yet another crucial way: in its exclusivist orientation. Christianity and Judaism each purported to have sole possession of ultimate truths and of the ways to bring personal, national, or world-wide salvation. Each held the other in mutually shared contempt and disdain. Medieval religious leaders of both systems sought sharply to define differences between the two in theological, liturgical, institutional, legal, and even calendrical terms, an effort made all the more sharp and compelling owing to the kindred origins of the two faiths.

Traditional Europe was also distingushed by the large extent to which it revered and utilized the past. Past-orientation displayed itself in the sacredness attached to ancient texts, customs, norms, and historic figures. Institutional or intellectual innovators legitimated their activities by claiming continuity with the respected thinkers of earlier times.

In another realm, as Edward Shorter's *The Making of the Modern Family* (1975) contends, only in the last two centuries or so have we seen the emergence of bourgeois domesticity, that is, the erection of a wall of privacy separating and insulating the nuclear family from the rest of society. Prior to that time, age/sex peer groups interpenetrated families throughout traditional Europe. The many ties of the individual to wider community-level allegiances coupled with the potent influences of religious institutions and social convention helped promote a powerful "collectivity-orientation," that is, a strong attachment to and involvement in the face-to-face community. As a corollary, many decisions that moderns now consider "personal" or "private," as subject solely to individual discretion, were legitimately influenced by such "public" institutions as family, community, law, and custom. Moreover, many expectations of personal conduct and opportunities for personal advancement derived from what sociologists call "ascribed" characteristics: age, sex, religion, parental background, and other immutable (or not "achievable") social traits.

Within this traditional world of Christian Europe, Jews constructed their religious culture and societies. Despite occasional outbreaks of severe persecution, they created a distinctive civilization which articulated a system of highly detailed rules of conduct, governing large portions of people's lives. It reflected, if not depended upon, many key features of the larger society: the face-to-face community, the centrality of religion, the determinist character of major life decisions, the significance of ascribed characteristics (religion, age, sex), reverence for the past, community-orientation, and personalization. All these features of traditional society served to engender and legitimate the normative and symbolic system Jews shaped in traditional times, but probably none were much more important in maintaining centuries of Jewish continuity than the mutually desired and enforced separation of Jew from Gentile.

TRADITIONAL JEWISH EXCLUSION

The wide social gulf between Jew and Christian, despite periods of expansion or contraction, endured in its essence from the reign of Constantine until the Enlightenment. One of its foundations and manifestations consisted of the separate juridical category Jews constituted throughout this period. As a distinct legal entity, they generally possessed rights inferior to those of merchants but superior to tenant serfs. They were subject to restriction in occupational choice as well as to special, usually onerous taxation. They had no political rights, although they were granted privileges through the favor of local political or clerical authorities.

Underlying these legal debilities was a theologically based rationale. According to Church doctrine, Jewish suffering bore testimony to their putative collective responsibility for rejecting Jesus. To ensure their emiseration, they were to be subject to restrictive legislation and social contempt; but, they were to be spared from physical extermination. The Church, in fact, often protected Jewish communities from popular antisemitic violence.

Jews also maintained a theological rationale for their oppression and social isolation. The rabbis helped perpetuate the collective consciousness of Exile according to which God expelled Jews from the Land of Israel to punish them for their sins. Rabbinic authorities paralleled their

Christian counterparts in other ways. Just as the Church obtained civil legislation barring many forms of Gentile contact with Jews, so too did rabbis erect barriers to intimate Jewish/Christian interaction. Though occasionally relaxed in instances of economic necessity, these rules helped maintain separation of Jew from non-Jew in medieval Europe (Katz, 1971).

Politically, too, Jews were separated from Gentiles. They were organized into *kehillot* (or "communities," autonomous Jewish governing units) which would not have come about were it not for the coincidence of Jewish/Gentile mutual disdain with the corporate nature of medieval Europe. Not only Jews, but also skilled craftspeople, the landed artistocracy, the Church, and peasants related to the larger society through corporate mediating structures. Thus, the *kehillah* (singular) was but one of several analogous structures; Jews were self-governing not only because they wanted to be, and not only because Christians wanted little to do with them, but because society was organized in a corporate manner.

The multi-faceted separation between Jews and Christians in traditional societies in turn generated distinctive Jewish residential, occupational, and familial patterns, all of which constituted a traditional Jewish demographic character.

TRADITIONAL JEWISH DEMOGRAPHIC CHARACTER

The most immediate demographic consequence of Jewish/Christian separation was manifest in spatial or residential terms. Most traditional Jews clustered in small to medium-sized concentrations. With only tenuous ties to particular locales (owing to their need to regularly renegotiate the right of domicile), they often had little opportunity or incentive to amass large land-holdings. As a result, most Jews lived in commercially oriented villages, towns, and cities. Late in the Middle Ages, many came to congregate on a "*Judengasse*" (Jewish street) or in ghettos. Jewish religious responsibilities also promoted residential concentration. These included the obligation to establish, support, and utilize such institutions as synagogues, ritual baths, local elementary religious schools, regional institutions of higher rabbinic learning, and ritual slaughterers. Moreover, as members of an insular and pariah subculture, Jews were simply more comfortable associating with one another than with those who held them and whom they held in contempt.

Traditional Jews' occupational concentration in turn paralleled their residential concentration. Many worked in such commercial occupations as itinerant peddlers, money lenders, and merchants, as well as financial agents and clerks for local noblemen. Still others practiced a variety of artisan skills which would lead them, in the modern period (i.e., by the nineteenth century), to enter Europe's urban proletariat.

Not only were medieval Jews residentially and occupationally distinctive; they also may have exhibited family patterns distinct from their Christian contemporaries. The evidence regarding traditional Jewish family life is sparse; however, we do have rabbinic responses, Yiddish folktales, anti-semitic tracts, and Gentile literature. Although somewhat unreliable and suspect, these sources portray consistent images of the Jewish family. They imply that Jews *probably* maintained better sanitary and hygienic practices and, as a result, experienced a somewhat lower infant mortality rate.

We do know that most traditional Jews had slightly lower birthrates than their Christian contemporaries (nineteenth-century Russian Jewry was an exception), perhaps as a result of their relatively greater urbanization and commercial concentration. They also enjoyed a reputation for marital fidelity and a lower incidence of pre-marital pregnancy. One should not infer from all this that Jewish family life was far more harmonious, healthy and idyllic than its Gentile counterpart; but lower levels of infant mortality, infidelity, and promiscuity do seem to have been present.

In the context of a traditional culture, mutually desired segregation of Jew and Christian, and distinctive patterns of residence, occupation, and family, pre-modern Jews established and maintained communities of a very special character with very significant control over their members' lives.

JEWISH COMMUNITY IN TRADITIONAL SOCIETIES

The formal local Jewish community in medieval Europe, the *kehillah*, fused what the West now regards as the separate concepts of church and state. Functioning with the tolerance and encouragement of secular authorities, these self-governing structures regulated Jewish life in intimate detail. *Kehillot* issued licenses for residence; they often influenced the granting of permits to pursue certain occupations; they assessed and collected taxes to finance elaborate communal services and to pay collective assessments levied by local authorities; and they also attended to the numerous religious functions in a time when such tasks took on a great significance. *Kehillot* hired rabbis, synagogue attendants, teachers, clerks, and other functionaries. Using such means as fines, gossip, and official ostracism, they enforced compliance with an incredible array of religious norms. These ranged from prescribing regular religious service attendance to prohibiting the wearing of opulent shoes, jewelry, and garments so as to minimize material ostentation and ill-feelings both within the Jewish community and on the part of Christian neighbors.

Kehillot also represented the corporate interests of the Jewish community to Gentile rulers with whom they regularly negotiated residential privileges contingent upon payment of tax levies. In fact, secular authorities had a stake in the *kehillah* precisely because it provided them with economic benefits. Courts headed by rabbis or prominent Jewish lay people adjudicated civil disputes among Jewish disputants and even held sway over internal criminal matters with the backing of the secular authorities.

A *kehillah* of sufficient population size would maintain a highly elaborate infrastructure of fraternal, charitable, social welfare, educational, and occupational associations, all of which were permeated with religious significance. Formally constituted groups attended to such functions as care for the sick, charity for the poor, burial of the dead, and the study of sacred texts. Communal celebrations took place around religious holidays and festivals, *rites de passage*, or upon completion of the study of a sacred volume by a learning circle. Jewish guilds paralleled their non-Jewish counterparts. They too took on religious significance with the establishment of their own burial societies, learning circles, welfare associations, and other groups sanctioned by religious law and customs.

The insularity of the medieval Jewish community meant that Jews constructed their own social hierarchies, they had their own criteria for who was to be accorded esteem, power, and prestige. According to Katz (1971), a combination of three qualities were employed: (1) wealth, (2) piety and religious scholarship, and (3) family honor (*yichus*, i.e., lineage, the quality of having ancestors or contemporaneous kin esteemed for their piety, scholarship, or wealth). These three status dimensions intertwined in several ways. Especially astute rabbinic students, even from modest social backgrounds, were sought after as grooms for the daughters of wealthy families. In turn, affluent families displayed their wealth in specifically religious settings, purchasing liturgical honors, supplying adornments for the synagogues, and patronizing the study of Talmud by needy students.

In short, the traditional Jewish community embraced all aspects of life, providing a specifically Jewish character to most important facets of the individual's identity.

JEWISH IDENTITY IN TRADITIONAL SOCIETY

Traditional Jewish identity was distinguished from its typical modern counterpart in several ways. It was more distinctive, more comprehensive, more integrated, and more inescapable.

These general analytic features of traditional Jewish identity stand in sharp contrast with the modern Jewish condition. As noted earlier, interactions of pre-modern Jews and Gentiles were carefully regulated, and were usually limited to economic interchange. Dress and language clearly demarcated Jew from Gentile. In short, traditional religious identity – as Christian or Jew – was a public as well as a private affair. Political life, the acquisition of social esteem and prestige, and spiritual concerns were defined by and conducted within the Jewish community rather than the larger society. A Jew's very sense of time – measured in days, weeks, seasons, festivals, or life-cycle events – was framed by a Jewish calendar with a rhythm distinct from its Christian counterpart. In addition, Jews developed their own cognitive and intellectual styles influenced by, but different from, those of neighboring Christian intelligentsia. Shunning much of the larger society's aesthetic expression and folklore which were suffused with Christian symbols, Jews still borrowed from the surrounding culture to create their own cultural forms. Amidst hostile surroundings, medieval Jews developed a sense of spiritual, moral, and historical superiority over their Christian neighbors.

All of these elements – the public nature of religious identity, the comprehensive character of community life and culture, and the profound sense of distinction – were special to Jewish identity in pre-modern Christian Europe. Both the semi-isolated subordinate position of Jews within traditional European society and the several features of traditional society discussed earlier helped sustain this traditional Jewish identity. Thus the past-orientation and religiosity of the surrounding culture lent legitimacy to a past-oriented and religious Jewish sub-society. The ascriptive nature of society validated the sharp differentiation of Jews from Christians, men from women, and old from young.

The face-to-face, intimate society underlay the Jewish community's many very detailed normative demands upon its members.

But what would happen to Jewish identification when cultural values and the structure of society underwent a thoroughgoing change? In moving from face-to-face communities to urban centers, religiosity to secularism, collectivity-orientation to individualism, past-orientation to futurity, ascription to achievement, determinism to liberation, local authority to the nation-state, and Jewish exclusion to conditional inclusion, Western society introduced a profoundly new set of influences upon the Jewish community and Jewish identity. The emergence of modern society and consciousness are at the root of contemporary Jewish social change; accordingly, we shall now review briefly the broad sociological concept of modernization, particularly as it has affected Jewish community and identity.

Modern society, modern consciousness

Whether through migration or social change at home, Jews in the West were compelled, sooner or later, to adjust to two broad sets of consequences of modernity.

First, modernity meant new social structures – such as cities, nation-states, and market capitalism – as well as new values. Second and as a result, modernity meant an end (whether swift or gradual) to the segregation and special treatment of the Jews, a process which historians refer to as the Emancipation. Modernity seriously altered the Jews' social and demographic characteristics and, in turn, their social structure and individual expression of Jewish identity.

The fundamental structural components of modernization in the eighteenth and nineteenth centuries are well known. As a result of the development of commercial agriculture and manufacturing, migrants from the countryside began concentrating in rapidly growing urban centers. After centuries of political struggle against loose networks of feudal principalities, central governments achieved the primacy of the nation-state. In place of the medieval mode of social organization in which political and social identity derived from corporate status, the modern nation-state became the nation of individual citizens. All citizens of the state, according to Enlightenment thinkers, should enjoy universal rights and privileges unaffected by ancient statuses (serf, lord, Jew, Christian), family history, or other "non-rational" distinctions. The modern state generated a growing bureaucracy charged with attending dispassionately, impersonally, and justly to the relationships between citizens and the state. Western modernization also witnessed – indeed was propelled by – accelerated technological advancement, and in particular, the improvement of communication and transportation between different regions, and between cities and the countryside.

The emergence of these new structural features gave rise to new values and cultural conditions which had profound effects upon the Jews' position within societies, as well as upon their religio-ethnic community and identification. The rise of the nation-state, the advance of capitalism, the abandonment of the corporate structure of modern society, and the emergence of citizenship, all worked to undermine the legal authority, autonomy, and legitimacy of the *kehillot* as autonomous Jewish communities. The United States and England never formally sanctioned *kehillot*. France abolished them after the Revolution of 1789. The German states steadily circumscribed their powers over several decades until they became shells of their former selves. Similar processes occurred in Poland, Russia, and elsewhere. Correlatively, modernization also meant the end (or curtailment) of influential Jewish courts, powerful Jewish communal officials, compulsory communal taxation, and in most Western countries, distinctive Jewish legal status.

But nation-states and universal citizenship went much further in undermining traditional Judaism. As the price of admission into society, the nation-state demanded that its citizens abandon traditional subgroup ties. To Enlightenment thinkers such ties were atavistic and absolute; and to political leaders they were a threat to national patriotism and allegiance. Where traditional authorities – either local rulers or national monarchs – made narrow and limited demands of Jews entailing primarily financial obligations, the modern nation demanded much more. Leaders in England, France, Germany, the US, the USSR, and elsewhere expected not only patriotic sentimental attachment to the State, but tangible evidence of a shift away from traditional ties; and almost everywhere this meant an implicit if not often explicit demand for reform of Jewish religious rites and communal doctrines, and changes in Jews' appearance, occupations (away from commerce), and cultural orientations (toward the larger society).

If the rise of the nation-state constituted a revolution in the organization of political authority, the rise of capitalism was such a phenomenon in the economic sphere.[2] The emergence of capitalism clearly meant the appearance of several new phenomena. Chief among these were: the triumph of the market economy over traditional restraints linked to ancient statuses; the rise of a powerful bourgeoisie urging the removal of obstacles to the operation of the market economy; and the creation of an industrial, wage-labor working class expressing varying degrees of class consciousness.

The effects of these changes upon Jews were several. When petty commerce and money lending were peripheral to the economy, they could be consigned to a pariah minority group. In the pre-capitalist economy of feudal Europe, Jews experienced both the hardships and advantages of limited markets and limited competition. With the rise of capitalism, Jews no longer retained a semi-protected position in the economy; as merchants, they were often shunted aside by the "native" bourgeoisie. However, they also benefited from experience in their historic occupational pursuits of possessing both the material capital and the cultural resources to adapt quickly to the capitalist economy. Most Jews entered Western economies as skilled workers, peddlers, or petit bourgeoisie. They and their children sought and generally quickly acquired middle-class status. Moreover, many assumed the interests, values, and concerns of the new social classes generated by capitalism; and since these classes were often antagonistic, the traditional notion of a unified, all-embracing, insular Jewish community ruled by an oligarchic alliance of the rich and the rabbis was severely damaged. The rise of capitalism, then, worked both to dislodge Jews from their traditional economic *loci* in traditional society and to fragment the Jewish community by sharpening class interests and antagonisms.

Aside from the emergence of the nation-state and capitalism, other structural changes intrinsic to Western modernization challenged traditional Jewish life and culture. The replacement of the face-to-face community by large urban centers curtailed the strict enforcement of religious norms; social sanctions were reduced to informal means such as gossip and mild social ostracism. Despite the persistence of a genuine sense of community and neighborliness in urban life, urbanization (and bureaucracy) meant the replacing of primarily personal social interaction with a large number of impersonal interactions, thereby contravening much of traditional Judaism's communitarian character.

Modern individuals interact with a wide variety of people in the different sectors of their lives. Neighbors, merchants, co-workers, family, and friends are often unknown to one another; they may easily hold contradictory cultural values. Correlatively, modern people tend to acquire fairly individualized combinations of "memberships" or loyalties associated with family, ethnicity, religion, race, residence, political party, social class, and occupation. These different affiliations often contradict one another, pulling individuals in different directions simultaneously, but also knitting together some members of such ancient "camps" as Jews and Gentiles. This situation has tended to diminish the allegiance of the individual to any one group affiliation — such as a religious one — if only because the group often consists of a socially and culturally heterogeneous mixture of members. Very concretely, when Jews came to hold competing class interests, different political affiliations, varied cultural orientations, and disparate regional attachments, their communal solidarity and commitment were subject to challenge.

Closely related to this experience has been a cardinal element of modern consciousness, the idea of individualism, a quintessentially modern notion advanced in several ways. For example, Enlightenment thinkers urged modern individuals to free themselves from external authority (such as rabbis) and traditions (such as those expressed in ancient sacred texts) in making important "personal" decisions. Elsewhere, in the family sphere, moderns erected barriers around their nuclear families against the larger community within which they conducted a private life free from the scrutiny of the public. For reasons and in ways beyond the scope of this work, modernity also split people into public and private persons, that is, differentiated the world of work, market, and politics from that of friends, family, neighbors, and religion.

On another plane, the technological and industrial aspects of modernization brought about a thoroughgoing re-orientation toward time. On the most minute level, modern industry demanded attention to scheduling in the way that traditional agricultural work did not. Technological advances and industrialization contributed to an orientation which saw the future as holding out hopes for material and spiritual progress. No longer was the past viewed as a source of legitimacy, but it came to be seen as primitive, confining, and worthy of transcendence. "Futurity" — adoration of the "new and improved" — replaced the veneration of the past as a central value; this shift had immediate consequences for the legitimacy and sacredness attached to ancient texts, customs, and religious symbols.

The decline of past-orientation, the rise of universalism, the erection of barriers between the family and community, the emergence of private and public spheres, the rise of individualism, and the waning of ecclesiastical institutional power in deference to the rising nation-state, all severely circumscribed religious authority.

Throughout society, religious myths and symbols diminished in significance as the influence of religious norms, institutions, and leaders declined. Thus arose secularism, a new feature of Western societies. For Jews secularism meant the possibility that their variant religious identification would no longer stigmatize them and keep them on the periphery of the larger society. It also meant that many components of their traditional identity and community could not persist. For only in a religious age could rabbis exert such a powerful influence on so many aspects of life; could a vast majority of Jews invest religious texts, myths, and symbols with such overriding significance; and could Jews living as a minority attach such positive meaning to their identity as a religious community that they would readily both accept and reinforce their separate status.

MODERN INCLUSION: THE EMANCIPATION

The transformation of several structural and cultural elements of traditional life perforce terminated the official exclusion of Jews from mainstream society. The ideals of an impersonal bureaucracy and a universalistic legal system collide with the notion of special juridical statuses for Jewish citizens. The principle of a national citizenry theoretically brought Christians, Jews, and atheists under the common rubric of the nation-state. Modern individualism militated against preserving the legal standing of the many groups and statuses central to medieval society. Thus, in the ideal modern society, religion was to become a voluntary, private affair of personal faith instead of the traditional, obligatory, public identity entailing responsibilities to the religious group. With such a goal in mind, progressive Europeans, those who saw themselves at the forefront of social change, urged limitations on, if not the elimination of, official recognition of religious differences. They often pressed for equal treatment of religious groups before the law, and for the virtual abolition of state involvement in establishing religion.

The modern structures and consciousness, then, logically compelled Emancipation, the end to Jewish exclusion from the polity, economy, and society. But Emancipation was offered conditionally. Political leaders, social thinkers, and other elites demanded that Jews adjust their communal structures, self-images, occupations, cultural orientations, and religious practices to comport with the new aesthetic, philosophical, and political premises of the modern society. To varying extents, all modern societies exerted pressure on the Jews to acculturate, if not assimilate. They also varied in the speed and comprehensiveness with which barriers separating Jews from Christians were removed.

What constitutes Jewish Emanicipation? For most historians, Emancipation has meant a legal evolution, entailing a series of linked developments removing the special legal restrictions long attached to being Jewish. Once prohibited from living in certain regions or larger cities (as in Germany or Russia), Jews were allowed to move into formerly restricted areas, first on a case-by-case basis and then without hindrance. Once barred from certain occupational endeavors, Jews received special licenses for these trades and were subsequently freed of any restrictions. Once excluded from the polity, Jews were begrudgingly given the rights accorded other citizens, even the right to hold public office.

But the eradication of legal restrictions was only one aspect of the Emancipation, only one result of the Enlightenment and the broader modernization of European society. In addition, writers, scientists, artists, and other intellectuals led the movement to create a neutral zone or at least a "semi-neutral society"[3] where religious distinctions were to be largely ignored. The qualified nature of the term reflects the very partial success of the drive to purge anti-semitism from even the most "progressive" segments of society. With remarkable consistency, Jews found that most Christians fell short of their professed ideals of tolerance; while, to the chagrin of even their most liberal Christian supporters, most Jews failed to acculturate fully as they retained significant vestiges of the insular, traditional Jewish community.

On the Christian side, "liberals" and "conservatives" in France, Germany, Poland, Russia, and other countries where Emancipation was a political issue, agreed that Jews should eventually disappear into the Enlightened society. They disagreed over the source of the Jews' pre-modern cultural traits and the likelihood for their successful assimilation. Liberals saw centuries of Christian oppression at the root of Jewish cultural "backwardness." In their view, removal of historic restrictions would eventuate in Jewish integration into mainstream society, if not their conversion to a humanistic Christianity. Conservatives were less "sanguine;" some suggested the Jews were inherently different and could never assimilate. Most demanded that Jews first prove themselves worthy of Emancipation prior to the relaxation of barriers to full participation in the larger society.

In response to European Gentiles' pressing them to acculturate, and as a result of their new opportunities to advance in the recently opened society, Jews underwent several interconnected changes. They acquired modern socio-demographic characteristics; they altered their patterns of conformity to traditional Jewish religious and cultural norms; and they reformulated their religious practices and beliefs to comport with the demands of modern thinking. These various linked developments comprise Jewish modernization, that is the package of Jewish responses to modernity.

MODERN JEWISH DEMOGRAPHY

The opening of Western societies to Jewish entry spurred several changes in many Jewish demographic characteristics including: generational status, residential mobility, social status, and family patterns. Wherever and whenever they integrated into modern societies, Ashkenazic Jews emerging from a traditional past displayed certain regularities in these four spheres.

Jews' transition to modernity – whether it occurred by way of indigenous change or migration – instigated a process of social change which largely unfolded in generational steps. Immigrants to the US or Western Europe from traditional Eastern Europe (the first generation) maintained many, although not all, of the traditional religious obligations while living in insular ethnic enclaves in the poorer sections of major cities (e.g., Berlin, Paris, Vienna, London, and New York). (This is not to deny that a significant minority of immigrants had, in fact, already begun to modernize before their arrival in the West.)

Their children, the second generation, Americanized (or Europeanized) more thoroughly than did their immigrant parents. In the US, turn-of-the-century immigrants were heavily Orthodox, while the second generation significantly advanced Conservative Judaism after 1920. Where the first generation in all major Western countries lived in virtual ethnic ghettos, the second generation typically moved into somewhat more mixed neighborhoods. Where most immigrants spoke Yiddish at home (or, many times, in the workplace) and an accented English (or other vernacular) in the street, the second generation used English (or German, French, etc.) almost exclusively. Many other contrasts can be drawn. But the point is that one can talk with some validity, conscious of the exceptions, of a broad distinction between traditionally oriented immigrant Jews, and their far more modernized and acculturated second-generation children.

The third generation, grandchildren of the immigrants, generally completed the process of acculturation. They displayed far fewer overt signs of ethnicity than did their parents although they still maintained ethnically homogeneous social networks of family, friends, neighbors, and co-workers. In so far as they express a denominational preference, a plurality of third- and fourth-generation Americans have been choosing Reform, the most modern, least traditional major option.

Again, these patterns are only gross generalizations. Sometimes the transition from traditional to fully modernized generations within particular families took longer (or shorter) than three generations. Nevertheless, much of the literature on the Jews of Europe and America in the last two centuries does convey the sense of steady declines in ethnic and religious Jewishness with significantly deeper declines occurring *between* generations rather than within them. In sum, the contact with modernity can be seen fruitfully in terms of "family time;" in this way modernity can be credited with creating a new axis of social differentiation: generation.

Settlement and mobility patterns also sharply changed with the Emancipation in Europe and with migration to the US. On both sides of the Atlantic, Jews quickly urbanized and did so to a greater extent than their Christian contemporaries. When they first moved to the cities they clustered heavily in their own quarters of town. Broadly speaking, in the US, successive waves of immigrants continually replenished the Jewish populations of the "old neighborhoods;" their children moved to more middle-class Jewish neighborhoods; and third and later generations moved to areas with smaller and more dispersed Jewish populations.

Alongside generational and residential trends, modernizing Jews displayed distinctive patterns of social and economic advancement. French, English, German, and American Jews moved through successive occupational concentrations and educational levels. Loosely speaking, Jewish immigrants arrived in the big cities to take jobs as skilled workers and very small entrepreneurs; their children began to professionalize and establish themselves as white-collar workers or in more lucrative and stable businesses than those of the prior generation; and the immigrants' grandchildren competed successfully for the most desirable educational and occupational positions (usually the professions) that their society had to offer.

Of all the dimensions of demographic modernization, the collection of behaviors subsumed under the fourth rubric, Jewish family patterns, is the most complicated, and the least amenable to classification in traditional or modern molds. As noted earlier, Jews historically have experienced slightly lower birthrates than their Gentile counterparts. When birthrates started falling in the eighteenth and nineteenth centuries, Jewish fertility plummeted sooner, faster, and further than that of non-Jews. The demographic transition affected Jews earlier than Christian Europeans and Jews retained a birth "deficit" relative to non-Jews even after everybody's birthrate reached lower levels.

Age at marriage varied considerably in traditional societies. The nineteenth century saw a gradual rise in the age at first marriage among the European bourgeoisie. Although evidence is scanty, Jews, especially the middle class, seem to have been situated on the forefront of this demographic trend and they tended to marry later than Gentiles. In this century, Americans' age at marriage has fluctuated considerably; in the last two decades, they have postponed their first marriage more than they have in the past. Over the years, probably owing to Jews' higher education, they apparently married slightly later than other Americans whether the latter were marrying relatively early (as in the 1950s) or later in life (as in the 1970s–80s).

One may generally associate low divorce rates with traditional (or religious) societies and high divorce rates with modern (or secular) societies. Consistent with this proposition, traditional Jews generally experienced less frequent marital dissolution than did their modern descendants. In this sense, recently rising Jewish divorce may be seen as another sign of "modernization." However, general American divorce rates have increased even faster and further than those of Jews (a datum borne out in the empirical chapter on the family below). In this respect, in so far as Jews divorce less frequently than others, they may have retained a cultural residue from their traditional past.

Underlying these seemingly diverse trends in generation, residence, social mobility, and family patterns are two central themes. First, in most societies – traditional or modern – Jews' demographic characteristics roughly approximated those of their non-Jewish neighbors. Second, where a traditional-modern continuum can be adduced, Jews were often in the forefront in adopting many "modern" characteristics as well. Without question, the encounter with modernity profoundly influenced Jews' demographic character and their group life as well.

JEWISH COMMUNITY AND IDENTITY IN MODERN SOCIETIES

When a wide social gulf separated Jew and Gentile, when society legitimized a comprehensive and detailed religious legal system, and when civil rulers encouraged an autonomous Jewish polity, traditional Jews constructed a comprehensive religious community and identity. When these conditions were undermined, so was traditional Judaism.

As noted, the Emancipation gave Jews a dual message. Those Jews who so desired would indeed be allowed entry into the social mainstream with all the rewards such entry would bring; but admission to the larger society was contingent upon their either completely abandoning group distinctiveness (i.e., assimilating) or, minimally, reconstructing their group definition so as to comport with the modern (read: Protestant) social constructs of the voluntary religious group.

This dual message in turn evoked a dual response. First, most Jews eagerly sought to end their centuries-long exclusion from the social and political mainstream. They rushed to integrate into the larger society with an extraordinary enthusiasm. In order to overcome their historic stigmatization, they embraced modernity in many forms. Many rapidly acculturated to higher-brow cultural pursuits and acquired the accoutrements of bourgeois civility; and many enlisted in distinctly modern, "progressive" political movements which seemed to support acceptance of acculturating Jews. But the *embrace of modernity* was only one half of the usual Jewish response to new opportunities. At the same time, Jews developed a deep-seated insecurity about their new social surroundings. In some ways, their anxieties were more complex and acute than the insecurities of their medieval ancestors. Their fears were heightened by the novelty of their situation, by the incomplete nature of their acceptance, and by their concern that some Western societies might revert to the historic exclusion and persecution of Jews.

These two ambivalence-producing sentiments – *the embrace of modernity* and *lingering insecurity* – underlay several substantively diverse ideological and individual responses to modernity. These responses generally entailed efforts to retain some aspects of the traditional heritage, even as Jews developed new modalities of identity and community consistent with and unique to modernity.

Although the several new modes of constructing Jewish community and expressing Jewish identity share pieces of a common genesis as well as some substantive similarity, the responses to the challenge of modernity were far from uniform. As individuals, Jews adopted solutions as variegated as active assimilation, ethnic inertia, and doctrinaire traditionalism. As communities, they constructed new movements and institutions that were alternately bitter antagonists and reluctant allies. Thus, the challenges modernity posed to Jewish continuity, which have been outlined in this chapter, generated diverse but classic responses.

2 The rise of modern Judaisms

Jews emerging from their historically segregated communities learned that their new-found freedom compelled them to choose the extent to which they would integrate into the larger society. For the vast majority who chose to remain Jewish while they integrated, a second forced choice emerged. Modernizing Jews found they had to refashion their Jewishness; that is, they had to abandon or modify different elements of the traditional way of life as well as innovate new symbols, myths, rituals, communal structures, and ideologies.

Two sorts of responses to the issue of integration lie outside the purview of this investigation. At one extreme were those who rejected integration. Chassidim and traditional Orthodox Jews (the latter are largely encompassed in the Agudath Israel movement) have viewed the open society as endangering Jewish continuity (see Shaffir, 1974; Mayer, 1979; Helmreich, 1982). They have tried to preserve as much of the traditional Jewish way of life as possible. They have done so by constructing socially and geographically insular, semi-isolated communities and by limiting involvement in the larger polity, society, economy, and culture.

This is not to imply that the lives of modern-day Chassidim and "right-wing" Orthodox Jews are virtually identical with those of their pre-modern forebears and predecessors. Most fundamentally, contemporary traditionalists must take into account the objective reality of the open society; the Christian (and now increasingly secular) world no longer encourages multi-faceted Jewish segregation. Thus, the traditional Orthodox Jews need to screen out vigilantly potentially pernicious influences of the larger society since unfettered social change can distort Jewish authenticity, as traditionalists understand it.

At the other extreme on the integration-segregation continuum are those who have chosen complete integration. Through combinations of formal conversion to Christianity, intermarriage, name-changing, and inertial assimilation, some unknown number of European and American Jews, over the last two centuries, detached themselves from the Jewish community. They thereby terminated their own Jewish identities as well as those of their descendants.

Between the two extremes of total integration and maximal segregation lie the vast majority of Western Jews. As political scientist Charles Liebman has noted, American Jews have tried to balance two competing impulses: the urge to *integrate* into modern America and the urge to *survive* as Jews. The combination of integrationist and survivalist impulses in turn have generated two broad types of change in Jewish life and culture. First, so as to integrate into the social mainstream, Jews sharply *reduced* the scope and intensity of their subcultural involvement. Second, so as to survive as Jews, they *innovated* new modes of Jewish identity and community.

The theme of reduction and innovation can be well illustrated by examining patterns of ritual modification typifying most Western Jewries. One finds that these Jews have abandoned or substantially modified those practices which they thought would inhibit their integration, while they retained certain modicum levels of observances so as to ensure group survival. The practices which were more readily abandoned included those which made large and repeated demands on time and energy (e.g., daily prayer), those which found little cultural support or understanding in the wider society (thus, in America, Passover celebration largely survives, Shavuoth does not), and, most importantly, those which tend to segregate Jews from their neighbors (dietary laws are a prime example) (see Sklare and Greenblum, 1979).

Social historian Todd Endelman, writing about the motivations for ritual change among late eighteenth-century English Jews, could have been writing about any of several Western Jewish communities in the last two centuries:

Among the Jewish middle class . . . many wanted to abandon the isolation of the legally autonomous, culturally self-sufficient Jewish community in order to participate in the life of the larger societies in which they lived. Their willingness to desert or refashion ancient patterns of life and thought was motivated in some cases by the conscious belief that Jewish traditions were outmoded and that the values and institutions of European culture were necessary for survival and success in the modern world. In other instances, the motive underlying the reordering of Jewish priorities was the unarticulated and more prosaic wish to conform to the way of life of the majority – the wish to reduce Jewish distinctiveness to blend in with the dominant group in society, to escape the stigma of being different.

(Endelman, 1979 : 118)

Not only were the integrationist- and survivalist-minded motives of those English Jews broadly analogous to those of recent American Jewry, so too were the ways they changed their patterns of ritual observance. Endelman reports radical drops in "synagogue attendance . . . over the course of the eighteenth century," and adds:

Some Jews . . . came to adopt an attitude toward the *mitzvot* (religious obligations) that was casual and selective, continuing to observe some *mitzvot* and ignoring others. An individual might close his business on the Sabbath, but eat nonkosher food when visiting Christian friends. He might attend synagogue on one Sabbath and stay home on the next. Overall, there was little consistency in how much was given up and how much retained. No doubt the vagaries of personality and the length of time spent in England were among the decisive factors in each case.

(Endelman, 1979 : 132)

These changes in ritual practice were one piece of a much larger transformation. Jews seeking acceptance by the larger society undertook to eliminate what they regarded as stigmatizing (and therefore segregating) cultural elements derived from their traditional past. They substituted the local vernacular for Yiddish; they replaced their traditional garb with modern clothing suitable to their class; and, in general, they undertook a variety of changes constituting what some denote as acculturation.

Complementing the many individual choices of how to reconcile integrationist and survivalist impulses were several competing and conflicting ideologies of modern Jewish life. Such diverse movements as secularist-socialist-Yiddishist-Bundist (a working-class movement of Eastern Europe), labor Zionism, German Reform, and American Conservatism, offer some sharp contrasts in substance, but they do share commonalities in form and origins. Despite their disagreement over what constituted the essential features of Jewishness, all modernist Jewish social movements contemplated substantial Jewish participation (integration) in the larger society. They have all sought to reconstruct Judaism so that it may comport with modern thought, culture, and social conditions. They all shared a "husk-and-kernel" imagery of traditional Judaism which divided traditional Jewish life into two spheres. One was defined as central, contemporary, and essential; the other was peripheral, outdated, and unnecessary. The husk was to be abandoned (reduction); the kernel was to be retained and recast (innovation). The several movements "merely" disagreed over what was husk, and what was kernel.

Examples of these processes are numerous. Modern American Orthodoxy has seen traditional dress as inessential; at the same time, it has utilized modernity's split of private and public spheres so as to compartmentalize religious life and practice and set it apart from public participation in the larger polity and economy. Jewish political liberals offer another illustration. They have interpreted certain values in the Jewish tradition not only as lending support to their political orientation; but some of them have also claimed that the very essence of Judaism is political liberalism (see Shorris, 1982). Similar husk-kernel imageries apply to contemporary pro-Israelism, East-European Zionism, Conservatism, German and American Reform, turn-of-the-century Yiddishist-socialism, and the several other post-Enlightenment Jewish social movements and ideologies.

By briefly examining just a few of the major movements that took root in America, we can gain some further insight into how reduction and innovation characterized Jewish responses to modernity. Although the masses have been less than totally responsive to the ideologies propounded by their elites (be they rabbis, organization leaders, or intellectuals), the elites' thought and activity do illustrate a range of solutions adopted by millions of individual American Jews. We shall review five major trends (or social movements, ideologies) in recent American Jewish life, chosen so as to elucidate elements of both diversity and commonality in the various major responses to the challenge of modernity. Three of these – Reform, Orthodoxy, and Conservatism – are best described as religious movements; the two others – liberalism and pro-Israelism – are most clearly political. All have evolved considerably over the last century; but each has retained enough of a common character to permit generalization and broad delineation.

Religious responses: Reform, Orthodoxy, and Conservatism

Reform Judaism owes its beginnings to early nineteenth-century upper middle-class German (and later, American) Jews who became dissatisfied with traditional Judaism in general and the worship service in particular. They undertook several liturgical changes which had the effect of bringing their service into closer conformity with its contemporaneous Protestant counterpart (see Glazer, 1972). Thus, Reform, over the years, introduced and expanded use of the vernacular (English or German) in the prayers while sharply limiting, or sometimes virtually eliminating, the use of Hebrew. To Westernized aesthetic sensibilities, traditional Jewish services appeared woefully chaotic and disorganized. As a result, Reform leaders instituted a sense of "decorum" in their services. They curtailed not only chatter, but also individually conducted worship, and greatly expanded structured, responsive readings directed from the pulpit. They sharply abbreviated the Saturday morning service from its traditional three- to four-hour duration. A few nineteenth-century American congregations went so far as to shift the traditional Sabbath commemoration from Saturday to Sunday. On both sides of the Atlantic, most Reform congregations introduced organs and choirs.

Along with these liturgical modifications, early Reform rabbinic thinkers introduced new theological formulations with implications for Jewish school curricula. They explicitly de-emphasized the Talmud (a uniquely Jewish text) and focused on the study of the Bible, a sacred text which Jews shared with Christians. They argued that the study of and compliance with the large body of traditional Jewish law would keep Jews tied to a very distinctively Jewish moral/legal system which would inhibit their integration, that is, their participation in the putatively progressive present and future.

Nineteenth-century German and American Reform so significantly diminished Jewish liturgical, ritualistic, and theological distinctiveness, that it was left with precious little with which to provide a collective Jewish purpose. Unwilling to maintain the traditional notion of the "Chosen People," Reform thinkers sought some other compelling justification for continuing the Jewish enterprise, for perpetuating a distinct communal entity when even Christian liberals persuasively urged modernizing Jews to convert to more "enlightened" and "progressive" (read: Christian) religions. To address this issue, Reform rabbis conceptualized Judaism as one of several enlightened religions whose chief purpose was to instruct Jews in the same universal moral principles embodied in Christianity. In so doing, they invested "Chosenness," with new meaning. The corporate Jewish *raison d'être* became a mission to bring higher moral ideals to the wider society by leading an exemplary ethical life and by participating extensively in socially useful causes and movements. (To this day, Reform Judaism is distinguished among the three major Jewish denominations in its numerous "social action" committees and programs by congregations and national bodies.) For only in laying special claim to leading an ethical life and doing justice could Reform thinkers argue for the continuity of a distinctive and identifiable Judaism that they had stripped of "unreasonable" features: its ancient legalisms, primitive rituals, outmoded symbols, as well as the historic quasi-national self-image.

By the mid-twentieth century, with integration more of a reality and integrationism less of an anxiety, American Reform retreated from its antecedents' anti-traditional stance to reintroduce several traditional elements. The Sunday Sabbath service, never typical of Reform congregations, completely dropped from sight. By 1972, all Reform congregations had lifted the ban on *bar mitzvahs*, no longer viewing them as primitive, embarrassing *rites de passage*. Once opposed to Zionism, Reform Judaism institutionally adopted a neutral stance to the Jewish national movement and eventually (by the mid-1970s) formally affiliated with the World Zionist Organization. New liturgical material published at the end of the 1970s provides further evidence of a traditionalizing direction, as Hebrew prayers were more numerous and prominent than they were previously. In time, American Reform Jews became less pre-occupied than their predecessors with demonstrating Judaism's and Jews' worthiness to participate fully in Western society. In essence, fewer integrationist anxieties meant less reduction. Thus, the religious denomination which once narrowly circumscribed the essential core of Jewish life, eventually broadened its understanding to incorporate once-excluded nationalist and Hebraic elements into the essential "kernel" of Judaism.

Leaders of American *Modern Orthodoxy* and neo-Orthodoxy, its German forerunner, have seen themselves as ideologically antithetical to Reform. In sharp contrast with Reform, Orthodoxy has regarded many aspects of Judaism's traditional legal, liturgical, and ritual system as still appropriate and binding. Orthodox synagogues and residential communities have maintained much of the communitarian quality of Jewish life (Heilman, 1976; Mayer and Waxman, 1977). Theologically,

Orthodoxy has retained the notion of a particularistic relationship between God and His Chosen People. Yet, despite all these substantive differences, Reform and Orthodoxy, both in their formative years and contemporaneously, have shared many structural similarities.

Historians date the recognizable beginnings of neo-Othodoxy to Central Europe at the turn of the nineteenth century. At the time, many Jews chose to pursue secular education and in other ways participate in the larger culture and economy even as they sought to retain such significant aspects of the traditional life as dietary law and Sabbath observance. Early Orthodox rabbis, thinkers, and other leaders appropriated and legitimated this bifurcation of life into public (secular) and private (Jewish) worlds. Within the private world, Orthodox Jews were to conform strictly to ancient law and custom. In their public spheres – with respect to their dress, language, secular education, occupational pursuits – they were permitted to conform to the norms and mores of the larger society. One leading rabbi's watchword for the new movement succinctly expressed these principles: "*Torah im derech eretz*" ("Jewish law with worldly involvement"). (The East-European Jewish Enlightenment movement generated a parallel expression: "Be a Jew at home, and a man in the street.") As noted earlier, in this fashion, Orthodoxy utilized the modern possibility of compartmentalization – the separation of private from public spheres. Over the years, it has emphasized both limited integration into the larger society and active membership in a tight-knit religious community.

At the same time as Orthodoxy certainly defined the essential "kernels" of Judaism, so too did it define a "husk" to be abandoned. In contrast with traditional Judaism, modern Orthodoxy understood aspects of the liturgy (e.g., the vernacular sermons, use of professionally trained choirs) and of the public sphere (dress, secular education, etc.) as discretionary, that is, beyond the purview of the mandatory *halacha* (religious law). In these areas, even the faithful Jew could Westernize. In short, where Modern Orthodox rabbis have seen the *halacha* as silent, they allowed modernity to fill the normative void created by the retreat of traditional law and custom. Modern Orthodoxy facilitated integration by relaxing controls over many areas of life which were formerly regulated by custom and social sanction. As a result of changing and differing interpretations of the discretionary zone, Orthodoxy has embraced far more diversity than many of its doctrinaire adherents or uninformed outside observers perceive.

Reform and Modern Orthodoxy, then, define two end points of a continuum representing a range of religious responses to modernity. At one end, Modern Orthodoxy seeks to retain significant portions of the tradition as essential to Jewish continuity. At the other is Reform which has drawn a smaller circle delimiting the essential core of Jewish existence, thereby consigning greater portions of the tradition to the inessential periphery.

Conservative Judaism has stood between Orthodoxy and Reform on that continuum. Thus, Conservative rabbis' innovations were less far-reaching and thoroughgoing than those of their Reform counterparts but were more removed from traditional practice than those Orthodoxy evolved. Their most notable changes included shifting the week's major worship service from Saturday morning to Friday evening, often after the traditional hour (sunset time) to facilitate attendance of the entire family, in contrast with the traditional emphasis on worship by adult males (Sklare, 1972). Many Conservative rabbis gave official sanction to the use of the automobile for the purpose of attending Sabbath services, which, according to Orthodoxy, constituted a clear violation of ancient religious law. They redesigned several ritual activities in harmony with American standards of aesthetics and spirituality.

Like Modern Orthodox and Reform rabbis, Conservative rabbinical innovators sought to conduct an orderly retreat of Jewish norms (although claiming continuity with the past), so that rapidly acculturating and partially assimilating Jews could remain loyal to and participate in a recognizable Jewish community. But similarities in motives did not guarantee identical results. In the sphere of Jewish law and its obligatory nature, for example, we find sharp disagreements. Thus, Modern Orthodoxy has argued that divine commandments are just as binding today as they were in the past, but that Jews could make use of the absence of specific religious legislation to modernize in many discretionary areas. Reform Judaism, on the other hand, especially in the early days, deliberately excised Judaism's historic mandatory legalistic character. Conservative rabbis, like their Reform counterparts, saw modernity as demanding a change not only in areas peripheral to the formal religious law but in the very content of the law itself. But, like the Orthodox, they rejected the notion that modern integration demanded the total abandonment of traditional regulations.

More than the theological temperament or particular ideological positions taken by the rabbis, the strikingly second-generation social character of the Conservative masses testifies to the movement's intermediate position between Orthodoxy and Reform. Studies relating generation to denominational preference document that the popularity of Conservative affiliation is paramount among the second generation, the children of the immigrants. As Sklare has amply demonstrated (1972), Conservative Judaism represented to its members an attractive compromise between the demands of Americanization (integration) and Jewish authenticity (survival). The appeal of particular rabbinic decisions and liturgical innovations lay not so much in some abstract theological approach, but rather in the balance they struck between traditional Judaism and modern social conditions. As a result of its generation-bound character, Conservative Judaism today has evolved into the branch with the oldest constituency, a circumstance causing much consternation to its leaders. It enjoys neither the high birthrates nor intergenerational loyalty of the Orthodox, nor has it been as attractive to young adult children of Conservative and Orthodox parents as Reform congregations have been of late.

In sum, rabbinic and lay leaders of the three major American religious movements have interacted with their constituencies alternately to expand and contract the scope and intensity of Jewish life within an arena of normative influence sharply reduced from its traditional antecedents. At the same time, both leaders and laity initiated liturgical, ritual, theological, and social innovations which utilized and incorporated elements of modernity. In this way, Jews of all three denominations responded to the conflicting urges to survive as Jews and integrate as Americans, albeit with somewhat differing solutions.

Political responses: pro-Israelism and liberalism

For many American Jews, politics – in particular pro-Israel and liberal activity – have come to constitute their principal working definition of Jewishness. In this sense modern Jewish political movements have served as functional alternatives to conventional religion. Like the religious movements, American Jews' political involvements – of which Zionism/pro-Israelism and liberalism have been among the most influential in recent years – also reflected the twin impulses to integrate and to survive; they too demonstrated the structural features of reduction and innovation.

Zionism, the movement for national Jewish regeneration and sovereignty in the Land of Israel, emerged in Europe in the late nineteenth and early twentieth century. Like the other reductionist/innovative responses to modernity, Zionists divided traditional Jewish life into a peripheral husk to be abandoned, and an essential kernel which it sought to retain through reinterpretation. Accordingly, they advanced a "folkist" or nationalist view of the Jewish People, clearly influenced by many analogous European models of the time. They also brought to their movement modern political overlays, usually socialist in character (with divisions between wings analogous to social Democrats and "scientific" Marxists), but sometimes of a bourgeois, classical liberal variety.

The husk most early Zionists sought to abandon consisted largely of those aspects of traditional Jewish life which they claimed reflected an unhealthy, minority-group Jewish consciousness. While they retained the traditional rabbinic view that Jews in Gentile countries were living in Exile, they rejected the rabbis' position that Jews must passively accept Exile as Divine punishment for their ancestors' collective sins. In striving to revolutionize the Jewish individual and group character, Zionists also rejected key elements of the culture that had been developed during centuries of Exile. They often substituted socialist "faith" and "ritual" for traditional religious tenets and practice. They resurrected Hebrew as a vernacular replacement for Yiddish, which they saw as the language of Exile, and of their ideological antagonists, the socialist Bundists (who sought cultural rights for Jews in Europe). They saw historic Jewish occupational pursuits – petty commerce and finance – as unhealthy (although inevitable) reactions to the demands of Gentile society. They envisaged an independent Jewish society in Palestine with a more "normal" occupational distribution replete with farmers and manual laborers.

Like modern movements generally, Zionism exemplified a rationalist faith: the Jewish problem could be solved through a large-scale nation-building enterprise. In order for Jews to participate in the world arena, for them to become, in effect, universalists, Zionists chose a nationalist program, a very particularist vehicle modeled after contemporary European movements. Where the religious movements and Zionism parted company was with regard to the promise of the Emancipation. European Reform and Orthodoxy agreed that were Jews to reformulate their group self-understanding, and acculturate as individuals, they would be granted the liberty to enter the larger society. Zionists were decidedly more pessimistic: either Christians would periodically revert to historic anti-semitism, or Jews would find the open society too alluring to retain a seemingly outmoded Judaism. They saw modernity as a threat to Jewish survival as well as a challenge to Jewish creativity; it compelled a more drastic response and a more wrenching break with the past than Reform or Orthodoxy seemed to propose.

In contrast, American "Zionists" have consistently and fundamentally differed with their European predecessors and counterparts. They have maintained that America is different from the rest of the Diaspora, that the twin threats of oppression and assimilation were not nearly as severe in the United States. Without this key element of classical Zionist ideology, the American "Zionist" movement has been primarily a support-for-Israel movement lacking any distinctive analysis of Jewish life in the United States. As such, American "pro-Israelism" (a term more accurate than American Zionism) has been able to inspire most of organized American Jews to lend considerable political and financial support for settlers in pre-state Palestine and for the State of Israel after 1948.

While American pro-Israelism is not as ideologically distinctive as Zionism, its European antecedent, they both share with the religious movements the four main themes of Jewish modernity. Pro-Israelism is survivalist; it clearly articulates a program for Jewish continuity in the United States and in the world through the State of Israel. It is integrationist; it presupposes and demands active Jewish participation in the larger polity. It is reductive; it focuses and enlarges upon the nationalist aspect of traditional Judaism. Finally, it is innovative; it adapts modern vehicles – pseudo-nationalism, harmonious with the demands of American multi-ethnic pluralism – to redefine Jewish identity and community.

Liberalism, an amorphous, ill-defined strain in American politics, also constitutes an American Jewish political response to modernity. Where pro-Israelism supposed integration into the larger society and set forth an agenda for group survival, one could say, without too much distortion, that Jewish liberalism presupposed group continuity in America and advanced a politics of integration.

That the integrationist impulse underlay American Jews' attraction to liberalism (and other leftist political movements in earlier times and in other Western societies) can be exemplified in a number of ways. Historically, liberals held out the explicit promise of acceptance. (Indeed, in Europe, the Jewish question divided liberals who favored Emancipation from conservatives who demanded prior Jewish acculturation, if not religious conversion, as the price of admission to the larger society.) In the United States, liberals were in the forefront of the civil rights struggles; for the Jews this meant an opportunity to join with others in a broad political coalition fighting for a cause which would make the society more committed to tolerance for all minority groups.

In international affairs, Americans saw liberalism as more internationalist, more conciliatory, less jingoist, and less militarist than alternative conservative philosophies; and Jews understood nationalism and international conflict as inherently threatening to their acceptance. Domestically, liberalism was most popular among minorities, urban-dwellers, the workers, and other outsider groups with whom Jews purported to share a common interest. Liberalism was also the predominant political orientation of the more highly educated, the "new class" of verbally oriented, free professionals whom Jews aspired successfully to join.

Additional qualities of American liberalism made it especially attractive to integrationist-oriented Jews. Liberals projected the understanding that social problems were inherently solvable, that the application of mankind's inherent goodwill and most advanced technology would, in time, cure most social ills. With the spread of education, Americans – and the world – would be liberated from ancient prejudices and intellectual backwardness. Certainly the generous social programs fostered by Democratic presidents, from Franklin Roosevelt to Lyndon Johnson, drew upon several cultural elements and perspectives which were particularly attractive to Jews eager to participate in the larger society.

As Jewish liberalism was integrationist, so too, in its own way was it survivalist. Not a small number of American Jews thoroughly identified liberal political and social activity with the struggle for ensuring the freedoms of Emancipation. Thus, through the 1960s, most major intergroup relations agencies placed the organized Jewish community solidly in the nationwide liberal coalition. They argued that an America free of social unrest, an America firmly committed to tolerance and opportunity for even its most oppressed minorities (particularly the blacks), and an America undeniably committed to civil liberties (and especially the separation of church and state) would also inevitably be hospitable to Jewish survival, continuity, and social aspirations.

But the identification of liberalism with Jewish survival went beyond a mere instrumental connection between the two. Many American Jews were raised with the understanding that liberalism or political radicalism constituted the very essence of Judaism, that all the rest – the rituals, liturgy, communal organizations – were outdated, vestigial trappings for a religion with a great moral and political message embodied in liberalism.

As Sklare and Greenblum found in their study of suburban, 1950s "Lakeville" Jewry (1979), young affluent Jews of the time equated being a "good Jew" with being an ethical and moral good person; one could add that both were in turn equated with being a good liberal. In this sense, Jewish liberals undertook their own version of the husk-and-kernel reformulation process. They were reductive in so far as many of them saw much of traditional Judaism's ritual and communal features as inessential; they were innovative in that they reinterpreted selected pieces of the tradition – that which lent Jewish authenticity and legitimation to liberal political values – into a modern lexicon and metaphor.

In some, American Jewish liberalism structurally resembled Orthodoxy, Conservatism, Reform, and Zionism. All tried to answer the same questions: How were Jews to integrate into the modern world and still retain some distinctiveness? How were they to reshape their Jewishness so as to retain some continuity with a real or imagined past and at the same time to respond to contemporary needs and realities?

As American Jews have integrated into the larger society, as time and generations have unfolded, many of the ideologies initially developed to cope with problems posed by the new circumstance of Emancipation have lost their compelling force. In a sense, the very success of these programs of adjustment, integration, and survival worked to undermine their vitality. For our purposes, then, the principal significance of the movements outlined above lies not in the limited extent to which they may have influenced American Jewish community and identity; rather, they are significant for what they *reflected*, namely, the range of principal behavioral options exercised by the bulk of American Jews.

Responses to modernity: a synthetic overview

The end of the last chapter noted two characteristic Jewish responses to modernity: the integrationist-inspired *embrace of modernity* and the survivalist-induced *lingering insecurity*. We can now elaborate on these two themes.

In light of their unprecedented opportunity to join the larger society, Jews avidly dedicated themselves to furthering those principles and institutions which seemed to promote and guarantee their wider social participation. The phenomenon of the Jewish *embrace of modernity* can be seen in a number of ways. Since public schools provided a vehicle for upward and horizontal social mobility (and thereby integration with non-Jews), Jewish parents and their children attended and supported the public schools and institutions of higher learning with extraordinary passion. Significantly, Jews, even more than other immigrants, attached special significance to voting. Entering the polling booth meant much more than exercising political influence; more important, it was a way of joining the larger polity. To this day, Jews still probably participate in the political process (as voters, technicians, contributors, and, in recent times, as candidates) more than one would expect on the basis of their education and social class (Isaacs, 1971; Alba and Moore, 1982). Jewish fervor for the modern legal system – the legislative and the judicial process – provides yet another illustration of the Jewish embrace of modernity. As lawyers, political activists, lobbyists, and intergroup relations specialists, Jews have exemplified a commitment to the legal process as a way of ensuring civil liberties and domestic tranquility.

American Jews' embrace of modernity has been closely linked with their *lingering insecurity* as an American minority. Persistent American anti-semitism, coupled with Jews' historically conditioned sensitivity to prejudice, has produced an insecurity which in turn generated strong attachments to various modern vehicles of social integration and acceptance. (Indeed, there is a temporal coincidence, if not some causal connection, between the speculation that Jews may be feeling more at home in America and suggestions that their involvement in liberalism, public schools, and voting has been declining.) In so far as Jews were to continue to identify as such, in so far as they retained a survivalist consciousness, they would continue to see themselves as real or potential outsiders.

The overarching proposition in this investigation is that integration into the larger society – modernization – compelled the reduction in the scope and intensity of traditional Judaism and provoked the innovation of new modes of Jewish practice, identity, and institutional life. The analysis essentially seeks to understand the link between integration and reduction/innovation in Jewish life.

A key preliminary problem this investigation faces is to measure the extent of integration into modern society. The last chapter suggested that the social, chronological, and metaphoric distance travelled from the traditional heritage into contemporary modernity can be indicated, if not actually measured, by four fundamental socio-demographic transformations. These are: (1) the passage of generations American- (or Western-) born; (2) residential mobility; (3) social mobility – educational attainment, professionalization, and affluence; and (4) adjustment to modern family patterns, particularly in the areas of marriage, fertility, divorce, and intermarriage. This investigation, then, relies on this premise to explore (1) how American Jews have changed along these dimensions; and (2) how each sort of change has been associated with reductions in

traditional expressions of Jewish identity as well as the rise (and sometimes subsequent declines) in innovative features of jewish community
and identity.

Plan of the remainder of the book

The next four chapters (3–6) explore how each dimension/indicator of
modern integration has been associated with changes in Jewish identification. We *generally* shall find that as Jews have become "more modern"
in terms of their generation, residence patterns, social status, and family
life, they have become "less traditional" in their ritual practices and
"more modern" in their institutional life.

The final two empirical chapters (7 and 8) shift the focus away from
the ritualistic and institutional activity of American Jewry to turn, in
essence, from the religious to the political realm. Chapter 7 assesses the
extent of recent changes in American Jewish liberalism, connecting
them to socio-demographic and religious trends. The last empirical
chapter examines pro-Israelism and how demographic, religious, and
political variations have also shaped this uniquely modern adaptation to
the twin impulses of survivalism and integrationism.

Since several issues are at stake and no single survey contains all the
requisite information, the analyses draw upon several local and national
data sets. By using information from various sources and setting them in
a theoretical context, the analyses try to make sense out of a wide variety
of seemingly disparate social trends among American Jewry. In this way,
this study seeks to elucidate how people emerging out of a traditional
society and culture have responded and adjusted to sweeping changes in
their social environment.

3 From generation to generation

Among major American white ethnic groups in general, and Jews in particular, advancing generation has consistently brought about several significant patterns of change. Later-generation white ethnics, for example, acquire more education, secure better jobs, and earn higher incomes than did their earlier generation counterparts (Lieberson 1963, 1980). And Jews, even more rapidly than other groups, have been upwardly mobile as their generations advanced (Goldstein and Goldscheider, 1968; Goldstein, 1981).

Not only is generation tied to social status; it is also associated with certain residential patterns (Lieberson, 1963). Most Southern and Eastern European immigrants to the US, in the late nineteenth and early twentieth centuries, clustered in America's urban ethnic enclaves. Their children, in turn, often moved to more affluent and ethnically mixed neighborhoods; and their children, the third generation, settled in even more desirable and ethnically integrated suburban and exurban areas. In this sphere as well, Jewish patterns paralleled those of others; in relatively short order, Jewish neighborhoods in Northern metropolises successively declined and re-emerged in line with generational and socio-economic transitions (Glazer and Moynihan, 1970).

Usually, along with increasing generational status, came more inter-group friendships and marriages (Alba, 1976; Cohen, 1980b). Accordingly, even though American Jews still have more "co-ethnic" close friends and spouses than most other white ethnics, later-generation Jews are increasingly finding friends, husbands, and wives outside their group (Sherrow, 1971; Massarik and Chenkin, 1973).

Finally, in the political realm, many have argued that ethnically motivated political mobilization, at least among whites, is predominantly – though not exclusively – a first- and second-generation phenomenon (see, for example, Dahl, 1963; for contrary arguments, see Glazer and Moynihan, 1970; Parenti, 1967; and Greeley, 1971, 1974). Since it is difficult to measure political mobilization, Jewish patterns are hard to discern; however, significant political mobilization even among today's later-generation Jews suggests an exception to the usual pattern of political assimilation. In short, ample evidence supports the generalization that, for major white American ethnic groups, later generations are in many diverse ways – socially, residentially, culturally, and politically – less ethnically identified (i.e., more assimilated) than earlier generations. Whether Jews fit this characterization is still subject to debate, and is a question central not only to this chapter but to this entire investigation.

The transition from one generation to the next has had significance and implications for Jews which set them apart from other white groups in the United States. In short, in several crucial ways, Jews are different.

First, unlike most large white ethnic groups, the Jewish subculture thoroughly combines ethnic and religious components. Sociologist Nathan Glazer writes:

> As against the Christian churches . . . Judaism is tied up organically with a specific people, indeed, a nation. . . . The ethnic element of their religion is essential to the Jews. . . . And so the assimilation of Jews – that is, the disappearance of Jews as an identifiable and distinct people – is a real threat to the Jewish religion.
>
> (Glazer, 1972 : 3, 5, 6, 7)

Jews' long pre-American experience as an autonomous, insular minority group afforded them with considerable survivalist resources when they arrived in the New World (Chapter 1). One such resource was their multi-purpose institutional infrastructure, transplanted from Europe and reshaped in the United States. The centuries of minority experience also imprinted fear, ambivalence, and a measure of disdain toward non-Jews, feelings which promoted self-segregation by American Jews. And, as Chapter 2 related, the minority experience also underlay the development of several survivalist ideologies or world-views. These approaches sought to accommodate the integration of modernizing Jews in the social mainstream while maintaining a modified group identity and coherence within an open society.

Finally, one other difference sharply distinguished Jews from other American immigrant groups. All immigrants encountered discrimination upon their arrival in the United States. However, significant anti-semitism in the US probably endured longer than prejudice directed at any other major white group. One study in the 1960s, for example, found greater interpersonal aversion toward Jews than toward any other white group (Hodge and Siegel, n.d., cited in Laumann, 1970). (Since then, popular anti-semitism has declined, although about a quarter of the population are judged still to hold unfavorable Jewish stereotypes (Yankelovich, Skelly, and White, 1981).)

Clearly the ethnic-cum-religious nature of the Jewish group, its extensive minority history which generated institutional and ideological resources, and enduring American anti-semitism all contributed to shaping a rather distinctive evolution of American Jewish life over the last century. It was an evolution which encompassed important changes in social and demographic character as well as in ethnic and religious identification.

A generational model of Jewish evolution

Distinctions based on historical or social categories (e.g., class, period, or generation) are never totally clean-cut; however, we can certainly elucidate overall trends and general tendencies. Accordingly, we can sketch a general portrait of each generation of American Jews, always bearing in mind that there are significant differences within generations, even as we focus on distinctions between them.

Generation is more than a measure of ancestral distance from the Old Country. It is also a social historical concept linked to specific periods. Jewish immigration from Eastern Europe to the United States first surged in 1881, peaked at the turn of the century, and slowed considerably after the passage of restrictive legislation in 1924. As a result, Jews of different generations in the United States were born, were socialized, and matured in different decades. Correlatively, in the mid-twentieth century, most surviving first-generation Jews were middle-aged or elderly, the second generation was predominantly middle-aged, and the third generation was overwhelmingly young. This correspondence of generations with particular age groups and historical periods allows one to describe each generation in terms of the institutions, thoughts, and activities of American Jews during the periods of cultural or demographic predominance of each generation.

The first generation of American Jews (predominant prior to 1930) differed from the others in that, by definition, all its members were born abroad.[1] Many were raised in a Jewish subsociety which was just beginning to modernize in Christian Eastern Europe; many came with fairly traditional views of religious practice and communal organization. They also came with significant institutional and ideological resources, derived from their long experience as a religio-cultural minority group. These helped them establish a largely segregated Jewish community in the US, owing in part to the suspicion of and disdain for non-Jews that they or their European ancestors had harbored. Although generally optimistic that the American promise of full Emancipation would be fulfilled, immigrants found good reasons in Americans' nativism and anti-semitism to feel insecure. With their quasi-traditional religious orientation, with their virtually unshakable foreignness in dress, diet, and language, with the larger society's ambivalence to their entry, and partially because of their limited economic skills and resources, first-generation Jews clustered together in immigrant residential enclaves. Their subsociety sustained many of the traditional mores of Eastern Europe even amidst the difficulties peculiar to starting life anew in unfamiliar surroundings.

Where many immigrants were preoccupied with material survival, their children, the second generation, could take advantage of a modicum of economic security and of an increasing adeptness in the larger social and political life. Second-generation Jews began to feel truly "At Home in America."[2] They shaped a group identity reflective not only of their ties to their traditional heritage, but also of their perceptions of what the "American Way of Life" demanded:

> Any group of newcomers (need not) be ashamed of a public display of its folkways . . . particularly, if such publicity makes other Americans familiar with them. . . . But anything which is closed off and private – any collective intimacy shared only by those of the same immigrant origin and not basically accessible to all others – is stamped as Old World clannishness. Such separatism is certainly permissible in the immigrant ghetto, but it signifies an unwillingness to be integrated into the real America.   (Halpern, 1956 : 35)

Integration ("into the real America") is the key to understanding how and why the second generation modified its religious and ethnic heritage. As in Europe, modernizing Jews abandoned or revised practices and modes of community which inhibited integration, while maintaining that which posed little hindrance to entry into the social mainstream:

> At the very outset of the European Emancipation, Jews were brusquely confronted with the price they must pay: for freedom of the individual, virtual dissolution of the group. The immigrant to these shores, too, found that the prize of Americanization was to be won at a price: by unresolved elasticity in discarding everything which America might find foreign. (Halpern, 1956 : 22)

To integrate, to partake of the pleasures of the open society, American Jews felt compelled to forego that which betokened "clannishness" or that "which America might find foreign." Which practices were these? "As full-fledged Americans, Jews were expected to mix with other Americans without reservation, often to the detriment of the observance of the Sabbath and religious festivals and almost certainly, kashruth" (Glazer, 1972 : 27).

Integration-minded Jews needed to create alternatives to traditional Judaism and community if they were to preserve some aspects of their heritage. The key solution to this problem was to develop a vast institutional network. The second generation established, expanded, and greatly enhanced hundreds of Americanized synagogues, scores of Jewish "Ys" or community centers, several national "defense" (community relations) agencies, a wide range of philanthropic and social welfare services, several social and fraternal organizations (B'nai B'rith is the largest), and a plethora of nationwide pro-Israel movements. All these had predecessors in the European past. Most, in fact, were initiated before the First World War, a period of first-generation predominance in American Jewish life. But their major growth in members and social significance coincided with the maturation of the second generation between 1920 and 1950.

Jewish institutional life in essence replaced declining ritual activity historically performed in the context of a tightly knit traditional community. As sociologists Marshall Sklare and Joseph Greenblum noted, "The significance of the Jewish organization must be understood: it partly fills the vacuum created by the erosion of the natural community of family and neighborhood" (Sklare and Greenblum, 1979 : 252). Political scientist Daniel Elazar goes a step further, asserting that the second generation established public affiliation – institutional Judaism – as a central mode of "being Jewish" in modern America:

> The American Jewish community is built upon as associational base to a far greater extent than any other in Jewish history. . . . To participate in any organized Jewish life in America one must make a voluntary association with some particular organization or institution, whether in the form of synagogue membership, contribution to the local Jewish Welfare fund . . . or affiliation with a B'nai B'rith lodge or Hadassah chapter. . . . In the past such activities have always been fitted into the framework of an organic community. . . . In the process of modernization these organic ties disappeared for Jews, as they have for other peoples who have gone through the same process. . . . Organized activity . . . has come to be the most common manifestation of Judaism, replacing prayer, study, and the normal private intercourse of kin as a means of being Jewish.   (Elazar, 1976 : 12)

Not only was the sheer quantity of organizational activity peculiar to the second generation. So too was the substance of their activities exemplified in five principal domains: Americanized synagogues; fighting anti-semitism; liberal and, in particular, civil rights activities; philanthropy; and "pro-Israelism." Each area demonstrates both integrationism, the urge to join the social mainstream, as well as survivalism, the simultaneous urge to retain some modified elements of traditional Jewishness.

To illustrate, social historian Deborah Dash Moore's study of second-generation New York Jews in the 1920s and 1930s aptly describes the Americanization of the synagogue (Moore, 1981a). The new institution departed in many ways from its immigrant predecessor. Not only did it maintain a worship service for adults, but it also sponsored adult education classes, a junior congregation, and a part-time Hebrew school for youngsters; it supported auxiliary associations such as the men's club and sisterhood, and an extensive and inherently secular recreational program; it hosted major family celebrations (weddings, *bar mitzvahs*), and cultural programs. Moreover, it was governed in bourgeois middle-class style by a board of directors who hired the professional staff (rabbi, cantor, executive director), balanced the budget, and made sure to confine their activities to those befitting "an American synagogue that would answer their middle class needs" (Moore, 1981a : 129). Moore also described what many earlier sociological investigations had demonstrated (see, in particular, Sklare, 1972; Sklare and Greenblum, 1979; and Gans, 1958): second- and later-generation Jews used the synagogue not so much for strictly religious purposes – Jewish religious service attendance has long been far below that of Catholics or Protestants – but more as an arena for ethnic-based socializing and group mobilization.

In 1956, a time of second-generation cultural and demographic predominance, sociologist-theologian Will Herberg articulated the centrality of institutionalized religious identification:

> People tend more and more to identify and locate themselves socially in terms of three great sub-communities – Protestant, Catholic, Jewish – defined in religious terms. . . . The mere fact that in order to be 'something' one must be either a Protestant, a Catholic, or a Jew means that one begins to think of oneself as religiously identified and affiliated . . . as somehow part of a church and involved in its activities and concerns. (Herberg, 1960 : 56)

In other words, and somewhat paradoxically, joining an Americanized synagogue for second-generation Jews was a way of joining the American mainstream.

The extraordinary commitment second-generation Jews brought to their fight against American anti-semitism also reflected their integrationist concerns. They greatly enlarged the American Jewish Committee, the American Jewish Congress, and the B'nai B'rith Anti-Defamation League, and built them into well-financed and professionally staffed defense agencies (Cohen, N.W., 1972; Moore, 1981b). No other religious or ethnic community could boast as elaborate an institutional network designed to advance its group interests. These agencies' activities have included lobbying, litigation, public relations campaigns, and coalition-building with other political and ethnic interest groups. Clearly, there are reasons why the second generation excelled in this functional area.

Their parents, the immigrant generation, were generally too segregated, too poor, and too insecure in their new country to directly encounter serious obstacles to their advancement. When they did, the same reasons inhibited them from mobilizing. But, with the second generation came extraordinary economic achievements which, no doubt, helped stir anti-semitism in college admissions, employment, hotels, and country clubs. In this context, though, unlike their parents, second-generation Jews also had the educational, financial, and psychological wherewithal to battle against what they saw as an un-modern and "un-American" assault on their rights.

Not only the fight against anti-semitism, but the way in which second-generation Jews pursued it, reflected their integrationist anxieties:

> There is a certain particularism . . . involved when a minority pleads with a majority not to hate it. Over and over again in the last century or so, in many countries, Jews have solved this problem by defining the battle against anti-semitism as one part of a wider issue that involves not only them but all of society, of the war on all social maladjustments. The battle thus becomes in various forms part of a 'popular front' in which the Jew is ranged by the side of many other forces.
>
> (Hertzberg, 1979 : 173)

In line with these observations, the second generation's combat with anti-semitism was situated in a larger political alignment with liberal political forces in the United States, particularly those working for black civil rights. As with the synagogue, activity which sprang from a particularist impulse became a vehicle to join the larger society.

Integrationism also deeply influenced the second generation's vast philanthropic network. In the early 1960s, a critic of this phenomenon wrote:

> There is classic Jewish warrant for the idea that . . . we must take care of the poor . . . without regard to race, creed, or color, but what has been happening has not been primarily rooted in a growing passion for this prophetic idea. The rapid rise of the Jewish community to economic affluence has decreased its own immediate needs; those services that remain . . . have become less and less specifically Jewish. . . . Charity, the very factor in Jewish life which began as an overarching form of Jewish identification and of Jewish separatism ('we take care of our own') . . . is increasingly a way of saying . . . that the Jews have an involvement in . . . doing social service work on the general scene.
>
> (Hertzberg, 1979 : 175)

By way of contrast, integrationist anxieties receded in the early 1970s as the newer, often younger third generation undertook a seismic shift in Jewish philanthropic priorities. They moved charitable funds in the direction of such particularist causes as Jewish education, culture, and religious outreach, as well as the defense of group interests in jobs, schools, and neighborhoods.

Integrationist concerns also influenced pro-Israel activities, the fifth major sphere of second-generation institutional life. American Zionism resembled but was not identical with its European counterpart (see Chapter 2). In fact, some have termed the American branch of the world

Zionist movement "pro-Israelism," or "pro-Palestinianism" in the pre-State period before 1948 (see Shapiro, 1971). In particular, American Zionists rejected a highly nationalist conceptualization, but they did feel comfortable supporting the building of a Jewish society in Palestine/Israel:

> A modified version of Zionism, the principle of Palestinianism, . . . provided an ideology of survival for the American Jewish group. . . . It served to justify the separate existence of the Jewish community in the United States and provided the ethnic status with a self-respect denied the group by the dominant society and its culture. At the same time . . . Palestinianism did not conflict with the duties and obligation of Jews as Americans. (Shapiro, 1971 : 251)

Thus, while pro-Palestinianism performed a vital function for Jews uneasy about their acceptance as Americans, an unadulterated highly nationalist Zionism would have hindered their entry into the larger society, or so most Jewish leaders believed:

> Acculturated Jews felt that acceptance of the Zionist version of Jewish nationalism would cut them off from the country to which they now belonged. Jews in Eastern Europe did not consider themselves Poles or Russians. The situation of American Jews was different; they considered themselves Americans though their belonging to America was never free of doubts. . . . Palestinianism . . . was interpreted . . . as being congruous with loyalty to the American nation. . . . Pro-Palestine sentiments of non-Jewish American leaders . . . encouraged many Jews to adopt Palestinianism. (Shapiro, 1971 : 253 : 4)

In sum, not only pro-Israelism, but the overall directions of the second generation's institutional activities aptly reflected ambivalent orientations to preserving European heritage and to integrating into the United States. In contrast with their parents, second-generation Jews acculturated sufficiently to give their Jewish survivalist sentiments multitudinous institutional forms, a process enhanced by the strong American penchant for voluntary organizations. But their integrationist concerns also shaped these institutional forms. As a result, a seemingly traditional and sectarian institution, the synagogue, became a way of joining the American middle class; the particularist fight against American anti-semitism became a fight against bigotry, intolerance, and the ills of society in general; Jewish philanthropic efforts were increasingly directed at non-sectarian ends, in part to demonstrate Jews' value to a society they feared might not fully accept them; and the most clear-cut expression of modern Jewish nationalism, Zionism, was understood as practically a charitable enterprise for refugee co-religionists.

The third generation, in contrast with its predecessors, is by definition most remote from the traditional European Jewish cultural heritage. Third-generation Jews were raised by acculturated, native-American parents; they have had comparatively fewer Jewish schoolmates, childhood friends, and neighbors; and they matured in a period when both ethnic allegiances and prejudices were less pronounced and, indeed, less legitimate than in their parents' time. Moreover, they have felt relatively secure; they came of age after the battles against blatant, overt social anti-semitism had been won. As a result, they have felt less need for integrationist-oriented institutional life, and, in so far as they have remained communally active, they have done so increasingly for survivalist reasons. This shift in motivations in turn underlies several recent significant developments within the Jewish institutional world.

For example, in so far as third-generation Jews have been involved in religious Judaism, many have rebelled against the alleged coldness and impersonal nature of the large synagogue. In their place, some have pioneered the small, intimate worship and study communities known as *havurot*, noted in the Introduction. In the political sphere, the fight against anti-semitism and for the liberal civil rights agenda no longer animates Jewish community relations agencies; and, in so far as they support elements of the liberal agenda – such as certain social welfare programs – they often do so because Jews themselves are direct beneficiaries of these services (Woocher, 1981b). As noted above, third-generation philanthropists have relegated old-line health and social welfare charities for the poor, Jewish or otherwise, to a somewhat lower priority, and have shown increasing concern for community-building activities among the Jewish middle class (Liebman, 1978). Pro-Israel activities have also changed. Today's lobbyists are less hesitant and apologetic than in the past and have adopted a self-assured, even strident approach toward American centers of power in matters affecting Israel's security. Moreover, the political dimension of Jewish identification – manifest most in concern and activities for Israel and Soviet Jewry – has assumed a significant place in many Jews' self-definition.

This overview of the generational evolution of American Jewry suggests certain empirical relationships between generation and key Jewish identificational activities. In particular, it suggests that ritual observance, especially practices which most betoken foreignness or demand separation, should decay most rapidly with advancing generation. Meanwhile, organizational activity might well increase in the second generation and then start to decline among younger third- and fourth-generation Jews who may feel less attached to Jewish life and less anxious about integrating into American society. As a result, they may be less motivated to affiliate with institutions which were particularly attuned to their parents' or grandparents' concerns.

Previous research: accepted findings and unresolved issues

Since the mid-1960s, a few sociologists and demographers undertaking several local and national Jewish population studies have made considerable progress in understanding how generation influences Jewish identification. From these several investigations, consensus emerges on four points:

1 Performance of traditional ritual practices, such as frequent worship, dietary law observance, and Sabbath candle lighting, declines significantly with each generation (Goldstein and Goldscheider, 1968; Himmelfarb, 1980, 1982).

2 Performance of practices supported by the wider culture, such as Passover Seder participation or Chanukah candle lighting, seem to stabilize or slightly increase with generational advancement.

3 Denominational affiliation shifts with generational progression: Orthodoxy declines precipitously after the immigrant generation; Conservativism predominates in the second generation; Reform gains considerable ground among third- and later-generation Jews; and many unaffiliated emerge in the fourth generation (Lazerwitz, 1979).

4 Intermarriage rises with each generation and its increase may accelerate particularly after the second generation (Sherrow, 1971; Goldstein, 1981; Farber and Gordon, 1982).

Against these points of consensus, we can discern several conflicting interpretations, the most crucial of which concerns the question of stabilization. Stabilization theorists claim that, at some point, the generation-linked erosion in Jewish identification comes to an end. Families who are going to assimilate have done so; others arrive and remain at a certain modicum of personal religious practice and public affiliation.

Sklare and Greenblum's study of Lakeville (suburban, late-1950s Jews), for example, locates most of the decline in Jewish practice between the first and second generation. It ceases afterwards and, in fact, some evidence suggested slightly more observance among the few fourth-generation respondents. The authors conclude, "In the more advanced generations, then, the trend toward declining religious observance is halted. . . . The overall trend is for stabilization to set in" (Sklare and Greenblum, 1979 : 83).

Sociologist Harold Himmelfarb collected survey data on the Jews of Chicago (1979). He too claims to discern stabilization in several measures of Jewish identification; but, in his data, stabilization occurs only in the fourth generation. While identification declines through the first three generations, the fourth is apparently as Jewishly identified as the third.

Stabilization implies the projection, if not the prediction, of a healthy Jewish community. As Sklare's recent survey of the literature concludes: "Assimilation has not proceeded as predicted. Jewish identity is far from disappearing. If anything, the Jewish community as an organized entity has gained in visibility in recent decades" (Sklare, 1978 : 170).

This optimistic projection, though, must be tempered by other evidence such as increases in intermarriage and residential dispersal, and declines in the number of Jewish youngsters obtaining any formal Jewish schooling. Social scientist Charles Liebman, for example, concludes his volume on American Jewry with a pessimistic forecast:

> Judaism, as I understand it, is threatened by contemporary currents in American life. . . . Literature, theatre, art, scholarship, politics – all seem to undermine what I consider to be the essentials of Judaism. More than ever before, the values of integration and survival are mutually contradictory. (Liebman, 1973 : 197)

A Jewish historian's perspective leads to no less gloomy prognostications:

> Wherever freedom has existed for several generations without a break, the Jews have never in the last two centuries settled down to be themselves. . . . In Central and Western Europe in the nineteenth century . . . the rate of falling-away was disastrous. In the third and fourth generation it began to approach one half. Today in America we are reaching the stage of the great-grandchildren of the Russian Jewish immigrants of less than a century ago, and all the indices of disintegration are beginning to rise. (Hertzberg, 1979 : 208)

In light of the conflicting evidence and theoretical considerations, the stabilization thesis bears further examination.

Some very recent literature on generation's impact upon Jewish identification raises another area of controversy. Himmelfarb and Loar (forthcoming) speak of a "polarization thesis," according to which Jews are dividing into a large, assimilated camp and a smaller, identified one; meanwhile, the number with intermediary Jewish identification is said to be shrinking. The last decade's trends in Jewish school enrollments illustrate and support this thesis. The number of children in part-time Jewish education (Hebrew schools, Talmud Torahs, Sunday schools) has been declining even as more are obtaining either no formal training or the most intensive, full-time education (yeshiva or day school) (Massarik, 1977; Ackerman, 1980).

The polarization thesis also finds support in the evidence suggesting a cessation in the shrinkage of Orthodox Jews and continued growth in numbers of Reform and non-denominational Jews (Himmelfarb, 1979; Lazerwitz, 1979). Moreover, Orthodoxy has experienced both an upsurge in institutionalization (perhaps because of its increasing affluence) and, as some informed observers tell us, a theological and legalistic move to the right (Liebman, 1979). These considerations suggest a growing rift between an increasingly observant and doctrinaire Orthodox group and growing numbers of religiously lax or indifferent American Jews.

Yet a third area of research lends credence to the polarization hypothesis. Over the last decade and a half, relatively assimilated Jews apparently have been leaving the circles of Jewish philanthropists. Charles Liebman's exploration of the New York Federation's leaders in 1968 and 1978 documents this trend on an elite level (Liebman, 1978). The ten years saw increases in the number of leaders who are Orthodox and who received a yeshiva or day school education. My own analyses of the surveys of Boston Jewry conducted in 1965 and 1975 showed similar trends on the mass level; ritually non-observant Jews in 1975 were less likely than their counterparts in 1965 to donate to Boston's central Jewish philanthropic drive (Cohen, 1980a; the same data are further explored below).

If the polarization thesis aptly describes current trends in American Jewish identification, we should find evidence of three patterns in the data, patterns which I term bimodality, denominational divergence, and consistency. *Bimodality* refers to increases in the number of Jews with very high or very low levels of Jewish identification at the expense of the middle ground. *Denominational divergence* refers to growing differences between Orthodoxy, Conservatism, and Reform. *Consistency* refers to the coalescence of various dimensions of Jewish identification.

Specifically, public and private forms of Jewish expression should converge as the non-observant abandon the organized community and the observant retain or even elevate their levels of communal activity.

Data, measures and methods

Much of the remainder of this chapter (and this book) is a secondary analysis of two surveys of Boston Jews conducted in 1965 (N = 1569) and 1975 (N = 934), and sponsored by the Combined Jewish Philanthropies of Greater Boston. The University of Massachusetts Survey Research Center collected the data via face-to-face interviews so as to represent the Jews in the Greater Boston area (Axelrod, Fowler, and Gurin, 1967; Fowler, 1977).

These data sets are particularly well-suited to the analysis of generation's impact on Jewish identification. In the decade separating the two surveys, Boston's Jewish community changed from one where the second generation predominated to one with a third-generation plurality. The mid-1960s was the last time we could find adequate numbers of middle-aged and elderly first-generation Jews in most community surveys to permit reasonable comparisons of immigrants with later generations. The mid-1970s, correlatively, was the first time when we would find a sizeable number of fourth-generation individuals in a Jewish community survey of a major Northeastern city.

The Boston surveys are particularly rich in measures of Jewish identification, some of which are behavioral, others attitudinal. The analysis below generally avoids attitudinal measures for several reasons. Judaism, in contrast with Christianity (particularly Protestantism), regards concrete behaviors as more central and significant than tenets, beliefs, or attitudes. (Sklare and Greenblum (1979) have referred to this feature as the "sacramental character" of Judaism.) Moreover, from a theological point of view, the measurement of attitudes is usually less reliable and more slippery than measuring behaviors, at least behaviors which are discrete, definable, and readily understood. Asking a respondent whether Jews should maintain traditional practices will probably elicit a more tentative and confused response than asking whether Sabbath candles are regularly lit in the home.

Among the vast domain of Jewish activities, this analysis focuses on four areas. It examines home rituals such as keeping kosher (dietary rules) in the house, lighting Sabbath candles, and participating in a Passover Seder. Second, it examines religious service attendance. Third, it examines three measures of institutional affiliation: synagogue membership, belonging to at least one Jewish organization, and contributing to Jewish charitable causes in minimal amounts ($25 in 1965 and $50 in 1975). (These Jewish affiliation variables are compared with analogous measures of wider social participation: belonging to at least one nonsectarian organization and contributing to non-sectarian charities.) The fourth area is primary group integration, in particular, the incidence of currently mixed marriage (indicated by the presence of a non-Jew in a married couple's household) and the proportion of friends who are Jewish.

The survey asked respondents about their nativity and paternal ancestry. Those born in a foreign country prior to 1920 were classified as first generation. Native-born respondents with foreign-born fathers comprised the second generation. Native-born respondents with native-born fathers and foreign-born grandfathers were third generation. Native-born respondents with native-born fathers and grandfathers constituted the fourth (or later) generation.[3]

The analysis aims to understand how frequencies of the several available behavioral indicators of Jewish identification change as generation advances. This objective is complicated in two ways. First, generation is of interest not only in its own right, but as a way of getting a handle on developments linked to Jewish modernization. Since this is our chief concern we will also be sensitive to changes associated both with history (that is, during the decade between the two surveys) and with age. Second, generation connotes several effects above and beyond family distance from the traditional heritage. Since generations vary so dramatically in age, they also vary in terms of period of socialization as well as life-cycle stage. Thus, part of the reason later generations may manifest low levels of Jewish identification is that young adults in general are less often ritually observant or communally affiliated, and later generations are disproportionately young. In short, generation's impact is confounded with life cycle and historical change; and so, differences between generations are magnified by their overlap with other influences such as period, birth cohort, and life cycle.

Basic characteristics of generations

Table 3(1) reports several fundamental social characteristics by generation in the 1965 and 1975 surveys. Taken together, they form the context in which to understand generational differences in Jewish identification.

Table 3(1)   Selected characteristics by generation

generation:	1965				1975					
	1st	2nd	3rd	all[a]	1st	2nd	3rd	4th	f.b.[b]	all[c]
mean age	66	47	35	49	71	52	32	27	31	42
mean education	9.3	14.1	15.9	13.6	11.6	14.6	16.3	16.1	15.8	15.2
% post-BA	8	21	30	20	12	23	42	30	41	31
% professional[d]	16	27	48	31	13	37	51	49	49	41
income ($1000s)	7.7	14.2	11.1	12.4	13.6	23.2	19.5	15.8	18.5	19.7
% reporting Orthodox parents	82	50	21	53	88	56	12	3	14	33
weighted N=	326	844	328	1569	79	319	373	89	74	934

Sources: 1965 and 1975 Boston Jewish Community Surveys.

Notes:
a Includes fourth generation and "no answers" to nativity questions.
b f.b. = foreign born.
c Includes "no answers" to nativity questions.
d Base excludes "no answers" and retirees.

Perhaps the most crucial difference between generations is their rather large age gaps. In 1965, the first generation averaged 66 years of age, the second generation was 19 years younger (mean = 47), and the third was still considerably younger (35 years old). The 1975 survey displays even sharper differences between the first and third generations (71 versus 32 years of age) with an even younger fourth generation (27).[4]

The educational attainment figures show a steady rise with generation. In 1965, nearly seven years of schooling separated first- and third-generation respondents. Ten years later, we find higher levels of education for each generation, with the fourth generation and foreign born approximating the high level of education found among third-generation respondents. Over 95 per cent of the fourth generation had a college degree (data not shown) and, in light of its youth, we may expect this generation eventually to surpass the educational attainment of the slightly older third generation.

This table also documents Jews' rapid and thoroughgoing professionalization. In 1965, only 8 per cent of employed immigrants in 1965 were professionals; in 1975, over two-fifths (42 per cent) of working third-generation respondents were so employed.

The income figures reflect the twin influences of Americanization and life cycle. There is a sharp rise between the first and second generation followed by a small decline in succeeding generations. Since earning power peaks around age fifty, the second generation bears the advantage of a favorable age distribution with respect to its income.

Finally, Jewish socialization changed dramatically over the generations. In 1965 over four-fifths (85 per cent) of all first-generation respondents reported having Orthodox parents, as compared with only 21 per cent of third-generation respondents. By 1975, only 12 per cent of the third generation and a mere 3 per cent of the fourth generation answered "Orthodox" to the question on their parents' denomination. There can be no doubt as to the large extent to which succeeding generations have moved away from traditional Jewish upbringing.

Stabilization or unceasing decline?

Stabilization theorists argue that by the third or fourth generation declines in Jewish identification should abate. Traditional religious practices may wither away but later-generation members should still perform several types of Jewish activities.

Tables 3(2) and *3(3)* report the data which test this thesis. The first table reports the frequency of several types of Jewish identificational behaviors by generation and time of survey (1965 or 1975); the latter presents the same information controlling for age. Since later generations are also younger, and younger people are less Jewishly active, controls for age should reduce initial differences between generations.

FROM THE FIRST TO THE SECOND GENERATION

The passage from first to second generation can best be examined with the 1965 data. (By 1975, only elderly – aged sixty-five or over – first-generation respondents were numerous enough for meaningful comparisons with comparably aged second-generation respondents.) We find a fairly consistent pattern of change as ritual practice declines substantially from the first to second generation. Moreover, the more traditional the practice, and the more it serves to separate Jews from the larger society, the steeper the decline. The middle-aged respondents in 1965 (middle columns, *Table 3(3)*) show this pattern most clearly. The decline in observance of kashruth from the first to the second generation is most precipitous (from 53 per cent to 23 per cent), that of Sabbath candle lighting is less severe (72 per cent versus 66 per cent), while Seder participation declines hardly at all (93 per cent versus 90 per cent). Frequent religious service attendance (more than high holidays), though,

Table 3(2)   Selected measures of Jewish identification and social participation by generation

| generation: | 1965 | | | | 1975 | | | | | |
	1st	2nd	3rd	all[a]	1st	2nd	3rd	4th	f.b.	all
kosher[b]	57	25	10	28	37	27	9	9	9	17
Sabbath candles	78	63	43	62	52	59	30	32	37	43
mezzuzah	—	—	—	—	55	74	42	42	44	54
Yom Kippur	—	—	—	—	44	64	49	55	61	55
chometz	—	—	—	—	62	68	53	46	39	57
Seder	92	89	84	88	80	88	84	83	77	85
service attendance	37	37	35	36	33	44	25	25	18	32
synagogue member	64	54	38	52	51	56	24	28	24	38
Jewish org. member	59	52	32	49	45	39	18	17	15	27
Jewish giving	36	51	25	42	49	53	32	21	27	39
non-sect. org. member	34	58	52	51	21	40	27	41	32	32
non-sect. giving	38	62	53	54	29	39	34	27	25	34
intermarried	1	2	5	3	1	9	19	17	19	14
Jewish friends	80	73	57	71	69	61	42	46	26	50
weighted N=	326	844	328	1569	79	319	373	89	74	934

Sources: 1965 and 1975 Boston Jewish Community Surveys.

Notes:

a Includes fourth generation and "no answers" to nativity questions.

b kosher = has "two sets of dishes for meat and dairy" products (1965); keeps "kosher at home" (1975).

Sabbath candles = lights Sabbath candles.

mezzuzah = "have a mezzuzah on" the door.

Yom Kippur = "you yourself usually fast on Yom Kippur."

chometz = "you yourself observe special dietary rules for Passover."

Seder = "take part in a Passover Seder."

service attendance = more often than high holidays.

synagogue member = "do you belong to a synagogue or temple?"

Jewish organization member = belong to Jewish organization(s) other than a synagogue sisterhood or brotherhood.

Jewish giving = "Over the past twelve months approximately how much did you and other members of your family give altogether to various charities (not counting what you gave to a synagogue or temple)? About how much of this was to Jewish causes (not counting what you gave to a synagogue or temple)?" Criterion = $25 in 1965 and $50 in 1975.

non-sectarian organization member = belong to a voluntary organization not under Jewish sponsorship.

non-sectarian giving = as above (see Jewish giving); total contributions of at least $25 in 1965 and $50 in 1975 to non-sectarian charities.

intermarried = percentage of currently married where one spouse now maintains a non-Jewish religious preference.

Jewish friends = "all" or "most" of "friends are Jewish."

Table 3(3)   Selected measures of Jewish identification and social participation by generation and age

age:	65+		40–64			18/21–39			
generation:	1st	2nd	1st	2nd	3rd	2nd	3rd	4th	f.b.
1965									
kosher	61	42	53	23	10	24	9	—	—
Sabbath candles	84	61	72	66	62	56	37	—	—
Seder	91	63	93	90	80	89	85	—	—
service attendance	36	30	37	39	51	35	30	—	—
synagogue member	63	48	65	61	63	40	29	—	—
Jewish org. member	68	51	49	57	44	42	26	—	—
Jewish giving ($25+)	26	49	48	57	51	36	16	—	—
non-sect. org. member	32	53	37	61	62	52	50	—	—
non-sect. giving	26	62	53	64	65	56	37	—	—
Jewish friends	86	68	74	74	68	74	52	—	—
intermarried	0	0	1	3	7	2	4	—	—
weighted N=	177	93	149	533	90	217	231		
1975									
kosher	34	25	—	29	7	22	9	8	2
Sabbath candles	58	61	—	60	47	56	27	31	31
mezzuzah	55	67	—	80	64	62	36	41	36
Yom Kippur	47	57	—	68	52	60	49	55	53
chometz	58	73	—	68	70	64	51	47	32
Seder	80	82	—	90	86	92	84	83	72
service attendance	31	32	—	51	37	34	22	27	10
synagogue member	55	39	—	64	59	50	16	28	18
Jewish org. member	38	50	—	42	45	14	11	17	12
Jewish giving ($50+)	44	43	—	62	62	35	25	18	10
non-sect. org. member	24	43	—	40	30	36	26	38	25
non-sect. giving	32	34	—	42	47	32	31	23	15
Jewish friends	64	75	—	63	63	35	37	45	20
intermarried	0	12	—	8	15	13	21	16	30
weighted N=	58	69	—	199	64	51	300	79	59

Sources: 1965 and 1975 Boston Jewish Community Surveys.

was the same for both generations (37 per cent; 39 per cent). The results among the elderly (65+, first two columns) are largely similar.

Institutional affiliation rates behave differently than do rituals. The second generation was only slightly less likely to join a synagogue than the immigrant generation (61 per cent versus 65 per cent among those aged 40–64). However, they were *more* likely than immigrant Jews to belong to a Jewish organization and to contribute to Jewish charities in the middle years (57 per cent versus 49 per cent and 57 per cent versus 48 per cent respectively). Moreover, the patterns of non-sectarian affiliation are also instructive. The frequencies of belonging to a non-sectarian organization and rates of contributing at least $25 to non-sectarian charities demonstrate that the second generation clearly participated in the non-sectarian world more often than the first generation. Moreover, in each instance, the rise in non-sectarian participation from first to second generation outstrips the comparable first to second generation increases in Jewish affiliation. In other words, part of the reason for the first generation's lower Jewish institutional activity is that many immigrants never fully acculturated to the world of American voluntarism. But, *relative* to their lower rates of non-sectarian activity, the first generation was, by comparison, *more* active in public Jewish life than the second generation.

To summarize, many second-generation members abandoned private ritualistic behaviors which reflected serious attachment to the traditional heritage. However, they shifted their energies to Jewish institutional life, particularly the more modern forms of institutional activity. Synagogue membership – the survey's most overtly religious institutional measure – modestly declined from the first to the second generation; Jewish organizational membership displays an ambiguous relationship with generation (declining by generation among the elderly, increasing by generation among the middle-aged); and support for organized Jewish philanthropy – a very modern and American creation – unmistakably rose in the second generation. Much as commentators in the 1950s and 1960s observed, the second generation had partially replaced personal, private, and traditional religious devotion – as manifest by such diverse activities as keeping kosher, lighting Sabbath candles, or attending services – with communal, public, and modern institutional life as displayed in synagogues, other formal organizations, or charitable drives.

In addition, as several observers of second- and third-generation Jewish communities before 1965 noted, most Jews of that period were largely segregated from intimate ties with non-Jews. At least three-quarters of all 1965 respondents, in all age-generation categories but one, reported that most or all of their friends were Jewish; in all age-generation categories but one, current mixed marriage (married couples where a spouse maintained a non-Jewish religious orientation) was under 5 per cent. That the two exceptions to these generalizations are among third-generation respondents suggests that the third generation, even in the

1960s, represented what a Jewish survivalist would regard as a "soft underbelly" of assimilation. By the 1970s the small distinctions between the third and previous generations in marriage, friendship, and the several other measures of Jewish identification would grow even larger.

FROM THE SECOND TO THE THIRD GENERATION

In general, comparisons of the third with the second generation demonstrate that the limited erosion in conventional forms of Jewish practice in the transition from the first to second generation broadened in the third generation. Almost all third-generation identification rates were significantly below those for the second generation. (Seder participation, with only minor declines between second and third generations in both surveys, constitutes the one unequivocal exception to this generalization.) But, more significant than the across-the-board declines in Jewish identification measures, the gap between second and third generations grew wider in the ten-year interval between surveys. Most second-generation Jewish identification measures remained steady between 1965 and 1975, but those of the third generation mostly declined.

The 1975 study asked about rituals not found in the earlier survey. These included whether the doorpost had a mezzuzah, whether the respondent fasted on Yom Kippur, and whether members of the household kept some of Passover's dietary rules (refraining from eating "chometz," leavened foods). Among middle-age Jews the first two of these measures declined in the third generation while virtually equal proportions of the second and third generations reported observing Passover dietary rules. Among those under forty, though, in both 1965 and 1975, the third generation was much less likely to perform religious rituals than the second generation.

The largest declines on a proportional basis from the second to third generation were in keeping kosher at home; the smallest were in Passover Seder participation; declines for the other activities – Sabbath candles, mezzuzah, Yom Kippur fasting, and observing Passover dietary rules – are generally in between the other two. In other words, as generations advanced, erosion of ritual observance occurred in stages; observance of dietary rules decayed first and fastest; other, less demanding and less segregation-inducing ritual observances eroded more slowly; and Passover Seder participation more or less held steady.

Among younger respondents, third-generation Jews were much less likely than the second generation to affiliate with a Jewish institution, be it a synagogue, philanthropic campaign, or organization. These patterns can be contrasted with those for non-sectarian organization membership and philanthropic giving. The third generation's rates of non-sectarian affiliation are roughly equal to or just slightly below those of the second generation. Clearly, the lower rates of young third-generation Jewish institutional affiliation derives not from a lack of propensity to affiliate in general, but from their diminished attachment to Jewish life.

Last, between 1965 and 1975, in-group friendship declined and intermarriage increased for comparably aged second- and third-generation respondents. The proportion of mixed marriages also rose along with advancing generation and declining age. The third generation was considerably more likely to report a mixed marriage than second-generation respondents of the same age category; and, younger respondents were more likely to be in a mixed marriage than middle-aged respondents of the same generation.

Reviewing these findings, one must conclude that rather than stabilizing, Jewish identification continued to decline into the third generation. Only in the institutional area, and then only among middle-aged respondents, was there evidence of intergenerational stabilization. In the ritual and interpersonal spheres of Jewish identification, the third generation was clearly more assimilated than its predecessor generations.

THE FOURTH GENERATION AND BEYOND

While the third generation fails to stabilize, perhaps the decline in Jewish identification is arrested in the fourth generation. The data allow for comparisons of the third and fourth generation in 1975. By and large, consistent with the stabilization thesis, we find few substantial differences between the two generations and even some increases in the fourth.

But, does the apparent leveling off in the decline in Jewish identification in the fourth generation imply the much broader conclusion that the past century's overall growth in assimilation among American Jews has come to an end? A further analysis of the evidence indicates a negative response. We focus our attention upon third-generation young people in the two surveys. Between 1965 and 1975, this group experienced sizable declines in almost all Jewish identification measures, the exceptions include keeping kosher and participating in a Seder. (By way of explanation, kashrut apparently has a rock bottom low of 9 per cent or so, and seems to have held steady; the Seder has been redefined as a general family celebration and is nearly universally practiced.) The only other activity not to decline significantly among the young third generation is Jewish giving. Most declines in Jewish activities over the ten years (1965–75) for the under-40 third generation are larger than for either the under-40 second-generation respondents or for the middle-aged third generation.[5]

These findings, then, suggest that generation-linked decline in Jewish identification may indeed terminate with the third generation. Young fourth-generation Jews in 1975, after all, are no less, if not more Jewishly identified than the young third generation in that year. But the end of generation-driven assimilation does not necessitate an end to growth in assimilation in the coming years. Younger birth cohorts have been socialized in milieus and periods which, taken as a whole, are historically and generationally more distant from the European traditional heritage than their elders. Therefore, apart from generation *per se*, they may well turn out more assimilated than their older predecessors.

Table 3(4) presents the frequencies of Jewish activities by ten-year age intervals in 1965 and 1975. Comparing each age-specific activity frequency in 1965 and 1975, we again find the overall patterns of decline observed previously. As in Table 3(3), respondents in the 1975 survey were less Jewishly identified, in most instances, than those in 1965. Philanthropy is the one exception to this generalization; giving held steady between 1965 and 1975.

Not only was there widespread decline in Jewish activity between 1965 and 1975, but most declines were more precipitous for young adults, those aged 25–34, than for others. In particular, declines in institutional affiliation (synagogue membership, organizational membership, and philanthropy), in-group marriage, and Jewish friendship among the 25–34 year olds outstripped lesser declines between 1965 and 1975 among the 35–44 year olds. In fact, the 1975 35–44 year olds were 10 per cent *more* likely to attend religious services frequently (52 per cent versus 42 per cent) while the 25–34 year olds were 6 per cent *less* likely to do so (22 per cent versus 28 per cent). In general, the gaps in Jewish identification measures between the 35–44 year old respondents and the immediately younger group (25–34) widened considerably between 1965 and 1975. Part of this differential decline in Jewish identification is due to a growing postponement of parenting occurring in the 1970s (see Chapter 6); but a good portion should be ascribed to the effects of having been reared ten years later and having been interviewed ten years later as well.

To some indeterminate extent, the lower levels of Jewish identification among the younger Jews result from enduring birth-cohort effects rather

Table 3(4)   Selected measures of Jewish identification and other characteristics

age:	65+	55–64	45–54	35–44	25–34	18/21–24
1965						
kosher	52	39	27	15	17	18
Sabbath candles	73	69	71	66	44	32
Seder	87	87	93	91	84	94
service attendance	33	31	45	42	28	42
synagogue member	56	59	65	60	24	37
Jewish org. member	61	47	56	52	32	32
Jewish giving ($25+)	32	54	58	49	23	0
Jewish friends	79	72	74	76	61	49
intermarried	0	3	3	4	2	2
weighted N=	288	245	354	293	276	87
1975						
kosher	28	34	25	11	9	9
Sabbath candles	56	54	57	50	31	26
mezzuzah	63	73	74	72	38	32
Yom Kippur	52	61	67	61	53	45
chometz	82	67	70	65	48	45
Seder	82	90	90	85	79	87
service attendance	31	42	50	52	22	15
synagogue member	45	54	62	63	11	26
Jewish org. member	46	50	40	31	12	9
Jewish giving ($50+)	45	59	67	61	21	13
Jewish friends	69	66	60	62	37	27
intermarried	6	1	9	13	26	26
weighted N=	139	110	120	116	250	181

Sources: 1965 and 1975 Boston Jewish Community Surveys.
See *Table 3(1)*, page 56, for explanation of the Jewish identification items.

than transitory life-cycle phenomena which may be vitiated by later marriage and childbearing. To that extent, we can expect continued erosion of Jewish ritual practice as younger, more assimilated birth cohorts replace their more identified elders. We find a parallel circumstance among American Christians:

> The rate of secularization since the 1950s has been more pronounced among younger than among older age-strata . . . both on religious practice and religious belief. It has been shown perforce that a "generation gap" exists in the religious data collected in recent years, whereas none existed in data collected in the late 1950s and early 1960s.   (Wuthnow, 1976 : 882)

In an environment where religious behavior in the larger society is declining, there is good reason to anticipate parallel declines among Jews as well. Conversely, where and when religious interest and practice increase, similar changes may be expected among Jews too.

Culturally significant, but demographically small movements of renewed Jewish interest in the 1970s and early 1980s testify to the plausibility of a revitalized commitment to traditional Jewish religious practice and communal organization (Silberman, 1981). But the 1975 Boston survey data fail to provide evidence that such renewal was at that time very influential or widespread among those aged thirty-nine and under.

In sum, if one takes a limited view of stabilization theory and casts the theory solely in terms of generation, we do find evidence of stabilization in the third/fourth generation. That is, after the third generation, generation loses the power meaningfully to predict the level of Jewish identification. If we take a somewhat broader view of stabilization, a view that looks at succeeding birth cohorts, American Jewish history and indeed the general direction of Jewishness in America, then some of the evidence refutes the stabilization thesis. On the contrary, over-time and birth-cohort data point to a continuing erosion in many of the conventional measures of Jewish identification. Putting matters simply, assimilation (in terms of the available measures) continues to advance, although it is no longer closely linked with generational status and it may be artificially induced in younger adults by family changes.

Bimodality

The analysis immediately above focused on changes in the central tendency of Jewish identification. Whether measured in terms of year of survey, generation, or birth cohort, the passage of time is associated with declines in many measures of Jewish identification.

But even though some of the mean scores point downward, the distribution of Jewish identification among later-generation or younger Jews might be assuming a different shape than in the past. Polarization theorists would argue that American Jewry is dividing into a large, assimilated and a small, highly identified camp, with the middle giving way to the two extremes. This particular consequence of polarization (the first of three we shall consider) may be termed the "bimodality hypothesis."

To test this hypothesis, two groups of respondents were defined so as to represent the two extreme wings on the Jewish identification continuum.[6]

Table 3(5)   Extremes in Jewish identification by generation, age, and age with generation

generation:	1st	2nd	3rd	4th	f.b.	all
1965						
high	23	23	15	—	—	21
low	4	8	21	—	—	10
1975						
high	27	28	8	9	9	17
low	19	14	30	25	37	24

age:	65+	55–64	45–54	35–44	25–34	18/21–24
1965						
high	21	17	32	26	12	0
low	7	3	9	2	19	32
1975						
high	20	32	31	29	5	3
low	15	12	10	13	40	31

age:	65+		40–64			18/21–39			
generation:	1st	2nd	1st	2nd	3rd	2nd	3rd	4th	f.b.
1965									
high	23	22	22	26	37	18	7	—	—
low	2	12	5	6	10	10	26	—	—
1975									
high	25	17	—	34	17	23	6	8	3
low	20	13	—	10	13	33	34	22	46

Sources: 1965 and 1975 Boston Jewish Community Surveys.

Table 3(5) reports the frequency of respondents with "high" and "low" levels of Jewish identification by generation, age, and age with generation for both 1965 and 1975. If the bimodality hypothesis is correct, then we should find that the proportions of respondents in the two extreme wings of Jewish identification should increase either between 1965 and 1975, or between the second and third generation, or between older and younger Jews.

Making such comparisons (between 1965 and 1975), we do find some support for the hypothesis. Specifically, second-generation respondents overall (top panel) and those under the age of sixty-five in particular (bottom panel) display the anticipated patterns. From 1965 to 1975 the proportion of such respondents in the two extremes of Jewish identification increased by a few percentage points.

While the bimodality hypothesis finds some supportive evidence among the second generation, the same cannot be said for the third generation. To understand the leading group, the third generation in 1975, we may make comparisons with their 1965 predecessors or with their second-generation counterparts in the same year (1975). Both sorts of comparisons show more Jews with low identification and fewer with high identification. Relative to its historic or generational predecessors, then, the third generation in 1975 is simply more assimilated, but clearly not more bimodal.

Comparing the ten-year age groups (middle panel) also shows limited and qualified support for the bimodality argument. Between 1965 and 1975, the proportions on the low end of the Jewish identification scale grew, albeit unevenly, for each age interval. At the same time, the proportions with high Jewish identification alternatively increased and diminished, depending upon the age group.

Overall, one must conclude that the bimodality hypothesis obtains some support from the data. Some findings support the thesis, and some do not. The historically most advanced Jews (those in 1975, who are younger, and third generation) reflect growth in the assimilated extreme when compared with less advanced groups (those in 1965, who are older, and second generation). But the highly identified wing is either holding steady or is diminishing and almost certainly is not expanding. In light of the growth in assimilated Jews, bimodality will hinge on whether the proportions in the upper reaches of Jewish identification stabilize or increase.

Consistency

People have many reasons for joining and participating in voluntary organizations. Some of the motivations for doing so are connected with the overt purposes of the organization. Thus, some workers join labor unions because they seek better working conditions; some join political parties, clubs, or associations because they believe in the ideals and aims of those groups; and some Jews join synagogues or Jewish organizations, or give to philanthropic drives out of religious or ethnic motivations.

But there are, unquestionably, other reasons for participating in voluntary organizations. People also join associations for the personal rewards they derive from membership: social status, respectability, or the pleasure of associating with others with like interests and background. Almost two decades ago, sociologist Erich Goode distinguished between two broad sets of motivations for participation in church life:

> Church activity . . . cannot be seen as an unambiguous reflection of religiosity, that is, as a measure of religious feeling [For] members of the white collar occupational level . . . church activity has become secularized to such an extent that it can be subsumed, at least partially under general associational activity.   (Goode, 1966 : 111)

Such a view of church participation (see also Lazerwitz, 1962) raises questions about Jewish institutional behavior. To what extent are synagogue membership, Jewish organizational affiliation, and philanthropic participation reflections of general affiliative tendencies typifying the middle class, and to what extent are they motivated by specifically Jewish ethnic or religious concerns? And to what extent have these types of motivations for joining shifted in recent years? Contrary to Goode's analysis of church life in the 1960s, various considerations strongly suggest that overall affiliative proclivities among Jews have become *less* crucial; while inherently Jewish motivations may have become *more* important in deciding whether to participate in synagogues, organizations, and philanthropy.

Goode's research linking middle-class affiliation with church participation was published only ten years after Herberg observed that joining a church or synagogue was a prerequisite to middle-class respectability in young adult suburban America. In fact, during the early 1960s spending on new church construction and the proportion of the US population belonging to churches hit their all-time historic highs, declining by the early 1970s (Wuthnow, 1976). Though accurate then, Goode's and Herberg's propositions may well have been time-bound.

As noted earlier in this chapter, Jews were following the larger society's trends in establishing and joining synagogues in record numbers. Moreover, the first and second generation, who constituted most of the 1965 Boston sample, as well as most of American Jewish adults at that time, retained considerable insecurity about their acceptance by mainstream society. For them, synagogues, Jewish organizations, and philanthropic agencies provided a sense of integration into respectable middle-class society. Thus, Jews who were "joiners" in general would be expected to join specifically Jewish organizations as well, since the motivations to affiliate with general or Jewish institutions were often similar.

Between 1965 and 1975, a number of historic events, demographic shifts, and changes in the larger society altered the reasons behind Jewish participation in their religious and ethnic institutions. First, church participation in general declined, signifying erosion in the expectation that respectable middle-class Americans would join and participate in their houses of worship (Wuthnow, 1976). Second, the adult Jewish population shifted from the second to the third generation. Commensurate with that shift, Jews became less concerned with marginality and more secure in their membership in middle-class America. No longer preoccupied with integration, their institutions less often appealed to them as vehicles of entry into the social mainstream.

Finally, the decade between the two Boston surveys were years of rising ethnic assertiveness among Jews and other minorities in the United States. For Jews, this period embraced two wars in the Middle East, raising renewed concerns for the security of Israel. They were years when the liberal political coalition unravelled and when Jews in many Northeastern metropolises felt themselves embattled with blacks and other minorities over jobs, neighborhoods, and political power. The new particularism manifested itself in changing philanthropic priorities – away from general purpose and toward more Jewishly oriented programs – and in changing political priorities – away from the liberal social agenda and toward specific Jewish concerns such as Israel and Soviet Jewry.

If this line of thinking is correct, then from 1965 to 1975 we would expect to observe several trends. Those with minimal Jewish identification but significant overall participation in voluntary organizations might be reasonably involved in Jewish institutional life in 1965; but they, or their successor counterparts, would be absent from the Jewish communal world by 1975. Indeed, such a prediction finds support in Charles Liebman's finding that the relatively assimilated and wealthy top leadership in the New York Federation of Jewish Philanthropies as of 1968 tended to drop out to be replaced, ten years later, by individuals with a stronger private and public commitment to traditional Jewish life (Liebman, 1978).

Second, as a corollary, the influence of overall affiliative tendencies upon the decision to join synagogues, organizations, or philanthropic drives should diminish over time. Correlatively, commitment to Jewish traditional practices should play more of a role in these decisions (see, for example, Cohen, 1978, 1980a).

Table 3(6) presents the data which test these propositions. Respondents were divided into "high" and "low" ritual observance groups based on their answers to questions on Seder participation, Sabbath candle lighting, and keeping kosher; "high" observance respondents performed at least two of these rituals. Respondents were also classified according to two measures of general affiliative tendencies. One was used in the analysis of synagogue and of organizational membership; it divides respondents who belonged to at least one non-sectarian organization from those who did not. The other affiliative measure was used in the analysis of Jewish philanthropy; it entails whether respondents made

Table 3(6) Three measures of Jewish affiliation by ritual observance and measures of non-sectarian affiliation

	1965			1975		
ritual observance:	low	high	% diff.	low	high	% diff.
	% members of synagogues					
non-sectarian org. member						
yes	44%	75%	31%	28%	73%	45%
	(305)	(492)		(153)	(146)	
no	16%	57%	41%	15%	59%	44%
	(303)	(461)		(393)	(232)	
% difference	29%	18%	—	13%	14%	—
	% members of Jewish orgs					
non-sectarian org. member						
yes	39%	71%	32%	18%	43%	25%
	(305)	(492)		(153)	(146)	
no	30%	46%	16%	18%	40%	22%
	(303)	(461)		(393)	(232)	
% difference	9%	25%	—	0%	3%	—
	% Jewish giving					
non-sectarian giving						
yes	50%	69%	19%	51%	88%	39%
	(352)	(492)		(166)	(146)	
no	14%	21%	7%	14%	39%	25%
	(261)	(463)		(377)	(239)	
% difference	36%	48%	—	37%	49%	—

Sources: 1965 and 1975 Boston Jewish Community Surveys.

minimal contributions of $25 in 1965 or $50 in 1975 to non-sectarian charitable causes.

The table examines how ritual observance and the appropriate measure of general affiliation simultaneously influenced each of the three measures of Jewish institutional participation we have been investigating: synagogue membership, belonging to a Jewish organization, and making a minimal contribution to Jewish philanthropic causes.

In 1965, both ritual observance and general affiliation influenced synagogue membership, although the former is a somewhat stronger predictor of belonging to a synagogue than the latter. Ten years later, the effects of ritual observance had grown larger while those of general observance had diminished. In particular, the major difference between the 1965 and 1975 findings is that those who belonged to a non-sectarian organization yet were not ritually observant were much less likely to belong to a synagogue in 1975 than in 1965 (only 28 per cent in 1975 versus 44 per cent ten years earlier). Clearly, during the decade between studies, private Jewish commitment became more of a prerequisite for synagogue membership, while the proclivity to join organizations in general waned in importance.

Similar results obtain in the case of Jewish organizations. In 1965, as with synagogue membership, religious motivations were somewhat more influential than general affiliative tendencies, but both factors influenced the decision to join Jewish organizations. By 1975 though, only ritual observance retained an influence over the likelihood of joining Jewish organizations. Those who were members of non-sectarian organizations in 1975 were no more likely to join Jewish organizations than those un-affiliated with non-sectarian groups, controlling for observance.

Unlike in the analyses of belonging to synagogues or Jewish organizations, the influence of general affiliative tendencies upon Jewish philanthropic giving remained constant over the ten-year period between the two Boston studies. In both 1965 and 1975, those who contributed to non-sectarian charities were substantially more likely to participate in Jewish charitable drives as well. However, over the ten-year period, ritual observance acquired a greater role in predicting Jewish philanthropic behavior. Essentially, the likelihood that ritually observant Jews would contribute to Jewish philanthropic causes increased substantially over the decade. By 1975, ritual observance became almost as important as participating in non-sectarian charities in predicting whether an individual would contribute at a minimal level to Jewish philanthropies.

In all three instances of Jewish association – synagogue membership, belonging to a Jewish organization, and contributing to Jewish philanthropies – we observed parallel shifts in the relative importance of the two types of motivation for participating in Jewish communal life. From 1965 to 1975, the importance of Jewish religiosity (as measured by ritual observance) increased relative to the importance of general affiliative tendencies (as measured by joining a non-sectarian organization or contributing to non-sectarian charities) as an influence on Jewish institutional participation.

In crude terms, we may say that Jewish affiliation became more of a purely "Jewish" and less of a general affiliative behavior. Thus we may speak of growing *consistency* between the ritual and affiliative dimensions of Jewish identification. The correspondence of these findings with qualitative observation strongly suggests the following: more and more so, those who were privately active as observant Jews became publicly active as organizational Jews; and those who were privately inactive became publicly inactive as well. The two dimensions of ritual observance and communal affiliation came into closer congruence with one another in the ten-year period between the two Boston surveys and, presumably, among American Jews generally in the last decade and a half as well.

Denominational divergence

To scholars and rabbis, the terms Orthodox, Conservative, and Reform connote significant theological and ideological distinctions. Yet to the layman, these terms serve primarily as a shorthand label for level of ritual observance. In study after study, those calling themselves Orthodox perform religious rituals more frequently than do Conservative Jews who in turn are more ritually active than their Reform counterparts (Lazerwitz and Harrison, 1979). Additionally, those who decline to categorize themselves in denominational terms – giving such answers as "just Jewish" – score even lower on most measures of Jewish identification.

Several observers have speculated that the constituencies of these four groups (the three denominations and the "unaffiliated") have begun to diverge in terms of ritual practice if not institutional affiliation as well. "Denominational divergence" maintains that the frequencies of Jewish activity among the Orthodox have been growing, or holding steady or even, and that those of the Reform and the unaffiliated have been diminishing. The reasons for such speculation are several.

Perhaps the simplest rationale entails the supposition that American Jews have become increasingly familiar and conversant with the denominational terminology. As a result, they may be using the denominational nomenclature to increasingly correspond with level of ritual observance. That such is the case with respect to Orthodoxy is clear to one observer:

> Many first generation American Jews who identified themselves as Orthodox in the past were not observant of Jewish law in their personal lives. . . . They may have identified themselves as Orthodox out of sympathy with Jewish tradition, for familial or social reasons, . . . or for any other number of reasons. That is much less true of second and probably even less true of third generation Orthodox Jews in America. Whereas fewer Jews identify with Orthodoxy today, those who do so are far more committed to its norms. (Liebman, 1979 : 20)

But aside from the clarification of denominational labels, there are reasons to adduce actual change in the ritual practices of the major denominations' constituencies. Those inside American Orthodoxy as well as outside observers agree that the most traditional American Jewish denomination "is moving to the right religiously." Liebman is useful in defining Orthodoxy's rightward shift: "First, Jews on the religious right interpret Jewish law more rigidly and prohibitively than Jews on the religious left. Secondly, they are less tolerant of deviations from Jewish law than are those of the left" (Liebman, 1979 : 20). Complementing Orthodoxy's move rightward, we have reason to anticipate a Reform move "leftward" or toward greater laxity in observance among its lay constituency. Lazerwitz has shown that Reform assumes its greatest popularity among third- and later-generation Jews (Lazerwitz, 1979). One may surmise that their denominational choice is in part influenced by the lower level of ritual observance typifying later generations relative to their predecessors and typifying Reform relative to Conservatism and Orthodoxy. As the previous section showed, third-generation Jews were somewhat less observant in 1975 than they were in 1965. Thus, if the third generation continued to supply the bulk of the Reform constituency, one would anticipate some decline in the level of religious observance among Reform.

The previous section's examination of consistency between private and public commitment to Jewish life suggests yet a third reason to anticipate denominational divergence. Increasing consistency in measures of Jewish identification may reflect a growth in Jewish ideological clarity. The ideologically committed should perform many prescribed ritual and affiliative behaviors while those who are not so committed should undertake few of them. The phenomenon of "cafeteria-style" Judaism where individuals pick those activities with idiosyncratic sentimental value may be supplanted by a more ordered environment where, for those who care at all about such things, some logic – linked to denomination – comes to govern such choices.

To determine whether the denominations have in fact moved apart from one another, we separate synagogue members from the totality of respondents. Changes among only those members of the denominations who belong to synagogues may more accurately reflect genuine ideological or institutional developments among the denominations; meanwhile, parallel changes among the totality of Jews may simply reflect changes in the way denominational labels are used in the Jewish public at large.

Table 3(7) reports frequencies for selected rituals and affiliative behaviors for members of different denominations (Orthodox, Conservative, Reform, and other), for both surveys (1965 and 1975), as well as for total samples and for synagogue members only. We may compare frequencies

Table 3(7) Selected measures of Jewish identification by denomination

	synagogue members and non-members							
	1965				1975			
	Orth.	Cons.	Ref.	other	Orth.	Cons.	Ref.	other
Sabbath candles	82	71	51	30	90	64	28	21
service attendance	41	46	47	6	57	54	22	8
synagogue	63	61	52	22	74	57	34	7
Jewish org. member	49	58	53	22	57	41	22	12
Jewish giving	30	45	50	30	64	52	38	17
weighted N=	224	690	416	183	47	321	325	208
	synagogue members only							
Sabbath candles	85	83	65	60	94	79	47	—
service attendance	42	60	55	13	68	30	55	—
Jewish org. member	58	71	69	57	69	53	43	—
Jewish giving	37	56	64	45	73	64	63	—
weighted N=	142	418	215	40	35	184	112	15

Sources: 1965 and 1975 Boston Jewish Community Surveys.
See *Table 3(1)*, page 56, for explanation of the Jewish identification items.

of a particular denomination in 1965 with the same denomination ten years later. Doing so, we find that among the Orthodox – among both the total sample and synagogue members – all measures of Jewish activity increased over the ten-year period. Increases range from the modest (e.g., 90 per cent – 82 per cent = 8 percentage point increase in candle lighting) to the substantial (e.g., from 30 per cent to 64 per cent for philanthropic giving); but there can be no doubt that, overall, the Orthodox of 1975 are more Jewishly active than their 1965 predecessors. Meanwhile, similar comparisons among Conservative Jews show hardly any change whatever. Reform and unaffiliated Jews, though, display several significant declines between the two surveys. Except for frequent religious service attendance – a measure which had fallen to a minimal level by 1965 – the other four measures declined deeply from 1965 to 1975. The synagogue members-only panel (lower half of *Table 3(7)* contains essentially the same patterns.

The preponderance of evidence clearly indicates that denominations are indeed diverging over time. Whether this pattern is attributable to a realignment and clarification of labels, or to genuine ideological changes cannot be determined from the available data. But the data do provide solid support for the notion that denominational distinctions have been growing.

Summary and conclusions

Generation has been a significant axis of social differentiation distinguishing American Jews in terms of social status and age as well as ritual observance and institutional affiliation. The earlier the generation the greater the likelihood the individual will undertake traditional ritual practices. While performance of most rituals declines almost uniformly from one generation to the next, participation in formal organizations assumes a different contour over the generations, generally peaking in the second generation and declining thereafter. Organized Jewish activity in the United States has been largely a creation of the second generation and appealed to that generation more than it did to the less acculturated immigrants.

The data generally refuted those who suggest that the decline in ritual activity during the transition from the first to second generation comes to a halt in the third or fourth generation. Rather, instead of stabilizing, many forms of Jewish activity decline through the third generation. While distinctions among later (third and fourth) generations are no longer major, succeeding birth cohorts may well be taking on the distinctions in Jewishness once born by generation. While we clearly saw stabilization in the fourth generation, declines in Jewish identification were evident in the passages from one young birth cohort to the next in the 1975 data, perhaps owing to family changes (see Chapter 6).

The notion that Jews are dividing into highly identified and highly assimilated camps found a little support in the data. While the number of non-observant, non-affiliated Jews does seem to be growing, little increase if any was found in more observant and communally active Jews. Fewer third-generation, younger Jews in 1975 met criteria for high ritual observance and institutional affiliation than did their predecessors or elders.

While one aspect of the polarization thesis – the bimodality prediction – finds a little support, the other two predictions – namely, consistency and denominational divergence – receive more substantiation. A modicum of ritual observance became more of a precondition for certain forms of public Jewish expression, particularly philanthropic giving and, possibly, synagogue affiliation. Those less ritually active inside the home were increasingly less likely to affiliate with formal institutions outside the home.

Differences between the denominations in religious observance and institutional affiliation grew in the ten years between the two Boston surveys (1965 and 1975). Those calling themselves Orthodox were somewhat more observant and communally active in 1975 than were their 1965 counterparts. Conservative Jews in the two surveys had similar levels of Jewish identification. Reform and denominationally unaffiliated Jews reported less frequent Jewish observance and voluntary activity in 1975 than did their predecessors in 1965. This is not to claim, necessarily, that members of these denominations actually changed in the ways indicated. A clarification of labels and a realignment of affiliation undoubtedly contributed to divergence. By 1975, a more select group of the more observant felt comfortable calling themselves Orthodox; meanwhile less identified Jews came to identify as Reform or unaffiliated, and "Conservative" had roughly the same meaning for respondents in 1975 as it did in 1965.

In sum, this analysis of the impact of generation upon Jewish identification points to how integration into modern society is a key to understanding broad changes in Jewish identification. Jews who are generationally close to the traditional heritage are most likely to express that closeness in concrete, ritual terms. As they integrate into society they may participate more extensively in formal institutions of the Jewish community even as their personal religiosity continues to decline. But, further integration – such as that experienced by third- and fourth-generation Jews – begins to erode participation in formal institutions as well. Without a personal religious commitment (expressed in high ritual observance) or a sustaining religious ideology (such as Orthodoxy), later-generation Jews exhibit less motivation than their elders or predecessors to affiliate with the conventional, organized Jewish community.

Comparisons across generations provide only a very crude picture of the assimilatory impact of integration. As generations have advanced, so too have American Jews advanced their integration into American society in several critical ways. Their rapid rise to the middle and upper rungs of the social and economic hierarchies has also influenced their Jewish identification and it has helped shape the particular forms in which that identification came to be expressed.

4 Dollars and diplomas: the impact of high social status upon Jewish identification

The extraordinary speed with which most American Jews have attained middle-class if not upper-class status in the last hundred years has been thoroughly documented. Observers (e.g., Goldstein, 1981) reckon that nearly all American Jews of college age attend college; that Jews have been entering the professions in highly disproportionate numbers since the 1920s, if not earlier; and that the average affluence of American Jews equals if not surpasses that of Episcopalians, the wealthiest major religious denomination, and exceeds that of all major US ethnic groups.[1] Despite large numbers of poor urban Jews, the overall high position of Jews' mean scores on standard measures of social status is undisputed. In fact, the most recent research reports that in the last ten years they have continued to advance, obtaining some of the most elite positions in society, as US Senators, corporate leaders, and heads of Ivy League universities and professional schools (Silberman, 1981).

While the fact of Jewish social mobility is not at issue, the underlying causes of that mobility have lately become a matter of debate. Conventional wisdom has long held that the Jews' cultural heritage was the key factor responsible for their remarkable success in this country (Glazer and Moynihan, 1970; Sowell, 1981). According to this view, the traditional heritage prized education, Jews were possessed of enormous drive and ambition, and they were adept at commerce and handling money. In contrast some have offered explanations which focus on certain structural features as the principal reasons for American Jewish mobility. They cite economic conditions and opportunities open to Jews when they arrived in the United States, and the occupational skills and financial resources they brought with them from the Old Country. (See, particularly, Steinberg, 1980 as well as Kessner, 1977, and Gorelick, 1981).

Rather than entering into the fascinating debate between competing explanations of Jewish social mobility, this chapter takes that mobility as a given. It asks how higher education, professional life, and affluence have influenced the quantity and quality of Jewish religious and ethnic identification.

The link between social mobility and Jewish identification can be formulated in several ways. Most central to this investigation is, of course, the notion that social mobility in American society signifies some measure of social integration into the modern world. People who have higher educational attainment, more prestigious jobs, and higher incomes are people who have generally moved more thoroughly into the mainstream of society. Thus, in asking whether rapid social mobility has eroded Jewish identification, then, we are also asking, more broadly, whether social integration into the larger society, signified by high social status, necessarily leads to ethnic and religious assimilation. Much of the literature on this larger issue is embraced by two research traditions: literature on American ethnicity, and the writing on the sociology of religion.

The ethnic perspective

Scholars and lay observers divide over whether an ethnic subculture can persist once the bulk of the group has attained middle-class status. Early twentieth-century sociologists held the 'melting-pot' expectation.[2] Accordingly, education, affluence, occupational advancement, residential dispersal, and generational distance from the Old Country inevitably combine to undermine in-group friendship and marriage, political mobilization, neighborhood turf, and the ethnic subculture.

In the 1960s and 1970s, though, many observers — among them social researchers, champions of ethnic survival, and political commentators — asserted that the demise of American ethnic groups is far from a foregone conclusion (e.g., Greeley, 1974). They pointed to numerous instances of ethnic survival in such spheres as the family, urban neighborhood, group politics, and the economy.

In reply, advocates of the melting-pot view contended that most of the evidence of ethnic persistence borders on the symbolic, anecdotal, or vestigial. Looking at the larger picture, they cited increasing inter-ethnic marriage and friendship accompanying generational advancement and social mobility among most if not all major American ethnic groups (Alba, 1976, 1981; Steinberg, 1980).

As for the immediate matter at hand – the relationship between social mobility and ethnic assimilation – the literature on American ethnicity, while not conclusive, is certainly suggestive. In most studies, social mobility leads to declines in several measures of ethnic identification.[3] This general finding suggests that middle-class status and high ethnic identification are usually in tension. In so far as Jews act like other groups, then, their middle- and upper-class status should damage their group solidarity and distinctive subculture.

But Jews may not behave as other white Americans. As noted earlier (Chapter 3), Jews, like other groups, have their points of distinction. One of them is that they constitute a religious as well as an ethnic group. For this reason the sociology of religion literature also bears upon the question of how social status affects Jewish identification.

The religious perspective

Investigations into American church membership and religious service attendance have uncovered a fairly uniform, but very modest influence of social class (Lenski, 1953; Burchinal, 1959; Lazerwitz, 1961; Dillingham, 1965, 1967; Mueller and Johnson, 1975; Alston and McIntosh, 1979). Middle-class people are somewhat more apt to join churches and attend worship services than working-class or lower-class people. (This generalization applies less to Roman Catholics than to most Protestant denominations.) Church activities, like those associated with other formal voluntary institutions in American society, are particularly attractive to the middle class (Goode, 1966; Estus and Overington, 1970). Not only do such activities contribute to the social standing of the middle-class person, but he or she is recruited by the church, or other formal organizations, for his or her skills, talents, and resources.

Despite the small direct relationship between class and church participation, class (in particular, education) is inversely related with both doctrinal orthodoxy and devotionalism (frequent and personal prayer and Bible readings). Although fewer working- and lower-class individuals participate in formal religious activities, more of them hold orthodox religious beliefs and perform private religious practices (Roof, 1976).

If we extend these findings, along with those from the ethnicity field, to Jews, we generate a variety of expectations: higher-status Jews should evidence (1) lower incidence of in-group marriage and friendship; (2) greater participation in the synagogue and other aspects of Jewish institutional life; and (3) fewer traditional religious beliefs and ritual practices.

To investigate these propositions in detail, one would need a certain conceptual and methodological precision. Social scientists have traditionally discerned three broad components of social status: educational attainment, occupation, and income. Accordingly, we turn to a more refined analysis of social status, one that considers the impact of education, professionalization, and affluence separately.

Educational attainment

Western Jews entering the modern world understood they had new opportunities for upward mobility; many saw educational attainment as a channel to the middle class. For American Jews, the perception of the instrumental value of education has been largely accurate.[4]

Vertical mobility, though, is only one type of mobility engendered by formal education. Jewish immigrants to the United States and their children also sought the "horizontal" consequences of formal schooling. That is, higher education often brings one into association with schoolmates from diverse ethnic backgrounds. At the same time, it imparts several values which undermine traditional religious commitment (Hyman, Wright, and Reed, 1975). These include cosmopolitanism, cultural relativism, toleration, individualism; in short, the many liberal Enlightenment values which adversely affect traditional Judaism (Chapter 1).

The integrative and liberalizing consequences of secular studies have long provoked concern by rabbinic and Jewish communal leaders. Historically, many traditional rabbis demanded that their followers immerse themselves as much as possible in sacred texts and avoid secular studies. In such a context rabbis saw such studies as a distraction from time better spent in traditional intellectual pursuits. However, in the modern period secular schooling came to represent something even worse: integration into the modern world and the potential for assimilation, if not outright conversion.

While the Jewish masses shared some traditionalists' perceptions of the likely consequences of secular schooling, they tended to place a different value on them. Some modernizing Jews saw education's assimilatory outcome as a small price to pay for its status-conferring effects.

Most, in fact, welcomed the opportunity to enter the social mainstream, to integrate, and to learn wordly values.

The twin effects of education – one on social status and the other on liberal values – suggest a complicated relationship between education and several dimensions of ethnicity and religiosity. Accordingly, the research in the area is somewhat contradictory; nonetheless, it reveals certain patterns. In a recent analysis of a national sample, researchers found a very modest direct relationship between education on Protestant church attendance after controlling for occupation and income (Mueller and Johnson, 1975).[5] A year later, Wade Clark Roof demonstrated that education has different effects on different dimensions of religiosity (Roof, 1976). In a local sample of American Protestants, he found that the better educated were more likely to attend church, to participate in its organizational life, and to have friends within the congregation; but they were less likely to hold orthodox beliefs about God, Jesus, the Bible, or afterlife and were less likely to pray privately or study the Bible on their own.

More critically, Roof was able to show that an index he called "local community reference" or "localism-cosmopolitanism" significantly mediated the effects of education and other background variables upon the several dimensions of religiosity. Better-educated respondents were more cosmopolitan, and cosmopolitans reported lower levels of religious identification in all its dimensions than did the locals. One may then differentiate education's status-conferring from its value-liberalizing effects. High social status fosters religious institutional participation; while liberal, cosmopolitan values undermine institutional and personal dimensions of religiosity.

Parallel research on American Jews has been far less sophisticated.[6] The most noteworthy study is Goldstein and Goldscheider's analysis (1968) of data on Providence Jews, collected in 1964. They found that education's influence was restricted to the first generation where it was associated with declines in ritual practice. Although the authors did not say so explicitly, education among first-generation Providence Jewry may be more of a vehicle (or a symbol) of acculturation than it was for later generations. Thus, education most thoroughly lowers traditional religious practice where its cosmopolitanizing influence is most pronounced, that is, among the first generation; but once acculturation is more advanced, as it is in the second and third generations, education has little effect on ritual observance. In fact, the two researchers uncovered a slight direct relationship between formal schooling and ritual observance in the third generation.

If these various findings can be extended to several dimensions of Jewish identification, we should find evidence both of education's status-conferring and its value-liberalizing effects. Specifically, those measures of Jewishness which depend upon a traditional and parochial world-view should most rapidly erode under the impact of education. Institutional measures of Jewish identification, though, might well benefit from education's status-conferring consequences.

Table 4(1) lays the foundation for this analysis by depicting the increase in educational attainment with each succeeding birth cohort.

The table may be read from right to left, from old to young, so as to convey a kind of educational history of American Jewry. We find, for example, that most of the oldest (aged 65 or over) respondents in 1965

Table 4(1)   Education by age

	1965						
age:	21–24	25–34	35–44	45–54	55–64	65+	all[a]
education							
low	0	2	10	15	25	51	19
high-school grad.	8	11	34	32	39	26	28
college grad.	87	38	38	31	22	7	31
grad. school	5	49	18	18	11	7	20
n.a.	0	0	0	4	2	9	3
	100%	100%	100%	100%	100%	100%	100%
weighted N=	87	276	293	354	245	288	1569
	1975						
age:	18–24	25–34	35–44	45–54	55–64	65+	all[a]
education							
low	4	3	0	3	6	9	9
high-school grad.	12	6	9	24	40	25	17
college grad.	68	34	50	40	38	26	43
grad. school	17	57	41	34	15	10	31
n.a.	0	0	0	0	0	0	0
	100%	100%	100%	100%	100%	100%	100%
weighted N=	181	250	116	120	110	139	934

Sources: 1965 and 1975 Boston Jewish Community Surveys.

Note:
a Includes "no answers."
All columns do not add up to 100 per cent because of rounding errors.

never obtained a high-school diploma. However, of those aged 25–34 in 1965, almost half (49 per cent) reported having received a post-graduate degree; fully 87 per cent had attended college. Similarly, spectacular growth rates in educational attainment are apparent in the 1975 data.[7]

Table 4(2) examines the impact of educational attainment upon various measures of Jewish identification. Since education is closely related to age, and therefore to generation and family life cycle, crude trends in Jewish identification by education would overstate the causal impact of education. For this reason, *Table 4(2)* reports Jewish identification scores after adjusting for education's principal antecedents which affect Jewish identification. These include age, generation and family life cycle.

The many broad continuities between the 1965 and 1975 findings lend confidence to the principal interpretations one may draw from the table. Net of other variables, education seems to have adversely influenced

Table 4(2)   Selected measures of Jewish identification and social participation by education, after adjusting for age, generation, and family life cycle[a]

education:	1965				1975			
	low	high school	college	post grad. degree	low	high school	college	post grad. degree
kosher	44	31	22	19	24	22	16	17
Sabbath candles	84	59	56	46	65	45	41	36
mezzuzah	—	—	—	—	55	59	54	50
chometz	—	—	—	—	61	59	56	56
Yom Kippur	—	—	—	—	56	50	51	63
Seder	81	88	92	87	70	89	85	87
service attendance	28	29	46	38	24	17	33	40
synagogue member	53	49	60	47	32	35	43	35
Jewish org. member	39	48	57	54	27	21	30	29
Jewish giving	28	31	52	52	21	32	42	44
non-sect. org. member	42	46	54	72	18	21	33	44
non-sect. giving ($25+/$50+)	31	48	66	72	15	19	33	44
Jewish friends	75	75	72	60	55	53	51	46
intermarried	3	2	3	4	13	13	13	12
weighted N=	296	433	480	314	80	157	402	293

Sources: 1965 and 1975 Boston Jewish Community Surveys.
See *Table 3(1)*, page 56, for explanation of Jewish identification items.

Note:
a Adjusted via Multiple Classification Analysis.

ritual observance. In 1965, for example, those without a high-school diploma were more than twice as likely to observe kashrut as those with post-graduate degrees (44 per cent versus 19 per cent). Similarly, the rate of Sabbath candle lighting declined precipitously from 84 per cent to 46 per cent. In 1975 the better educated were also generally less likely to have a mezzuzah on their doorposts, to observe the dietary rules of Passover, or to fast on Yom Kippur.[8]

While education diminished ritual observance, it had the opposite effect on Jewish institutional affiliation, but only to a limited degree and in the case of synagogue membership only up to a point. To varying extents, synagogue and organizational membership and Jewish philanthropic giving generally increased as we move from the least educated, to those with a high-school diploma, to those with some college experience. However, the most highly educated, those with a post-graduate degree, had slightly lower rates of synagogue affiliation than those with just a BA or some college attendance.

These results may be interpreted as reflecting the twin components of education. On the one hand, education confers status, facilitating one's entry into the middle class. And as we have seen (Chapter 3), joining Jewish institutions is promoted by affiliative proclivities in general. But since the better educated initially possess, or by virtue of their education come to obtain, certain values and social networks which undermine religiosity, they have fewer of the purely religious motivations either to practice rituals or to join religious institutions. Since religious motivations are crucial to performing traditional practices, the latter erode most clearly with advancing education. Since both religious motivations and the desire to affiliate with middle-class institutions promote participation in Jewish organizational life, such participation climbs only slowly with rises in education and stops at a certain point. After the BA, additional education may have relatively less of an impact upon bringing one into middle-class life as compared with its effect on (or reflection of) acquiring those cosmopolitan values and social networks which depress religious motivation.[9]

Occupations: professionalism and self-employment

As a concomittant to advancing generation and educational attainment, American Jews underwent rapid changes in the ways in which they earned their livelihoods. The third and fourth generations entered graduate and professional schools in substantial numbers to emerge as teachers, doctors, lawyers, engineers, accountants, academics, and social workers. In doing so, they took up occupations which unmistakably signified their successful integration into modernity.

More to the point, for the analysis of Jewish identity, professions are potential communities; and, as such, they might serve as surrogates and replacements for religious communities (Goode, 1957; Wilensky and Ladinsky, 1967; Wolf, 1970). Their community-like qualities are several. Professions often demand a high degree of specialized skills which can be obtained only through a lengthy period of formal training. Correlatively, they also may demand a lifelong commitment. In fact, relatively few who enter a particular profession abandon their careers for other occupations.

Other community-like qualities of many professions include their tendency to develop their own rules of conduct often embodied in formal codes of professional ethics. Moreover, professionals usually seek autonomy; they try to insulate their practitioners from public scrutiny and to control recruitment, training, advancement, and compensation. Many professions take up considerable time, much of it in frequent professional and social interaction with colleagues. Formal associations, journals, and newsletters further provide the associative basis for the communities that readily grow up around professional occupations.

In addition, members of certain professions speak to each other in a distinctive language replete with arcane terms and jargon. They often see themselves as separate from, if not superior to, the larger society. They may share common political and economic interests, social values, experiences, and commitments to one another. As might be expected, the influence of the professional community sometimes spills over to spheres of life outside the workplace. Members of some professions are known for distinctive cultural tastes, leisure pursuits, political views, styles of dress, consumer preferences, and family life.

As communities, as sources of prestige and self-esteem, some professions could conceivably rival ethnic and religious communities in many ways. The public service orientation of many professions makes them logical candidates for fulfilling their members' needs for meaning and purpose in life, a function often performed by religion. Professionals often feel that they contribute to the creation, development, or sustenance of justice, beauty, truth, knowledge, health, comfort, and the public's well-being. Many feel involved in a noble, spiritually uplifting, and ultimately significant task with intrinsic rewards complementing the benefits of high income and social prestige that often accompany professional status.

In the course of arguing for ethnic persistence, Nathan Glazer and Daniel Moynihan proposed that ethnicity may take over "some of the task in self-definition by others that occupational identities have generally played" (Glazer and Moynihan, 1970 : xxxiv). If so, then the reverse may also be true. Members of prestigious, fulfilling, and economically rewarding professions may shift their sense of personal identity and of social location from their religious or ethnic group to their profession.

Were all professions to conform to the above idealized description, they would indeed stand a good chance of virtually supplanting religion or ethnicity. However, the research literature reports considerable variation among both professions and professionals in precisely those characteristics which most militate against religious or ethnic attachment (Becker and Carper, 1956; Gerstl, 1961).

For example, professionals who work in a bureaucratic setting have been contrasted with those who work either free-lance or in a firm with professional colleagues. Of all settings, the bureaucratic one is least autonomous, permits less self-regulation, and is less insulated; hence it most inhibits the feeling of belonging to a bounded professional community.

Not only work setting, but professions themselves vary. Not all are equally prestigious, not all depend upon arcane knowledge and skills, not all make significant contributions to the larger public good, and not all make severe value and time demands beyond the workplace. Professions and professionals also vary in the extent to which local or cosmopolitan networks influence advancement, remuneration, reputation, and social prestige. (Presumably, locally oriented professions might promote religious involvement; cosmopolitan professions might inhibit religious participation.) Furthermore, individual professions differ in the commitment they engender, and in how much involvement with professional colleagues they create.

Aside from the varying abilities of different professions to serve as bases for communities, there are other reasons to question the expectation that professional status should supplant religious and ethnic identities. All professions qualify their incumbents for middle-class membership. In so far as the middle class over-participates in organized religion, professionals may likewise be expected to join churches or synagogues, to participate in their auxiliary groups, and to attend religious services more than non-professionals.

The fact is that the modern Jewish community has learned not merely to cope with, but even successfully to utilize professional and occupational commitments; and this is not a new phenomenon. In the pre-modern *kehillah*, Jews established voluntary societies built around occupational identities; these societies attended to such diverse functions as text study, life-cycle celebrations, and organized philanthropy (Katz, 1971). More recently, the major Jewish philanthropic drives in the United States have been organized around particular trades, professions, and industries. The campaigns depend heavily upon reputational networks and commercial ties to turn out philanthropic givers at fund-raising dinners and to inform solicitors of the financial means and gift-giving potential of prospective donors. In this way, the Jewish community manipulates strong occupational and professional identities.

In line with this last argument, the most recent research on church participation among major American religious groups reports that those with high-prestige occupations and professional status actually over-participate in organized religious life (Goode, 1966; Alston, 1971; Mueller and Johnson, 1975). However, these results are somewhat inconsistent and in all cases they are weak to moderate in magnitude.

If Jews behave as do American Christians, then Jewish professionals and such established members of the middle class as self-employed business-people should over-participate in the organized community. However, no major study has examined whether professionals observe religious rituals or affiliate institutionally more or less frequently than do others.

To address these unresolved issues, the analysis below examines the ritual and affiliative behavior of four major occupational categories: self-employed and salaried professionals, business-people, and salaried employees. Since individual professions vary considerably in the extent to which they conform to the idealized description offered earlier, the analysis proceeds beyond a consideration of professions generally to assess the effects of particular professions upon several dimensions of Jewish identification.

Table 4(3) presents the occupational distributions of the 1965 and 1975 Boston samples by age.

Heads of households were classified in five categories: self-employed and salaried professionals, self-employed business-people, salaried employees of all sorts (people who are working but are neither professional nor self-employed), and a residual category consisting of retirees, students, homemakers, and the inevitable "no answers."[10]

While almost a quarter (23 per cent) of the 1965 heads of household were self-employed outside the professions ("business-people" in the

Table 4(3)   Occupation by age

| age: | 1965 | | | | | | |
	21–24	*25–34*	*35–44*	*45–54*	*55–64*	*65+*	*all*
occupation							
ret./n.a.[a]	32	4	6	7	11	63	18
salaried worker	34	28	43	43	36	13	34
business-people	1	10	28	27	39	14	23
sal. professional	33	51	17	15	7	4	19
self-emp. prof'l	0	7	6	8	6	6	6
	100%	100%	100%	100%	100%	100%	100%

| age: | 1975 | | | | | | |
	18–24	*25–34*	*35–44*	*45–54*	*55–64*	*65+*	*all*
occupation							
ret./n.a.	30	8	9	2	19	67	22
salaried worker	41	27	31	33	33	18	30
business-people	2	11	20	29	24	7	14
sal. professional	20	45	23	26	10	5	25
self-emp. prof'l	8	9	17	11	15	3	10
	100%	100%	100%	100%	100%	100%	100%

Sources: 1965 and 1975 Boston Jewish Community Surveys.

Note:

a   ret./n.a. = retirees and "no answers."

table) only one in seven (14 per cent) were so employed in 1975. Simultaneously, the ten-year interval saw a dramatic increase in professionals generally and from 6 per cent to 10 per cent for the self-employed variety. Consistent with the changes in the totals over the ten-year period, in both surveys more young people were professionals than were older people.[11]

These trends in Jews' occupational distribution are well-known. Less understood are how they might be affecting Jewish identification. *Table 4(4)* sheds some light on this issue.

The table reports several Jewish identification measures for the five occupational categories, for both surveys, adjusted for age, generation, family life cycle, and education via Multiple Classification Analysis.

We find that the professionals' ritual observance and service attendance scores generally *exceeded* those of analogous non-professionals (that is,

Table 4(4)   Selected measures of Jewish identification and social participation by occupation, after adjusting for age, generation, family life cycle, and education[a]

| | 1965 | | | | | 1975 | | | | |
| | ret./ n.a. | sal. | bus. | sal. prof. | self-emp. prof. | ret./ n.a. | sal. | bus. | sal. prof. | self-emp. prof. |
occupation:										
kosher	31	25	27	31	28	16	11	19	23	30
Sabbath candles	70	58	62	59	73	35	34	46	49	57
mezzuzah	—	—	—	—	—	50	51	53	62	57
chometz	—	—	—	—	—	51	56	55	64	64
Yom Kippur	—	—	—	—	—	38	54	51	71	63
Seder	90	88	91	84	89	85	85	80	90	79
service attendance	42	27	45	38	44	31	28	32	35	41
synagogue member	64	46	62	43	57	34	35	48	34	54
Jewish org. member	53	44	55	43	61	28	29	31	24	30
Jewish giving	32	43	54	40	42	27	37	47	37	53
non-sect. org. member	54	48	55	51	44	28	26	36	39	47
non-sect. giving	39	56	56	56	52	22	33	37	37	45
Jewish friends	73	69	73	69	79	45	53	59	45	49
intermarried	5	3	4	1	3	19	20	9	8	13
weighted N=	288	527	354	301	98	207	279	127	230	90

Sources: 1965 and 1975 Boston Jewish Community Surveys.
See *Table 3(1)*, page 56, for explanation of Jewish identification items.

Note: ret./n.a. = retirees and "no answers."
sal. = salaried workers.
bus. = business-people (self-employed).
sal. prof. = salaried professionals.
self-emp. prof. = self-employed professionals.
a Adjusted via Multiple Classification Analysis.

comparing within either the salaried or the non-salaried groups). Sabbath candle lighting in 1975 is just one example; here, salaried professionals exceed their non-professional counterparts by 15 percentage points (48 per cent versus 34 per cent); while among the self-employed, professionals exceed non-professionals by 11 percentage points (57 per cent versus 46 per cent). Similar though generally smaller differences obtain in almost every other ritual practice.

In the institutional arena, differences between professionals and non-professionals are both smaller than they are in the ritual area and, more important, they are often contradictory. In other words, professional status as a general category does not seem either to inhibit or promote affiliation with voluntary institutions in the Jewish community. Similarly, no consistent patterns can be discerned with respect to friendship or marriage.

While the influence of professional status *per se* is confined to a positive effect in the ritual area, that of self-employment is limited almost entirely to organizational affiliation. In almost all instances, the self-employed reported slightly more institutional affiliation than did their salaried peers. Synagogue membership in 1975 provides an excellent illustration of this effect. The self-employed professional was 20 percentage points more likely to belong to a synagogue than the salaried professional (54 per cent versus 34 per cent).

Taken in their entirety, these results refute the notion that professionalism in general competes with and undermines religious identification. As a whole, professionals are slightly *more* ritually observant. Curiously, though, in the institutional area where one would expect professional status to have its most pronounced effect, no consistency was found. These findings suggest that while professional occupations may offer collegial communities which compete with the ethnic or religious community, they apparently also offer the social status which promotes institutional affiliation. Clearly, professional status does not incontrovertibly and necessarily inhibit participation in the organized religious community, and it may even promote private ritual practice.

The small but consistent positive impact of self-employment upon affiliation suggests that slightly declining entrepreneurship rather than greatly increasing professionalism poses a greater challenge to future Jewish affiliation rates. Self-employment provides one with flexible time, discretionary income, and sometimes, a stake in one's reputation in a localistic social network upon whom entrepreneurs, professional or not, often depend for their livelihood.

One other reason why professions have little impact on Jewish identification is that, as noted earlier, many of them substantially differ from the idealized model offered at the outset of this section. Some professional occupations simply lack the potential either to influence values significantly outside the workplace or to offer a surrogate community. The training and work experiences of their incumbents may fail to separate them physically or psychically from the larger public. Alternatively, they may offer little in the way of social prestige, sense of fulfillment, income, or other rewards which would command extraordinary devotion and commitment on the part of their practitioners.

The professions which do impinge upon their members' values, norms, friends, and affiliations outside the workplace may influence Jewish identification in either of two directions. Some may create collegial communities which serve to separate the individual from religious or ethnic life in any of several ways noted earlier. Alternatively, others may actually further integrate their practitioners – particularly self-employed professionals – into an organized community which values professionals' participation and rewards it with social esteem, professional contacts, enhanced reputation, or simply a larger pool of prospective clients.

Among Jewish communal activists, attorneys are reputed to over-participate in voluntary organizations. Lawyers active in the Jewish community report that the work of running formal bureaucracies, sitting on committees, reviewing budgets, and holding staff accountable appeals to their interests, talents, and sense of civic duty. At the other extreme, physicians and academics have acquired reputations for under-participating in Jewish communal life. Physicians comprise a distinct subcommunity founded on the basis of the many professional characteristics noted earlier: extensive and intensive training, severe demands on time and energy, a sense of social superiority, and, not least, a sense of contributing to the larger good by way of their profession thereby fulfilling their altruistic needs. Professors, who share many of the structural characteristics of physicians, are most likely to maintain those universalist, cosmopolitan, and upper-brow social attitudes which look askance at religious or ethnic involvement, or, for that matter, at any engagement in a middle-class community dominated by businessmen's ethos.

The data on specific professions presented in *Table 4(5)* address the question of whether certain specific professions influence various dimensions of Jewish identification. (Since the number of respondents in these and other specific professions is necessarily small, the data should be seen as merely suggestive.)

One professional group emerges as somewhat more ritually observant than the rest (see top six rows). These are the attorneys who score at or above average on most ritual observance measures. At the same time, both varieties of physicians – salaried or self-employed – are generally less observant than the other professions. Accountants, teachers, professors, and engineers report moderate levels of ritual observance, or, more precisely, scores which are alternatively above, below, or near the means for the six rituals.

The reasons for these variations are not immediately obvious but some speculation is in order. Perhaps most striking are the divergent influences of the academic and medical worlds. Professors attain average to

Table 4(5) Selected measures of Jewish identification by selected professions, after adjusting for age, generation, family life cycle, and education[a]

profession:	prof.	sal. MD	self-emp. MD	acct	school-teacher	sal. atty	self-emp. atty	engineer
kosher	18	6	8	18	24	22	21	15
Sabbath candles	54	20	22	59	55	43	48	40
mezzuzah	56	54	56	69	53	32	68	78
chometz	75	33	42	64	55	71	64	79
Yom Kippur	73	34	44	63	69	77	80	80
Seder	99	76	80	84	87	93	89	83
service attendance	39	38	41	27	46	24	70	63
synagogue member	25	6	39	40	48	31	47	56
Jewish org. member	15	12	24	18	45	18	45	25
Jewish giving	33	16	73	38	57	50	64	44
non-sect. org. member	47	22	60	29	54	36	66	31
non-sect. giving	37	26	60	43	58	19	59	42
Jewish friends	54	49	77	46	56	51	60	39
weighted N=	43	30	18	21	75	16	20	37

Source: Boston 1975 Jewish Community Survey.
See *Table 3(1)*, page 56, for explanation of Jewish identification items.

Note:
Sal. MD = salaried physician or dentist.
self-emp. MD = self-employed physician or dentist.
acct = accountant, mostly self-employed.
sal. atty = salaried attorney.
self-emp. attorney = self-employed attorney.
engineer, mostly salaried.
a Adjusted via Multiple Classification Analysis.

high levels of ritual observance, while physicians are the least ritually observant. Perhaps the highly demanding medical world consumes so much psychic energy that physicians are less able to attend to areas of life – such as religious observance – outside their professional interest. Professors, on the other hand, have a reputation for under-involvement in Jewish life. But this reputation may derive more from their failure actively to participate in institutional affairs (see discussion immediately below) rather than extraordinary under-performance of traditional rituals.

In the institutional domain, differences among professions are both more unambiguous and readily interpretable. Two professional groups stand out as the most active in synagogues, Jewish organizations, and philanthropic campaigns: self-employed attorneys and school teachers. Simultaneously, professors and salaried physicians are especially prone to under-affiliate, while other professions' affiliation scores are near or slightly below the mean.

Here we again observe the influence of self-employment upon institutional involvement. The large and fairly consistent differences between salaried and self-employed members of the same profession (be it medicine or law) suggest that the organized Jewish community is especially appealing to entrepreneurs.

The under-participation of professors and salaried physicians comes as no surprise. Both conventional wisdom and the professions-as-surrogate-communities argument presented earlier would lead one to anticipate these findings. Members of these professions see themselves as set apart from the larger middle-class world of religious, voluntary institutions and have little material or social incentive for bridging the social and psychological gap that divides them from the rest of middle-class society.

In conclusion, inspection of Jewish identification scores by specific professions reveals influences of professional status which were not observable in the aggregate. In particular, some professions serve to integrate their members into Jewish institutional life. Their members' values, interests, and cultural styles are compatible with religious affiliation. Other professions, in effect, pull or keep their members out of synagogues, Jewish organizations, and philanthropic campaigns. The organized community probably offers them few material or social rewards for participating; its business-oriented ambience conflicts with certain professional subcultures; and, undoubtedly, certain professions are, in fact, able to serve as surrogate communities in place of the religious or ethnic group.

Income

For several reasons we would expect income to influence various dimensions of Jewish identification. Most fundamentally, higher income reduces the relative costs of participating in synagogues, Jewish organizations, and philanthropic campaigns. Richer people simply have more discretionary income and are more able to bear the expense of institutional life.

But income has implications other than material ones. Differences in income relate to differences in class and cultural style. Both voluntary associational life in general, and religious institutional life in particular, are associated with the middle- and upper-class cultures in American society. Accordingly, several studies report increases in church membership associated with increasing income; one study documents a direct relationship between income and church contributions, but, simultaneously, an inverse relationship between income and the proportion of income people donate to church-related causes (Hodge and Carroll, 1978). On the other hand, other research reports more muddied relationships between income and church attendance. Gallup polls show highly inconsistent patterns of rises and falls in church attendance associated with changes in income among American Protestants and Catholics (Alston, 1971). Of three socio-economic status measures, Mueller and Johnson found income to have the weakest relationship with church participation (1975). Not much research has explored income's relationship with personal religiosity.[12]

For reference purposes, *Table 4(6)* reports the distribution of income by age for both the 1965 and 1975 Boston studies. Consistent with the

Table 4(6) Income by age

	1965						
age:	*21–24*	*25–34*	*35–44*	*45–54*	*55–64*	*65+*	*all*
income							
low (under $6000)	39	26	12	15	19	45	24
medium ($6000–$15,000)	30	57	46	42	31	18	38
high (over $15,000)	0	14	31	29	24	9	21
n.a.	31	3	10	14	26	27	17
	100%	100%	100%	100%	100%	100%	100%
	1975						
age:	*18–24*	*25–34*	*35–44*	*45–54*	*55–64*	*65+*	*all*
income							
low (under $15,000)	66	41	13	18	33	47	39
medium ($15,000–$30,000)	11	34	31	24	19	15	23
high (over $30,000)	5	16	32	38	17	2	17
n.a.	18	9	25	20	32	36	21
	100%	100%	100%	100%	100%	100%	100%

Sources: 1965 and 1975 Boston Jewish Community Surveys.

widely documented relationship between age and income, the income of the Boston respondents rises and then falls as we proceed from young to middle-aged to elderly families.

Table 4(7) permits examination of the influence of income upon various dimensions of Jewish identification, net of controls for age, generation, family life cycle, education, and occupation. These findings indicate that income has varying influences upon different aspects of Jewish identification.

Wealthier Jews were less likely to keep kosher (see the top row of the table for either survey) and somewhat less likely to light Sabbath candles or keep some of Passover's dietary rules ("chometz"). On the other hand, as we read across the rows we find rises in income associated with slight increases in displaying a mezzuzah and in Seder participation,

Table 4(7)   Selected measures of Jewish identification and social participation by income, after adjusting for age, generation, family life cycle, education, and occupation[a]

income:	1965			1975		
	low	medium	high	low	medium	high
kosher	38	23	21	24	18	10
Sabbath candles	66	63	53	43	47	37
mezzuzah	—	—	—	53	56	60
chometz	—	—	—	61	57	49
Yom Kippur	—	—	—	57	58	58
Seder	89	86	90	85	83	88
service attendance	33	38	37	35	28	33
synagogue member	51	47	68	39	34	43
Jewish org. member	46	46	55	30	28	23
Jewish giving	27	47	64	32	44	67
non-sect. org. member	46	55	58	28	33	50
non-sect. giving	48	61	65	20	47	60
Jewish friends	67	68	79	49	49	52
intermarried	1	2	7	6	23	15
weighted N=	381	600	328	368	213	154

Sources: 1965 and 1975 Boston Jewish Community Surveys.
See *Table 3(1)*, page 56, for explanation of Jewish identification items.

Note:
low = under $6000 (1965); under $15,000 (1975).
medium = $6000–$15,000 (1965); $15,000–$30,000 (1975).
high = over $15,000 (1965); over $30,000 (1975).
a Adjusted via Multiple Classification Analysis.

while we find nearly perfect stability in Yom Kippur fasting and service attendance over the three income groups in 1975.

The most one can infer from these contradictory tendencies is that income – net of education, occupation, age, family cycle and generation – erodes the least frequently practiced and presumably most traditional ritual practices (kashrut and Sabbath candles) to a small but noticeable extent. Other forms of religious practice, more frequently observed, are either enhanced or unaffected by integration into middle-class or upper middle-class society as signified by higher incomes.

In the institutional sphere, the relationships with income are more clear-cut and readily interpretable. With the exception of one measure in one survey (Jewish organizational belonging, 1975) all measures of institutional affiliation reached their zeniths among the highest income families. For most types of participation middle-income households more often affiliated with Jewish institutions than did their lower-income counterparts.

Income's effects on Jewish philanthropic giving were more pronounced than they were for synagogue or organizational membership. Since philanthropic giving is more closely related to economic means than is either synagogue or organizational membership, the stronger relationship of contributions with income is perfectly understandable. As might be expected, rates of non-sectarian voluntary activity (organizational membership and philanthropy) also increased with income.

In both surveys, the highest income group was the one most deeply embedded in a network of Jewish friends, although the differences with the two lower income groups were rather small. The relationships of income with intermarriage were inconsistent, and, as a result, are difficult to interpret substantively.

Income, then, influences Jewish identification in ways which parallel earlier findings for the two other forms of status attainment. Less dramatically and consistently than education, income diminishes some forms of private religious observance; at the same time it appears to exert a small effect in the direction of integrating people into an American Jewish norm which demands a modicum of religious observance. In other words, wealthier Jews may be less likely to practice the least popular rituals, but they are also somewhat more likely to practice the most widespread observances. Increasing income then, advances Jews toward a vast middle ground of religious practice, although there are still considerable variations among the most affluent Jews.

Income, like all other forms of social status, generally elevates all forms of institutional affiliation. Higher income, like self-employed status and education, increases rates of synagogue and Jewish organizational membership as well as philanthropic activity.

Summary and conclusions

Wending our way through the relationships between education, occupation, and income on the one hand, and several dimensions of Jewish identification on the other, we can discern a small number of fundamental themes.

Of the three aspects of social status, education has the most substantial and consistent effect upon ritual practice. Better-educated respondents were less likely to observe religious practices. The reasons for this effect can be ascribed, with caution, to the cosmopolitanizing influence (or significance) of education on (or for) both values and social networks. With one small qualification, we may say that income – as opposed to education – has little or no net impact upon ritual practice. The qualification consists of a slight tendency for upper-income respondents to adopt a modicum of religious practice, one which de-emphasizes the least widely practiced rituals and entails more frequent observance of the most widely practiced rituals.

The three aspects of social status have a fairly consistent impact upon participation in Jewish institutional life. Although higher-status individuals are generally more likely to join synagogues and Jewish organizations and to contribute to Jewish charities, each social status dimension has a distinctive relationship with each measure of Jewish affiliation. Thus, for example, only up to a point does education increase synagogue belonging. After the BA, synagogue affiliation slightly declines, probably because those with a post-graduate degree are somewhat less likely to participate in the localistic, middle-class oriented culture which emphasizes participation in conventional religious and ethnic institutions. The middle-class character of such institutions is further exemplified by the consistent and unambiguous positive effects of income and of self-employed status upon institutional affiliation. Finally, while professions broadly conceived have little impact upon affiliation, members of certain professional occupations either under- or over-participate in Jewish institutional life.

Almost all of the results in this chapter are small ones. Yet the patterns of consistency observed within the two major domains of Jewish identification – ritual practice and institutional affiliation – support the conclusion that social status, and by extension, Jews' considerable social mobility, has had a noticeable influence upon the ways in which Jews express their religious and ethnic identification.

In summing up the effects of social mobility upon Jewish identification, we note two contradictory trends: (1) upward mobility generally erodes traditional ritual practice, even as (2) it promotes institutional affiliation. Interestingly, as we saw in the last chapter, these trends can be said to characterize generational mobility as well – later generations are less ritually active, but more (or at least, not too much less) institutionally affiliated. Whether similar trends also flow from changes in Jewish migration and residence patterns will be examined in the next chapter.

5   Mobility and community[1]

From traditional stability to modern mobility

In the late eighteenth and nineteenth centuries, the opening of new economic and residential opportunities caused by the European Emancipation stimulated a dramatic surge in Jewish residential mobility. In particular, Jews moved from traditional, historic areas of residence and continued to experience high residential mobility within the new cities and countries in which they settled.

The sheer number of instances in which Jews of different modernizing societies followed similar patterns of mobility testifies to the distinctive ability of Jewish modernization to induce migration. Throughout eighteenth- and nineteenth-century Europe, Jews left the rural towns and villages where they and their ancestors had long resided and headed for major metropolitan centers. They left Alsace-Lorraine for Paris; they left the German and Polish countryside for Berlin and other large and growing German cities; they came from Bohemia, Galicia, and other parts of Austria-Hungry to swell the Jewish communities of Vienna and Budapest; and within Poland, Russia, and Eastern Europe, nineteenth-century Jews greatly enlarged the Jewish communities of Warsaw, Odessa, St Petersburg, and numerous other major urban centers.

Failing to find economic security in their local regional cities, Russian, Polish, and other East European Jews repeated on a large scale the migration patterns of their West European counterparts in one of Jewish history's largest and swiftest migrations ever. Within forty years (1881–1921), close to two million Jews migrated to the United States where, like their European Jewish counterparts, they settled in major metropolitan centers (Diamond, 1977; Halevy, 1978).

Once settled, the immigrants to America and their descendants began classic processes of concentration, migration, reconcentration, and, eventually, dispersal. The history of Jews of Greater New York illustrates these patterns. (It also represents the actual experiences of most American Jewish families in that the New York area has been home, at one time or another, to most American Jews throughout the last century.)

When turn-of-the-century Jewish immigrants to New York first arrived, they crowded the poor neighborhoods of the Lower East Side (in Manhattan) and Brooklyn's Brownsville section. Their children (the second generation), in turn, acquired the means to rent the thousands of apartments built for them (many by Jewish builders) in new middle-class areas of Brooklyn (Flatbush) and the Bronx (Grand Concourse, Pelham Parkway) (Moore, 1981a). After the Second World War, young third-generation Jewish families joined in middle-class America's move to the suburbs as they bought homes in Nassau County (Long Island), West-chester, Southeastern Connecticut, and Northern New Jersey. In the last two and three decades, large numbers of third- and fourth-generation Jews have left the New York area and the Northeast metropolitan region entirely, settling in the exurbs and the middle-size cities of the nation's Sunbelt (Newman and Halvorson, 1979; Goldstein, 1982). Each of these moves – from immigrant enclave, to middle-class neighborhood, to suburb, and, finally, to the exurbs or Sunbelt – further dispersed the Jewish population.[2]

This point can be graphically illustrated. Immigrant Brownsville in the early twentieth century had a Jewish population density which, at times, exceeded 80 per cent. Neighborhoods of second settlement, like Flatbush in the 1920s and 1930s, were only one-half to two-thirds Jewish. Most post-war suburbs where Jews settled in large numbers were no more than one-half Jewish, and often quite less. The areas of most recent Jewish settlement – such as Phoenix, Denver, or Suffolk County, New York – are even less densely Jewish. If the European Emancipation stimulated the move from traditional semi-rural community to modern urban enclave, the ongoing experience of American modernity has meant frequent migrations from well-established, more densely settled Jewish neighborhoods to initially younger, less institutionalized communities with (and, again, initially) smaller numbers and concentrations of Jewish inhabitants.

For this reason and others, rabbis and other communal leaders have been concerned about Jewish mobility, fearing several adverse consequences. These include the potential for disaffiliation from the organized community by the migrants, for weakened institutions situated in areas undergoing abandonment by out-migrants, and for the huge costs entailed in erecting institutions in new areas of settlement. That survivalists' fears of lower affiliation rates by recent movers has some validity is easily demonstrated by the 1975 Boston Jewish Community Survey data. *Table 5(1)* reports that affiliation rises with residential stability. Most graphically, those who have moved within the last 4 years were about one-third as likely to belong to a synagogue as were residential veterans who had lived at least 18 years in their respective communities. Only 21 per cent of those living in their town or neighborhood 4 years or less were synagogue members, as compared with 37 per cent of those resident 5–8 years, 51 per cent of those with 9–17 years of continuous residence, and fully 59 per cent of those with 18 or more years in their communities. The table reports parallel findings for Jewish philanthropic giving. Only 20 per cent of the newcomers (0–4 years of residence) reported making substantial contributions ($50 or more) to Jewish charities as opposed to at least half of those with 9 or more years of stable residence.

Clearly, the residentially mobile are less communally affiliated than the residentially stable; the question is why. Three sorts of reasons can be advanced. First, there may be an element of *self-selection*. That is,

Table 5(1) Synagogue membership and Jewish philanthropic giving[a] by length of residence[b]

length of residence	synagogue membership	Jewish philanthropic giving	weighted N
0– 4 years	21	20	388
5– 8 years	37	46	119
9–17 years	51	59	176
18+ years	59	52	240

Source: 1975 Boston Jewish Community Survey.

Notes:

a Those who reported contributions of at least $50 *in toto* the previous year.

b Length of residence is determined by responses to the question: "How many years have you lived in (city/town/part of Boston)?"

those who move may also be the types of people who would have been less often affiliated in any event. Second, the very act of moving may *disrupt* formal and informal ties to family, friends, local institutions and years may pass before they are reconstituted, if they ever are (see Jaret, 1978). Third, since Jewish movers often move to new areas of Jewish settlement, they may experience a *contextual impact* of their new residential locale. To appreciate more fully the three plausible links between mobility and affiliation – i.e., self-selection, disruption, and residential context – we need to situate these three processes in larger historical and theoretical contexts and to examine the pertinent data.

Self-selection

In the United States as elsewhere, movers are different from non-movers; in particular, the mobile are younger and tend to have smaller families (Sandefur and Scott, 1981). Among Jews, these characteristics are associated with lower levels of ritual practice and communal affiliation (see Chapters 3 and 6). Hence, in so far as Jewish movers are similar to other mobile Americans, they will tend to derive from the more assimilated segments of the Jewish population.

Aside from these demographic considerations, cultural factors also suggest that Jewish migrants should maintain lower levels of Jewish identification even prior to moving. By virtue of their commitment to Jewish communal life, Orthodox and other observant Jews often develop strong ties to local Jewish institutions. In addition, Orthodox religious doctrine demands that worshippers reside within walking distance of the synagogue. For these and other reasons, the religiously observant or ethnically identified might be more reluctant to relocate (especially to new Jewish communities) than those whose involvement with and commitment to fellow Jews is much less pronounced.

These generalizations, while meant to apply to contemporary American Jews, have historical precedents in the nineteenth century and earlier. As a rule, European Jewish migrants with weaker ties to traditional Jewish life and community were more willing to move to areas lacking in heavy concentrations of Jewish population or in established communal institutions. The mass migration to the United States, for example, led rabbis and other East European traditionalists to brand the destination of many of their contemporaries as a *"treyfe medinah"* ("unholy land"). Observers of the time contended that migrants were more secularized and assimilated than those who chose to stay behind (Howe, 1976).

Nineteenth-century French Jewry offers yet another example of self-selection influencing the decision to migrate. The Jews who left the traditional areas of settlement in Alsace-Lorraine for Paris were disproportionately drawn from the affluent merchant class (Hyman, forthcoming). More indigent Jews were probably less aware of emerging opportunities in new areas of settlement, or they were less capable of taking advantage of these opportunities, or they were simply more attached to their traditional communities.

American patterns of ongoing mobility and resettlement following the initial international migration has replicated many aspects of earlier European migratory behavior. Each new area of American Jewish settlement – second-generation neighborhood; third-generation suburb; third- and fourth-generation Sunbelt community – was probably first settled by Jews who were younger, more affluent, and generally more assimilated than those they left behind. *Table 5(2)* reporting the determinants of being a "newcomer," examines the extent to which recent movers in the 1975 Boston area shared these distinctive characteristics. (A "newcomer" or "recent mover" is defined as one who has lived in the same town or neighborhood four years or less.)

The table's first column reports bivariate relationships between several independent variables and newcomer status. The second column reports the effects of adjusting for all these predictor variables simultaneously.

We find that newcomers are indeed significantly younger; as a corollary, they are also much more likely than veteran residents to be single or to be without children. Very few of them are parents with children at home, older couples with no children, older singles, or widowed. We also find that recent movers are well educated (BA or post-graduate degrees) and earn lower incomes.[3]

Of all these variables, age is the sole powerful determinant of residential mobility (see column 2). Accordingly, those in early stages of the family life cycle, those with lower incomes, and those who are ritually non-observant are mobile largely because these types of people are young and it is youthfulness which promotes geographic mobility.

Since movers do differ from others in terms of age and other characteristics associated with communal affiliation, part of the reason newcomers are less affiliated than veterans may well derive from "self-selection," that is, factors antecedent to the decision to move. To the extent that age and the other predictors of moving fail to explain totally why movers less often affiliate than do the geographically stable, we could attribute a

Table 5(2) Newcomers[a] by age, family life cycle, education, income, and ritual observance (Multiple Classification Analysis)

	unadjusted[b]	adjusted[b]	weighted N
age			
18–24	77	63	181
25–34	75	66	244
35–44	16	25	114
45–54	9	22	120
55–64	16	24	110
65+	11	20	138
n.a.	26	21	16
eta/beta	0.63	0.43	
family life cycle			
single	79	53	257
young childless couple	70	45	72
child(ren) under 6	52	46	67
children home	8	26	137
older couple, no children home	14	39	166
widow, older single	13	35	118
divorced, separated	32	28	36
intermarried (all family stages)	55	51	67
n.a.	—	—	4
eta/beta	0.61	0.19	
education/income			
less than high-school grad.	12	31	50
high-school grad., under $15,000	35	46	65
high-school grad., $15,000 and over	3	16	36
college, under $15,000	68	53	163
college, $15,000–$30,000	41	42	99
college, $30,000 and over	36	41	49
post-BA, under $15,000	77	54	98
post-BA, $15,000–$30,000	54	42	78
post-BA, $30,000 and over	29	41	86
all other/n.a.	23	33	199
eta/beta	0.44	0.19	
ritual observance[c]			
0 none	55	47	119
1 low	50	41	419
2 medium	28	35	251
3 high	33	49	133
eta/beta	0.22	0.08	
R		0.68	
R^2		0.46	

Source: 1975 Boston Jewish Community Survey.

Cont. overleaf

---

good part of the remaining linkage between mobility and (non)affiliation to mobility's disruptive effects.

Disruption

The notion that moving disrupts or suspends links to the formal Jewish community − such as the synagogue or philanthropic campaigns − entails two interrelated propositions: (1) religious affiliation is primarily a "group phenomenon;" and (2) it is also a "localistic" one.

That religious participation reflects group ties and not merely commitment to tenets of a faith has long been readily apparent to both religious practitioners and observers. Rabbis, church fathers, classic sociological thinkers (Emile Durkheim being the most noted), and contemporary researchers have all recognized the social dimension to religious life and activity. One recent researcher provides a useful summary of this perspective:

> The religious group . . . is composed of people in interaction with one another. [It] is characterized by normative expectations . . . enforced by sanction, ranging all the way from resounding approval to rejection

from the group in disgrace. . . . [They] are both socialized into the children . . . and continually reinforced by the members of the group.

(White, 1968 : 25–6)

The recent work of sociologist of religion Wade Clark Roof has demonstrated the localist quality to religious participation in America (Roof, 1976). Those who maintain localistic rather than cosmopolitan orientations and who are involved in local formal associations and informal networks, are also more likely, Roof finds, to participate in the locally based religious community. Writing about Protestant residents of a North Carolina town, Roof concludes that localism is a key link between residential stability and church involvement. In other words, veteran residents are more active in the church in large measure because they are more localistic than newcomers.

Other previous research in these and related areas is also highly suggestive. Recent migrants generally need at least five years of stable residence to attain the higher social participation levels of veteran residents (Zimmer, 1955). With regard to religious participation in particular, a recent study of Protestant and Catholic church-going reported lower levels of service attendance during the first five years of residence in a new community (Wuthnow and Christiano, 1979).

The research on mobility and Jewish affiliation in particular is rather sparse. One recent study of Chicago-area Jews finds different effects for different denominations (Jaret, 1978). The analysis contends that Orthodox and Conservative Jews – presumably with greater commitment to Jewish communal life – retain high levels of involvement in spite of recent relocation. Other Jews – Reform and non-denominational – exhibited the anticipated adverse impact of residential mobility upon affiliation.

The extent to which mobility depresses affiliation even after taking into account self-selection (especially the youthfulness of newcomers) can be seen in *Table 5(3)*. The unadjusted columns (1 and 3) repeat *Table 5(1)* where we learned that fewer newcomers than veterans either belong to a synagogue or contribute significant amounts to Jewish philanthropy. The adjusted columns (2 and 4) report the impact of length of residence upon synagogue belonging and philanthropic giving after controlling for age, education, income, family life cycle, and ritual observance.

The results indicate that self-selection and disruption (or some other consequence of moving into a new neighborhood context) both play vital

Table 5(3) Synagogue membership and Jewish philanthropic giving[a] by length of residence, unadjusted and adjusted for age, education, income, family life cycle, and ritual observance (Multiple Classification Analysis)

length of residence	synagogue membership		Jewish giving		
	unadjusted	adjusted	unadjusted	adjusted	weighted N
0– 4 years	19	31	20	33	388
5– 8 years	37	38	46	44	119
9–17 years	51	38	58	46	176
18+ years	59	48	52	40	239

Source: 1975 Boston Jewish Community Survey.

Note:
a Percentage who reported giving at least $50, in the prior year, to Jewish philanthropic causes other than the synagogue.

roles in explaining the link between high mobility and low affiliation. Moreover, the importance of self-selection differs for the two measures of affiliation, for reasons which will be made apparent.

Length of residence continues to exert a noticeable influence upon synagogue membership even after controls are introduced. Controlling for age and the other antecedent variables, only 31 per cent of the newcomers (residents for 4 years or less) are synagogue members as opposed to 48 per cent of the most established veteran residents (18 years or more of continued residence). On the other hand, the adjusted column for philanthropic giving shows a very ambiguous pattern. It suggests that self-selection almost totally explains the initial relationship between mobility and giving, and that disruption is of little if any significance.

Putting things in their simplest terms, we have found thus far:

1 Both synagogue membership and philanthropic giving are less frequent among the residentially mobile than among their more stable counterparts.
2 Self-selection (that is, the association of moving with age and other factors which influence affiliation) is a significant explanation of the link between mobility and lower synagogue membership, and it is virtually the total explanation for the link between mobility and lower philanthropic activity.
3 Apparently, disruption – or some other consequences or *sequelae* of mobility – operates above and beyond self-selection to depress synagogue membership but it (or they) has little effect upon philanthropic

giving after the special character (youth, for example) of movers has been factored out.

These findings immediately raise the question of why one type of affiliation, synagogue membership, responds to the disruptive impact of moving while the other, philanthropy, does not. The most plausible explanation lies in the synagogue's localistic character (typifying American houses of worship generally) relative to that of philanthropy. Synagogues draw most of their congregants from local catchment areas. Like churches, synagogues are identified with the particular communities in which they are located; they provide services – such as religious training for youngsters, worship services, facilities for celebrating major life-cycle events – for which residence in the vicinity is desirable. For these reasons and others, the synagogue community is indeed almost always a highly local one.

Philanthropic giving, on the other hand, entails a much less pronounced localistic dimension. Many donors to major Jewish charities are solicited through their business by leading members of industry-wide or city-wide informal Jewish networks. Donors who move from one neighborhood or town to another within a metropolitan area will probably maintain their philanthropic contacts and visibility. As a result, mobile Jews seem no less likely than stable residents to contribute significantly to Jewish causes once we take into account their lower ritual observance, younger age, earlier family life cycle, higher education, and lower income.

In sum, we find evidence of mobility's disruptive impact only upon joining a synagogue, a highly localistic institution. Self-selection does not entirely explain why fewer newcomers join synagogues than do veteran residents, although it does largely encompass why the former are less philanthropically active than the latter.

Undoubtedly, some component of mobility's disruptive impact can be regarded as entailing the types of neighborhoods in which the mobile choose to reside. In other words, not only does residential mobility disrupt ties with some formal Jewish institutions (such as synagogues) and informal Jewish networks, it also frequently brings one into a setting where few such ties characterize one's neighbors.

Contextual effects

By their very nature, the neighborhoods or towns to which many geographically mobile Jews move differ from areas where Jewish residence is more established (for comparison, see Zimmer and Hawley, 1959). The former are distinctive in four major ways: (1) in their residents' aggregate characteristics – age, social class, family life cycle; (2) in the maturity of their Jewish institutions; (3) in the density of their Jewish populations; and (4) in their proximity to major Jewish communities and central institutions.

To elaborate, movers often move to locales with many other recent migrants. Within metropolitan regions these areas often include gentrifying center-city neighborhoods, or recent housing developments, or, in an earlier era, newly developed suburbs. On the national level, many recently booming Sunbelt communities have experienced a huge inflow of Jewish migrants. A recent study of the Denver Jewish population, for example, reports that about half of Denver's Jewish residents as of 1981 had come to that city in the last decade (Allied Jewish Federation of Denver, 1982.) Areas which contain many recent migrants are also apt to consist of people who are young, in early stages of family development, and ritually less observant, for these are the characteristics associated with moving. Thus, a person who moves to an area attractive to other movers is likely to have Jewish neighbors (in so far as there are Jewish neighbors) with characteristics associated with low levels of communal affiliation.

Aside from the aggregate characteristics of the Jewish population in new areas of Jewish settlement, these areas are also likely to be deficient in well-established communal institutions. Since a critical mass of settled Jewish residents is often required to establish a synagogue, Jewish schools, Jewish shopping facilities (particularly kosher butchers), community-wide organizations (such as charitable campaigns), new areas of Jewish settlement are often under-institutionalized on a *per capita* basis. (Conversely, it is worth noting that one sign of a declining Jewish neighborhood is the presence of an over-abundance of institutions relative to the number of Jews – usually elderly – who remain in the old neighborhood.)[4]

The third aspect of new areas of Jewish settlement which militates against communal affiliation entails their Jewish population size. By definition, new areas of Jewish settlement contain – at least initially – both small numbers and small proportions of Jews. While small Jewish communities could survive under medieval Christendom where wide social and political gulfs separated Jew from Gentile, the small community in an open society can often erect few barriers against assimilation. However, it should be noted that the limited amount of research on small-town American Jewry suggests countervailing sources of strength and weakness. The small size of these communities promotes a certain intimacy, solidarity,visibility, and coherence absent in larger communities. On the other hand, they can neither support many major institutions nor can they provide a large enough marriage market to preclude significant religious intermarriage (see, for example, Allied Jewish Federation of Denver, 1982).

Finally, new areas of Jewish settlement are often remote both from major institutions of Jewish life and the well-established networks of family and friends who help sustain Jewish identification. This remoteness may be seen either in metropolitan or in national terms. On the metropolitan level, neighborhoods or suburbs of new settlement are often quite distant from major areas of historic Jewish concentration, where large proportions of densely settled Jews can be found.[5] On a national level, Jews migrating to California or other Sunbelt destinations – particularly if they are young – often leave parents and grandparents behind in the older Northeastern metropolises along with mature synagogues, religious schools, Jewish community centers, and social service agencies. The very distance of family, friends, and formal institutions from migrants living in new areas of settlement precludes their having significant influence upon the Jewish identification of recent movers.

A detailed and thorough analysis of the contextual effects of area of settlement upon Jewish identification would aim at isolating the influence of each of the four factors noted immediately above. Undoubtedly, the character of the indigenous Jewish population in these areas, their small size and density, the relative immaturity of the organized community, and remoteness from centers of Jewish life should all influence individuals' levels of communal affiliation. Unfortunately, these factors are so inextricably intertwined – they often characterize the same neighborhoods and communities – that only a prodigious research effort with detailed historical and contemporary data on dozens of Jewish communities across the United States could even hope to tackle the task properly.[6]

Although the available data precluded such an effort, a more modest analysis was feasible. I categorized twenty Boston area localities by the proportion of newcomers (those who moved within the last four years). The twenty localities (each consisting of one or more contiguous towns or neighborhoods) were then divided into three groups: those with high, medium, and low residential turnover (or conversely, those with low, medium, and high residential stability). By comparing people of similar durations of residence residing in different types of neighborhoods, we can get some inkling of whether neighborhood context – or at least one crucial aspect of that context – influences communal affiliation.[7]

Table 5(4) reports synagogue membership rates by length of residence of individuals and residential turnover of their localities. The left panel reports unadjusted figures; the right presents membership rates adjusted for age, education, income, family life cycle, and ritual observance.

Holding recency of migration constant, we find few, if any, consistent differences in synagogue membership between the "medium" and "low" residential turnover areas. However, we do find that newcomers in "high" turnover localities are considerably less likely than other recent movers (i.e., those who chose "medium" or "low" turnover areas) to belong to a synagogue. Only 9 per cent of high turnover area movers had joined a synagogue as opposed to 27 per cent and 24 per cent of newcomers in more residentially stable areas.[8]

Clearly, then, some quality relating to residential turnover in a town or neighborhood has some influence (either before or after the move) on a mover's likelihood of joining a synagogue. The degree to which Jewish movers select their new neighborhoods on the basis of the availability of Jewish communal institutions is unknown. To illustrate, in a recent survey, nearly 40 per cent of New York area Jews reported that it was

Table 5(4) Synagogue membership by length of residence and neighborhood residential turnover[a], unadjusted and adjusted[b] for age, education, income, family life cycle, and ritual observance

neighborhood turnover:	unadjusted			adjusted			weighted N		
	high	med.	low	high	med.	low	high	med.	low
length of residence									
0– 4 years	9	27	24	26	37	36	166	222	21
5– 8 years	—	35	50	—	38	36	—	71	39
9–17 years	—	51	59	—	40	43	—	105	54
18+ years	—	63	60	—	52	47	—	132	89

Source: 1975 Boston Jewish Community Survey.

Notes:

a Turnover is measured by the proportion of area residents who have moved within the last four years. Areas – twenty in all – consist of individual Boston area towns and cities and collections of contiguous locales with small Jewish populations. "High" turnover areas include: Brighton, Somerville, West Roxbury, and Back Bay. "Low" turnover areas include: Newton, Marblehead, Swampscott, Winthrop, and Hyde Park. "Medium" turnover areas include the rest of metropolitan Boston.

b Adjusted through Multiple Classification Analysis.

"very important" for them to live "near a synagogue that appeals to you" and more than half said it was "very important" for them to have "a sizeable number of Jews in the neighborhood" (Ritterband and Cohen, 1982).

The Boston or New York data are insufficiently detailed to sort out the pre-moving from the post-moving influences of neighborhood context. Nevertheless, the data do indicate that, all other things being equal, newcomers with the same characteristics (age, family, etc.) but moving to different neighborhoods will have different propensities to join a synagogue because of the areas they choose. To some small, but noticeable extent, then, the neighborhood context affects Jewish communal affiliation above and beyond the individual characteristics of the people in those neighborhoods; and, since movers are more prone to choose neighborhoods with larger proportions of recent migrants, they are also prone to choose areas which are less likely to promote communal affiliation. Precisely why and how these neighborhoods exert their influence – whether their aggregate population characteristics, Jewish population density, organizational immaturity, or remoteness from centers of Jewish life are most important – remains beyond the limits of the available data to determine.

Concluding discussion

This chapter's analysis has demonstrated that high residential mobility – a distinctive Jewish behavioral response to modernity – is a crucial factor influencing communal affiliation. Movers are indeed less often affiliated than non-movers. In part this is so because movers are initially different from – primarily younger than – the residentially stable. Indeed, this process of self-selection is the principal reason why recent movers contribute less often to Jewish philanthropic causes. However, joining a synagogue is a much more localistic activity than participating in Jewish charitable drives. As a result, synagogue membership is adversely affected by residential mobility as well as by the antecedents of mobility (especially age and family life cycle).

In particular, the residentially mobile disrupt their ties to family, friends, and formal institutions; and they take five or more years to reestablish those ties in their new residential locales. Moreover, they are likely to move to those areas where residential mobility is high and where, as a consequence, established Jewish informal networks and mature communal institutions are relatively rare.

In sum, large-scale residential mobility, like other forms of demographic change brought about by Jews' encounter with modernity, is associated with a complex variety of consequences for Jewish identification in modern America. On the one hand, it betokens successful integration into the social mainstream, the acquisition of absolute freedom in selecting where to live and when to move. These were freedoms generally denied Jews in pre-modern times. Nevertheless, residential and other forms of mobility and change, typifying much of Jewish life in the modern era, also generally reduce selected forms of Jewish practice and affiliation. As significant, though, as are the consequences of generational change, social mobility, and residential mobility for Jewish identification, none of these are as unambiguous and profound as those associated with the Jewish family life cycle and with the last one to two decades of changes in American Jewish families.

6 Singlehood, childlessness, divorce, and intermarriage: the meaning of recent family trends for Jewish identification[1]

The dual nature of the Jewish family

Throughout history, Jewish families have been subject to two sorts of influences. The first consists of those which affect not only Jews, but indeed all members of society in which they live. Thus, in many ways, Jewish families resemble those of contemporaneous non-Jews in similar social circumstances. When families in the larger society change, so too do Jewish families change in parallel (though not identical) fashion. At the same time, though, Jewish families have also been subject to sets of influences largely distinctive to Jews. This is not to say that Jewish families in different societies have always varied from comparable non-Jewish families in precisely the same way; it is to say that we can observe both general and secular as well as particular and distinctive features in the Jewish family. To appreciate more fully how the contemporary American Jewish family has changed in line both with changes in the larger society and with a distinctive Jewish dynamic, we would do well briefly to review the historic antecedents to the American Jewish family.

Although studies on Jewish family history are both sparse and uneven, we do know that pre-modern Ashkenazic Jewish families differed from their Christian counterparts in many ways (Cohen and Hyman, 1983). Of the several distinguishing features of the pre-modern Jewish family, four are especially pertinent to this study of today's American Jewish family. First, Jews generally married at least as often as others such that rates of Jewish bachelorhood and spinsterhood were no higher, if not usually lower, than those of Christian contemporaries. Second, Jewish couples generally bore fewer children than others, probably owing to the disproportionate number of Jewish village-dwelling merchants in contrast with the large proportions of Christians who were rural farmers and peasants (Goldscheider, 1966, 1967). The possibly lower rates of Jewish infant mortality also may have diminished the Jewish birthrate. Third, traditional Jews were reputed to experience lower divorce and infidelity rates. (If true, then the insecurity of minority-group status, the intimacy and coherence of closer-knit Jewish communities, and a strong cultural inhibition against adultery are logical candidates for explaining these distinctive Jewish family traits.) Fourth and finally, formally sanctioned Jewish-Gentile intermarriage without prior conversion by one of the partners was rare, if not virtually non-existent, in the medieval world.

The modern period – roughly, the last two centuries – saw profound changes in each of these four areas, changes which would affect Western Jews and Gentiles in similar, but somewhat varying fashion. In this period, marriage as a formal institution became more widespread and articulated as the nuclear family took on tasks formerly handled by the wider community and extended family. (Edward Shorter (1975) has written of the rise of "bourgeois domesticity," with its barriers of privacy encapsulating a self-contained, nuclear family household removed from the age-sex peer groups which once penetrated the family.) Second, for the last two centuries, Western fertility has experienced a broad-based almost monotonic decline (Westoff, 1978). (A momentary rise in the decade after the Second World War constitutes the sole exception to this pattern; ever since, birthrates have resumed their nearly steady drop.) Third, in recent decades, divorce in Europe and America has risen, partially as a result of such factors as a decline in the efficacy of religious and cultural opprobrium of divorce and of expanding economic opportunities for women to be financially independent (Cherlin, 1981). Fourth, the entry of Jews into the social mainstream and the lowering of barriers to Jewish-Gentile social intimacy have helped bring about steady increases in Jewish-Gentile intermarriages throughout the West (Rosenthal, 1963; Sherrow, 1971; Goldstein, 1981).

Many of these long-term trends in the family have accelerated and taken on greater significance in the last decade or more. Since 1970, or thereabouts, the American family has undergone such dramatic changes as to spark a popular and scholarly debate about whether it is in fact disintegrating (see, for example, Bane, 1976; Cherlin, 1981; Hacker, 1982). While the validity of such a far-reaching conclusion is still at issue, none can dispute the significant recent changes charted by demographers and the US Census Bureau. Without doubt, Americans are marrying at a later age than in the past (Michael, Fuchs, and Scott, 1980). Those who do marry, especially those in their twenties, are divorcing more frequently than was the case just ten or fifteen years ago (Michael, 1978). In just ten years, between 1970 and 1980, the number of "people who are separated or divorced and live" alone rose by 122 per cent for men and 79 per cent for women (more divorced women than men continue to live with their children) (Hacker, 1982 : 37). As a corollary of those trends, the number of single-person households grew by 74 per cent, "which was more than six times that for the overall population" (Hacker, 1982 : 37; see also Kobrin, 1976a and b). The number of young adult households without children has also risen as a result of sharply declining birthrates (Kobrin, 1976a and b). Married couples are not only having fewer children, but they are bearing them at a later age (Westoff and Jones, 1979).

The historic connection between Jews' family patterns and those of their neighbors leads one to anticipate parallel trends among American Jews. Indeed, Jewish federations and family service agencies report many more young Jewish singles, divorced people, and single parents among their clients (Waxman, 1980, 1982). Jewish communal surveys in the last two decades indicate declining Jewish birthrates (Goldstein, 1981), a decline also observable in the 1970–71 National Jewish Population Study (DellaPergola, 1980). Similar evidence supports the incontrovertible observation that many more Jews are marrying non-Jews (Goldstein, 1981).

To the extent that Jewish families are indeed changing in the ways suggested above, we can readily anticipate profound consequences for Jewish identification (Goldscheider 1978, 1982). A considerable body of evidence testifies to the centrality of the Jewish family for the transmission and expression of Jewishness (for cross-religious comparisons, see Caplovitz and Sherrow, 1977). To illustrate, only when parents are themselves ritually observant does full-time Jewish education (i.e., yeshiva or day school) significantly promote high levels of observance (Cohen, 1974). Moreover, even though children's ritual practices largely repeat those of their parents (Cohen, 1974), spouses have even greater influence than do parents upon adult Jewish identification (Himmelfarb, 1977). In addition the presence of children at home elevates Christian and Jewish religious practice and institutional involvement (Nash and Berger, 1962; Nash, 1968; Goldscheider, 1973; Sklare and Greenblum, 1979). In light of these many connections between family and group life, recent increases in Jewish singlehood, childlessness, divorce, and inter-marriage, should all help erode Jewish identification, at least so long as conventional family life and Jewish identity are closely linked together. This chapter attempts to assess the scope and nature of these demo-graphic trends. Moreover, by examining changes both in the relation-ship between Jewish identification and the family life cycle and in the distribution of the types of Jewish family, it explores the extent to which recent family changes have in fact influenced Jewish identification.

Later marriage, more singlehood

Since roughly 1950, middle-class Americans have been marrying at a later age, contributing to rising numbers of singles in their twenties and thirties. *Table 6(1)*, which reports the percentage ever-married by major religious groups, confirms this widely noted growth in singles.[2]

During the 1960s, roughly three-quarters of Protestants and Cath-olics, 18–24 years old had married; in the 25–34 age group, the ever-married proportion reached 90 per cent or more. By the 1970s, however, the ever-married rates for both young adult age groups dropped considerably. Among 18–24-year-old Protestants and Catholics only half (as opposed to three-quarters in the 1960s) had married. For the 25–34 year olds the drop is less precipitous, falling to 87/88 per cent.

More important than confirming well-documented trends for the gen-eral population, these data allow us to examine Jewish marriage patterns in particular. Here we find parallel trends, with Jews marrying later than the two major Christian groups in both the 1960s and 1970s. While three-quarters of 18–24-year-old white Christians had been married in the 1960s, less than half of the comparable Jews had married. Similarly, in the 1970s, the ever-married rate among 18–24-year-old Jews is fully 20 percentage points beneath those of the Protestants and Catholics. Among 25–34 year olds, the ever-married deficit of Jews compared with other 25–34 year olds also grew considerably from the 1960s to the 1970s, from only 3–7 percentage points to a gap of at least 13 percentage points ten years later.[3]

The Western decline in fertility accompanying industrialization has been taken by demographers as a measure of integration into the modern world, as an adaptation to city living, and as a consequence of entry into

Table 6(1)   Percentage ever-married by religion, age, and time of survey

age:[a]	18–24	25–34	35–44	45–54	55–64	65+
1960s						
Protestants[b]	79	94	95	96	94	94
	(409)	(1253)	(1436)	(1326)	(985)	(1080)
Catholics	73	90	95	95	95	91
	(143)	(455)	(472)	(346)	(219)	(202)
Jews	46	87	97	96	95	97
	(13)	(46)	(69)	(69)	(40)	(30)
Jews (1965)[c]	37	87	94	90	85	91
	(86)[d]	(271)	(289)	(348)	(241)	(283)
1970s						
Protestants	51	87	96	97	95	95
	(1481)	(2475)	(1939)	(1980)	(1923)	(2349)
Catholics	48	88	96	95	95	93
	(777)	(1364)	(968)	(897)	(712)	(645)
Jews	29	74	91	94	99	91
	(45)	(113)	(81)	(83)	(72)	(82)
Jews (1975)[c]	12	60	97	95	87	86
	(160)	(247)	(132)	(125)	(117)	(139)

Sources: Pooling of National Opinion Research Center (NORC) General Social Surveys, other NORC National Surveys, and Michigan Survey Research Center (SRC) Electoral Surveys; whites only (except as otherwise noted).

Notes:

a Age of respondent; unit of analysis is the household, so that currently married respondents represent two adults. Entries therefore somewhat understate percentage of individuals who are ever-married.

b All respondents are white.

c Boston Jewish Community surveys.

d Aged 21–24.

the educated middle class. Similarly, today's postponement (if not outright eschewal) of marriage may also be seen as an adaptation to "modernity." Young singles have higher education and they live in certain parts of major metropolitan areas known for their cosmopolitan character. In so far as Jews are better educated, more professionalized, more urbanized, and more cosmopolitan than other Americans, they are also more likely to postpone or, perhaps, even to avoid marriage altogether. In this sense, recent Jewish marital trends may be seen as part of the larger phenomenon of Jewish entry into the modern world.

The delay or avoidance of marriage is but one of many factors which may lower Jewish birthrates, yet another dimension of Jewish family behavior with potentially significant consequences for ritual practice and communal affiliation.

The Jewish birth dearth

Table 6(2) charts the widely noted nation-wide decline in birthrates.[4] All major religious groups – Protestants, Catholics, and Jews – reported fewer children in the 1970s than they did in the 1960s. Moreover, since the table includes only those respondents who were married, and since fewer young adults in the 1970s were married than in the 1960s, it even understates fertility declines. Among Jews, the understatement is most pronounced since they, more than Christian Americans, experienced a sharp decline in the proportion ever-married.

At any age, and in both decades (1960s, 1970s), married Jews had fewer children than married Christians. And, just as nation-wide birthrates fell in the last decade, so too did those of the Jews. As an example, in the 1960s, married Jews aged 25–34 had averages of 2.1 and 1.5 children in the national and Boston data respectively. Ten years later, those figures had dropped to as little as 1.2 and 0.7, about half of what they were in the 1960s.

No one can accurately predict the total number of children today's couples will eventually bear, but, on the basis of past experience, it does seem safe to say that the completed Jewish birthrate for today's Jewish parents may remain well below the number needed for replacement. (Replacement requires an average of more than two children per married couple since some people never marry and some couples are unable to bear children, particularly those marrying late in life.) Barring a significant rise in national fertility, Jewish birthrates – if they follow historic patterns – should continue to reside in the region of NPG (Negative Population Growth).

The reasons for the low Jewish birthrate are both complicated and not totally clear. Several complementary explanations come to mind (see Goldscheider, 1966, 1967, 1973, 1978, 1982, 1983; DellaPergola, 1980). Most fundamentally, Jews are heavily urbanized and highly educated; and these are factors which usually depress birthrates. As a corollary of widespread urbanization and higher education, more Jewish women are not only employed, but are pursuing professional careers; these two employment patterns also slightly depress birthrates. While it is true that later marriage and fewer births are only loosely connected (most of those marrying later are still capable of having more than two children), later marriers do bear fewer children than early marriers. As we have seen, Jews are distinguished from others in that they tend to stay single longer.

Table 6(2) Number of children ever-born by age, religion, and time of survey (ever-married respondents only)

age:	18–24	25–34	35–44	45–54	55–64	65+
1960s						
Protestants	1.3	2.3	2.2	—	—	—
	(253)	(900)	(1001)			
Catholics	1.3	2.5	2.8	—	—	—
	(78)	(310)	(323)			
Jews	—	2.1	1.9	—	—	—
		(29)	(44)			
Jews (1965)[a]	0.6	1.5	2.5	—	—	—
	(31)[b]	(224)	(164)			
1970s						
Protestants	0.9	1.9	2.9	3.0	2.6	2.5
	(625)	(1822)	(1576)	(1618)	(1560)	(1913)
Catholics	0.9	1.9	3.2	3.2	2.4	2.5
	(315)	(1060)	(815)	(739)	(602)	(543)
Jews	—	1.2	2.3	2.4	1.9	1.9
	—	(75)	(66)	(67)	(61)	(66)
Jews (1975)[a]	0.3	0.7	2.3	2.5	—	—
	(20)	(149)	(128)	(119)		

Sources: NORC General Social Surveys, conducted annually, 1972–78; whites only (except as otherwise noted).

Notes:
a 1965 and 1975 Boston Jewish Community Surveys. Number of children ever-born was not ascertained for married respondents where the wife was more than 40 years old in 1965 or 45 in 1975.
b Aged 21–24.
Fertility behavior was not determined for women over 45 on many surveys.

Yet another reason to expect low Jewish fertility to continue entails the increasing secularity of American Jews. Previous research has demonstrated an association between synagogue attendance (as an indicator of religiosity) and fertility desires in the 1960s, as close a connection as, in fact, existed between Catholic church attendance and Catholic fertility desires (Cohen and Ritterband, 1981). The researchers interpreted these findings to mean that the higher fertility of religiously active Jews (or Catholics) reflects their pro-natalist heritage and subculture. In so far as Jewish involvement in the traditional religious subculture wanes, Jews may be expected to bear fewer children owing in part to their increasing remoteness from their pro-natalist religious tradition.

Closely connected to this argument are the fertility patterns of those

Jews who marry out of the faith. Some studies have found lower birth-rates among intermarriers. However, none has comprehended whether religious intermarriage is a cause or merely a correlate of fewer births. Hence, in so far as religious exogamy continues to rise, it may either stimulate or simply indicate continuing declines in the Jewish birthrate. (An alternate view, though, suggests that rising intermarriage would signify no such thing (Goldscheider, 1983). Rather, in so far as intermarriage becomes more common, intermarriers may come to resemble more closely those who marry within the group. According to such a view, intermarriage would have little causal connection, if any, with the continuance of low Jewish birthrates.)

Undoubtedly, these several aspects of Jewish distinctiveness aside, so long as middle-class, urbanized Americans experience low birthrates, so will comparable Jews. Jewish birth patterns will generally follow those of the larger society as they have in the past. If anything, advancing assimilation may well bring Jewish fertility behavior into even closer alignment with that of their non-Jewish contemporaries.

More Jewish divorce, but still less than others

Over the years popular stereotypes have credited Jews with enjoying stable families. Whether in Europe or the United States, both Jews and Gentiles have maintained images of a typical Jewish family as one often infused with passionate conflicts and tensions, but one nevertheless able to withstand serious challenges to marital harmony and endure as an intact unit (Hyman, forthcoming). In contrast with this romantic image, historians investigating periods of grave social dislocation – such as the mass migration from Eastern Europe to the United States – have un-covered considerable evidence of abandonment, infidelity, and marital breakup. However, the paucity of accurate data as well as considerable conceptual and theoretical difficulties preclude drawing hard and fast conclusions as to whether Jewish marital dissolution during these periods was relatively low or high, whether it testifies to the mythic strength or to some heretofore hidden weakness in Jewish family coherence.

Conceptual and measurement problems have also hampered efforts to study Jewish divorce rates in contemporary times. In a period of generally rising American divorce rates, professional family workers as well as some communal agencies (such as YMHAs and summer camps) report scattered impressions of an increasing incidence of Jewish divorce. Even

Orthodox rabbis and lay leaders have demonstrated rising anxiety over divorce within the Orthodox community which they had thought was immune from adverse influences of the larger society. In light of these impressions, one wonders whether American Jews are retaining their ostensible historic "advantage" relative to non-Jewish divorce rates.

Table 6(3) reports ever-divorced rates by age and religion for white, ever-married respondents.[4]

Table 6(3)   Percentage ever-divorced by age and religion

age:	18–24	25–34	35–44	45–54	55–64	65+
Protestants	5	15	20	20	16	17
	(328)	(988)	(875)	(895)	(876)	(1106)
Catholics	4	10	15	13	18	11
	(230)	(712)	(574)	(501)	(398)	(365)
Jews	—	8	10	7	5	8
		(53)	(40)	(43)	(39)	(45)

Sources: NORC General Social Surveys, conducted annually, 1972–78; white, ever-married respondents only.

If the divorce frequency had remained constant over time, the ever-divorced rate would rise steadily as people age. After all, older people have been "at risk" of divorcing longer than younger people. Contrary to this hypothetical stationary pattern, the older groups in *Table 6(3)* have divorced generally less frequently than some younger groups, particularly the middle-aged. Since some young and middle-aged people will eventually divorce between the time of the survey and when they die, their ever-divorced rates when they attain old age will surpass the rates for those who are now elderly. Thus, the table clearly documents rising divorce in recent years, especially among younger Americans.

We also note a certain constancy in the relationship amongst divorce frequencies for the three major religious groups. Using white Protestants as a standard point of reference we find that Catholics generally divorced about two-thirds to three-quarters as frequently as did the Protestants. Similarly, Jews seem to have divorced only about one-half as frequently as comparably aged Protestants, and that relationship characterizes younger as well as older people.

In short, Jewish and Christian divorces have indeed become more frequent in recent years. However, Jews are maintaining their historic "advantage" of a "divorce deficit" relative to Protestants and Catholics.

As a proportion of the larger society's rising divorce rate, Jewish divorce – though rising in absolute terms – is still as infrequent today as it has been for the last several decades.

Intermarriage: ever upward

No precise and accurate estimates of the current rate of American Jewish intermarriage are available. The lack of such statistics owes, in part, to confusion over how to measure the phenomenon. Some researchers speak of couple rates (comparing the number of marriages between two Jews with those entailing one Jewish and one non-Jewish spouse); others use individual rates (how many Jews marry non-Jews versus how many marry fellow Jews). Moreover, intermarriage alternately refers to the religious upbringing of the partners, or to their religion at marriage, or to their current religious affiliation. Despite these measurement problems, observers uniformly concur that the trend in intermarriage incidence, however defined, is unambiguously upward (Goldstein, 1981).

As with the other family characteristics – fertility, age at marriage, and divorce – Jews' marital choices, specifically their increasing tendency toward exogamy, reflect both general societal trends as well as a distinctive internal dynamic. Most fundamentally, all white American ethnic groups experience increasing out-group marriage with advancing generational status. Jews are certainly no exception to this generalization, but they do out-marry somewhat less frequently than other major white ethnic groups (such as Italian or Irish Catholics) in similar generational, social class, and residential circumstances (Cohen, 1980b). In short, with increasing generational distance from the traditional European heritage, American Jews – like their West-European predecessors in the late nineteenth and early twentieth centuries – may well experience high and increasing intermarriage rates as they disperse socially and geographically.

Yet another reason to expect continuity in high or rising intermarriage rates entails the changing sex ratio of intermarriers. Historically Jewish men have out-married something like twice as often as Jewish women. Several reasons for this circumstance come to mind. Most principally, Jewish sons have been afforded a greater amount of geographic, psychic, and social independence than have Jewish daughters. Also, certainly in the past, a daughter's parents have had greater opportunity to screen her dates and thereby her prospective marriage partners as well, whereas the simple logistics of American middle-class dating patterns have provided for more freedom of opportunity for young Jewish men.

The modern feminist movement, in challenging traditional sex roles and socialization practices, has contributed to removing some parental restraints formerly imposed upon middle-class daughters. In many ways, young women are attaining a level of geographic and social freedom heretofore reserved for their male counterparts. As a result, we may expect to witness a narrowing of Jewish intermarriers' sex ratio as female intermarriage rises to levels of Jewish male intermarriage.

Yet other reasons to anticipate a high and climbing rate of intermarriage entails changes in the timing of marriage. Previous research has demonstrated higher intermarriage among those who are psychically or geographically distant from their parents, among those who marry late in life, and, as a corollary, among those who remarry (Sherrow, 1971). The increase in age at marriage and the increase in divorce documented above both increase the likelihood that Jews will be marrying at older ages, times which have historically been associated with higher intermarriage.

Finally, the most crucial and fundamental trend leading one to anticipate growing frequencies of intermarriage entails the growth in assimilation generally. For Jews, as for other major American religious groups, religious commitment is closely associated with the likelihood of marrying within the faith. Hence, declining commitment to the ethnic as well as to the religious aspects of Jewish identity will serve to lower barriers to intermarriage. Indeed, studies have demonstrated an increasing acceptance by both Jews and Gentiles of interreligious marriage owing to increasing secularity and intergroup tolerance (Goldscheider, 1983).

Although increasing intermarriage certainly bodes ill for Jewish continuity broadly conceived, the effects of out-group marriage upon the religious affiliation of spouses and children are far from uniform. Not all Jewish intermarriers and not all children of exogamous unions fail to identify as Jews. A study of intermarriers in the 1960s (the last date when such research was completed) showed that spouses move to harmonize their initial religious differences (Sherrow, 1971). Typically, one of them converts (formally or informally) to the religion of the other partner; or else, either or both drop their original religious affiliations, assuming the "other" or "none" categories when asked to check off their religious affiliation on social surveys. In this dynamic, Jews gain more converts than do either major Christian groups, but all three major faiths lose to the "other" religion or "no" religion categories. Interestingly, initial adherents of a major faith are more likely to abandon that faith when they marry a spouse with no religious preference than if they marry an affirming Protestant, Catholic, or Jew.

This pattern of intermarriage-induced conversion and religious change certainly casts a new light upon historic Jewish attitudes toward Christianity. Traditionally, Jews have regarded Christianity as a dangerous rival for the loyalty of Jews by birth. In today's secularized society, Judaism may be more vulnerable to threats from forces promoting indifference to religion than to the allure of competing major religions. In other words, Christianity and Judaism in America paradoxically may be natural allies in a struggle against secularity which may hold greater peril for all major faiths than do the ostensibly competing religious systems for one another.

While the adverse demographic impact of intermarriage may be ameliorated by conversion or a Jewish upbringing for the children, there is no gainsaying the observation that the religiously intermarried maintain lower levels of communal affiliation and ritual practice. (However, the extent to which exogamy is a symptom or cause of assimilation is difficult to determine (Massarik and Chenkin, 1973).) The rise in intermarriage, then, along with postponed marriage, lower birthrates, and increasing divorce, may both reflect and stimulate lower levels of Jewish identification.

Jewishness and the family life cycle

In pre-modern times, the responsibility for assuring conformity with the normative demands of the Jewish tradition and community lay largely with the larger community. The community provided the setting in which group identity was learned and practiced. Its governing structures – the *kehillot* – enforced compliance with religious norms. Formal and informal age/sex peer-group associations provided individuals with their sense of location in society, performing many of the psychic functions which would later be taken up by the nuclear family. In these last respects, the traditional Jewish community resembled that of surrounding Christian society.

With the rise of "bourgeois domesticity" – the ideal of the nuclear family separated from the community – the nuclear Jewish family assumed a greater measure of centrality in the expression and maintenance of Jewish identity. Almost all American Jews who join synagogues and contribute to central philanthropic campaigns do so as family units. The most frequently practiced ritual observances – the Passover Seder, lighting Chanukah candles, and, to a lesser extent, attending Yom Kippur services – are family events. Writing of third-generation suburban Jews in the 1950s, sociologist Herbert Gans noted the child-centeredness of Jewish affiliation and ritual practice (Gans, 1958). Like Christian Americans, Jews then, as now, focused much of their communal and ritual activity upon their children. Critics of this phenomenon were led to remark that assimilating American Jews had become so child-centered in their practice, that children could rightly adduce that Jewish activity was something one does only as a child and not as an adult.

If in fact Jewish expression in contemporary America is as closely tied to family circumstances as previous observers have suggested, we should find that several forms of affiliation and ritual observance should rise and fall along with changes in the family life cycle. In particular, those living in conventional family settings, such as couples who have school-age children, should be most closely tied to the Jewish community and undertake various ritual practices most frequently. Those in alternate family stages, who deviate from the conventional model, should less often express Jewish identification.

Table 6(4) reports the frequency with which people in various stages of the family life cycle observed selected ritual practices or affiliated with formal institutions of the Jewish community. As one would expect from the family-centeredness literature, parents with children either of school age or older are the most active in Jewish life no matter what the measure. Older couples, the widowed, older singles, and parents of preschoolers are somewhat less active; the singles, childless couples, divorcees and intermarried are uniformly the least active.

If we focus our attention on just three sequential groups in family life cycle – childless couples, parents of pre-schoolers, and parents of school-age children (columns 2, 4, 5) – we can readily glean some understanding of how much family life cycle influences Jewish identification. In the transition from childless couple to one with a baby or tot, affiliation with Jewish institutions in the 1975 survey rose in the order of 10 to 25 percentage points. Increases in ritual performance are somewhat less dramatic, and not totally uniform. The next transition – from parents of pre-schoolers to parents of school-age children – results in even more substantial rises in all measures of Jewish identification. Affiliation rates increase by 20 to over 30 percentage points, roughly doubling in the instance of synagogue affiliation and Jewish organization belonging. Ritual performance also increases substantially, by about 15 percentage points in most cases. Clearly, these findings provide unambiguous evidence of the positive impact bearing children exerts upon ritual

Table 6(4) Jewish activities by family life cycle and time of survey

family life cycle:	young singles[a]	young couples[a]	divorced/ separated[a]	pre-schoolers	parents	older couples[a]	widowed, older singles[a]	inter-married[b]
1965								
kosher	13	16	65	18	18	43	42	6
Sabbath candles	23	41	58	46	74	72	62	41
Seder	95	82	89	85	92	89	83	81
service attendance	43	32	25	22	46	36	28	39
synagogue member	39	24	7	14	71	62	46	49
Jewish org. member	23	30	48	41	59	56	44	44
Jewish giving	12	26	36	28	51	51	32	70
weighted N=	110	92	28	153	528	349	276	29
1975								
kosher	8	21	8	7	19	34	31	0
Sabbath candles	18	49	31	53	63	63	52	18
Seder	85	76	68	90	97	94	78	58
service attendance	12	35	35	36	54	42	37	13
synagogue member	16	14	30	41	73	60	43	8
Jewish org. member	9	10	26	19	41	52	48	6
Jewish giving	13	28	31	53	72	60	47	12
weighted N=	258	72	36	71	139	167	118	70

Sources: 1965 and 1975 Boston Jewish Community Surveys.
See *Table 3(1)*, page 56, for explanation of Jewish identification items.

Notes:
a No children at home, "young" = under 45; "older" = over 45.
b Includes all family life cycle stages.

practice and communal affiliation. Like American Christians, American Jews are led to their houses of worship and to private religious practice by their children.

Alongside the relatively high rates of Jewish identification by conventional families are the complementary low rates of Jewish identification among alternative households – the singles, childless, dovorcees, and intermarrieds. In so far as these family situations result in diminished Jewish identification, the growth in their numbers suggests that family change is itself a significant factor in explaining the overall decline in Jewish identification in recent years.

But the change in Jewish identification occasioned by the shrinkage in the sheer number of conventional families constitutes only one major family-linked component in recent declines in Jewish identification. We may use the tools of demographers who divide the components of social change into "compositional" and "rate" effects. As a simple example, birthrates can change due to changes in the number of women of childbearing age in the population (a composition effect) as well as because of changes in the number of births per woman in each age-group (a rate effect). Similarly, family-linked changes in Jewish identification derive not only from a shrinking proportion of conventional families, but also from changes in the extent to which conventional or alternative families undertake Jewish activities.

In particular, not only have alternative households grown in number, they have become more distant from Jewish life as well. When adults were single for just a few years, when they bore children fairly soon after leaving their parental homes, when few divorced, and few intermarried, alternative family stages were often viewed as both transitional and deviant. Jews in most alternative stages could anticipate rejoining the Jewish community of conventional families fairly rapidly. In recent years, though, the sheer growth in alternative households means that they have come to be seen as less transitional and more permanent, less deviant and more accepted (if not celebrated). In effect, singles, childless couples, divorcees, and the intermarried have created their own communities, subcultures, and counter-norms to support and legitimate their once-deviant status. As a result, they may have less use for, or feel more excluded from, a conventional family-based Jewish community. The end result of this process is not only more alternative households, but greater remoteness of such households from Jewish concerns and activities.

To appreciate the extent to which compositional and rate effects have

Table 6(5)   Decomposition of components of family-linked changes over time in Jewish identification

A alternative households[a] by age and year

	18/21–24	*25–34*	*35–44*	*45–54*	*55–64*	*65+*	*total*
1965	80	36	13	7	6	5	17%
1975	100	76	22	16	6	5	47%

B selected measures of Jewish identification by household type and year

	conventional[b]			*intermediate[c]*			*alternative*			*all*		
	1965	*1975*	*diff.[d]*	*1965*	*1975*	*diff.*	*1965*	*1975*	*diff.*	*1965*	*1975*	*diff.*
kosher	28	27	−1	33	22	−10	22	9	−13	28	17	−11
Sabbath candles	73	63	−10	56	52	−4	35	24	−11	62	43	−19
Seder	91	96	+5	84	82	−2	88	78	−10	88	85	−3
Syn. member	67	67	0	35	42	+7	31	16	−15	52	38	−14
J. org. member	58	47	−11	43	37	−6	31	10	−21	49	27	−22
J. giving	51	66	+14	31	49	+18	26	17	−9	42	39	−3
weighted N=	877	436		430	189		260	306		1569	934	

C comparison of actual and hypothetical 1975 total rates of Jewish activity

	(1) actual	*(2) hyp.-1**	*(3) hyp.-2***	*differences*		*total change*
				(1)–(2)	*(1)–(3)*	
kosher	17	22	23	−5	−6	−11
Sabbath candles	42	52	47	−9	−4	−19
Seder	85	89	89	−4	−4	−3
syn. member	38	52	45	−14	−7	−14
J. org. member	27	38	37	−11	−10	−22
J. giving	39	54	44	−15	−5	−3

 * Hypothesis-1 assumes 1975 rates of Jewish activity and 1965 distribution of household types. The first difference column reports the impact of changing household composition, particularly the growing number of alternative households, upon Jewish identification.

 ** Hypothesis-2 assumes 1975 household type distribution (composition), 1975 rates of activity for conventional and intermediate households, and 1965 rates of activity for alternative households. The second difference column, therefore, reports the impact of 1965–75 declines in alternative households' rates of Jewish activity upon the 1975 total rates of activity.

Sources: 1965 and 1975 Boston Jewish Community Surveys.
See *Table 3(1)*, page 56, for explanation of Jewish identification items.

Notes:
a Young singles, childless and married, divorced, and intermarried are "alternative" households.
b Parents of school-age children and couples or singles over 45 are "conventional" households.
c Parents of pre-school children, widowed, and over-45 singles are "intermediate" households.
d dif. = difference between 1975 and 1965 rates.
e Compositional effects are changes in Jewish identification from 1965 to 1975 due solely to changes in the distribution of Jewish household types, assuming no change in the rates at which they perform Jewish activities. That is, we multiply the 1965 rates for each household type by the 1975 distributions of household types, yielding a new total rate for each Jewish activity. The figures reported are the differences between this new, hypothetical rate of activity and the actual rate in the total 1965 sample.
f Rate effects are changes in Jewish identification from 1965 to 1975 due solely to changes in the rate at which Jewish households performed Jewish activities, that is assuming no change in the distribution of Jewish household types. That is, we multiply the proportion in a household type in 1965 by the difference between 1975 and 1965 rates for that type, yielding the figures reported.

---

contributed to the family-linked changes in Jewish identification in recent years, we need to comprehend changes in the types of households as well as changes in the Jewish identification of the different types of families. *Table 6(5)* compares the data from the 1965 and 1975 Boston Jewish Community Surveys and allows us to assess the extent to which different sorts of change contributed to declines in Jewish identification in the Boston area over the ten-year interval between the surveys. The top panel reports the percentages of "alternative" households – singles, childless couples, divorcees, and intermarrieds – by age for both surveys. Clearly, between 1965 and 1975 there was a dramatic rise in the proportion of alternative families, particularly among those under 35. Postponement of both marriage and childbearing were the principal factors responsible for the huge increase in alternative households.

The second panel reports on selected measures of Jewish identification by household type and year (1965 or 1975). Household type has been constructed so as to consist of three categories. Alternative households are the singles, married but childless, divorced, and intermarried; conventional households consist of parents with school-age children or marrieds over forty-five where children are now absent from the home; the intermediate families are those couples with pre-school children as well as older singles and widowed individuals.

In virtually every instance, for both years, we find that conventional households have higher Jewish identification scores than do intermediate families. Some comparisons reveal only small differences or none at all, while a few, particularly in the institutional domain, show that conventional families were as much as 30 percentage points more likely to affiliate than were intermediate households. Meanwhile, alternative families, particularly in the 1975 survey, scored much lower on Jewish identification measures than did either of the other two types of households.

More to the point, the 1965/1975 comparisons within household types reveal strikingly different patterns of change for the different families over the ten-year period (see "difference" columns, panel *B*). Both conventional and intermediate families report mixed patterns, although overall, the level of Jewish activity for these households slightly declined. For the alternative families, though, the patterns are much less ambiguous. From 1965 to 1975 all measures of Jewish activity for this group declined. The drops range from 9 to 21 percentage points. These declines are at least as steep, if not much steeper, than that experienced by conventional and intermediate families. Perhaps most dramatically, while Jewish philanthropy increased by 14 to 18 percentage points among the conventional and intermediate families, it actually fell by 9 percentage points among the alternative households. Similar but less startling results obtain elsewhere.

Clearly, alternative households – singles, childless, divorcees, and intermarrieds – moved away considerably from Jewish concerns between 1965 and 1975, falling well below their initially low levels of 1965. The implications of these findings for Jewish activity generally is conveyed in the bottom panel *C* of *Table 6(5)*.

The panel reports what the overall level of each particular type of Jewish activity would have been had not each of two processes taken place. The column labelled "hypothesis-1" assumes that the rates of Jewish activity for each family type declined from 1965 to 1975 as in fact they did, but it also assumes that the distribution of household types remained unaltered. That is, it assumes that the explosion of alternative households and the shrinkage of conventional households did not take place. The column labelled "hypothesis-2" assesses the effect of the huge drops in Jewish activity among the alternative households. It assumes that the rates of Jewish activity for this group alone remained steady from 1965 to 1975 even as the alternatives grew in number, and the rates of activity for the other family types moved either up, down, or not at all.

The results of comparing hypothetical with actual 1975 rates (column 1) are found in columns 4 and 5 labelled "differences." By way of further comparison, the last column presents the actual decline in overall rates of Jewish activity between 1965 and 1975.

Clearly both processes – the growth in alternative households and their increasing remoteness from Jewish life – account for much if not all of the decline in Jewish activity for the larger population. The impact of growing numbers of alternative households (the composition effect) is in most instances larger than the disproportionate drops in Jewish activity among alternative households (the rate effect); but both effects contributed substantially to the overall decline in activity.

Although one cannot precisely allocate over-time change to these and other components, this analysis does nevertheless point to the centrality of family change for inducing (and generally diminishing) Jewish identification. In sum, while singlehood, childlessness, divorce, and intermarriage are helping to diminish American Jewish population size, these trends have also diminished Jewish identification among those who remain identifiably Jewish.

Discussions and implications

The recent growth in Jewish singles, smaller families, divorcees, and intermarrieds along with their increasing remoteness from Jewish life have not gone unnoticed within organized Jewry. Many synagogues, community centers, family agencies, and federations have initiated a variety of programs to address these ever-increasing groups of unaffiliated, primarily younger Jews. Such programs can often be subsumed under the rubric of "policies of containment," in that they are aimed at containing the rise in alternative households. Some are designed to promote early marriage between Jewish men and women; some seek to encourage couples to bear more children; and still others try to keep strained Jewish marriages intact.

Putting aside the moral value some may attach to communal efforts to relieve the economic and psychic burden of having many children, to reduce marital discord, and to promote early marriage (or remarriage) among Jews, such efforts are highly unlikely to significantly influence the family behavior of most American Jews. Generally, formal institutions in modern societies – be they governmental or voluntary – have had little success in altering people's family decisions. The organized Jewish community, with its limited resources and tenuous connections with most American Jews, can do little on its own to stimulate early marriage, higher birthrates, and marital harmony.

While one cannot reasonably expect reductions in the number of alternative Jewish households unless the larger society experiences parallel reductions, one may well anticipate certain changes in Jewish communal institutions. Although alternative household members disproportionately under-participate in communal life currently, we should recall that institutions generally lag behind changing demographic circumstances. As the number of alternative households continues to grow, synagogues and other institutions will inevitably move to accommodate the new types of Jewish families. Just as in the larger society structures with special appeal to singles, childless couples, and divorcees emerged in the 1970s, so too has the Jewish community begun to create structures specially geared to attract members of alternative Jewish households.

These structures take on several sorts of relationships with the established communal institutions ranging from complete separation to total integration. At one extreme are new structures established by alternative household members outside pre-existing institutions. Examples of these include a handful of gay synagogues as well as a small number of *chavurot* – worship and study communities – consisting primarily of single and childless young people. More closely integrated with synagogues and community centers are groups organized especially for singles or divorcees. Special programs for intermarried couples – discussion groups and special outreach efforts – also fall within this intermediate category, between total integration into pre-existing institutions and total segregation from them. At the integrative extreme are efforts fully to incorporate alternative household members into the ongoing programs of local Jewish institutions.

The impulse to accommodate growing numbers of alternative households will, no doubt, be tempered by cultural and religious inhibitions. In particular, one can expect increasingly sharp debates over accommodating both intermarried and homosexual households. In so far as the organized community resists efforts to incorporate these and other types of alternative households, and in so far as alternative household Jews retain an interest in Jewish community life, the latter may be expected to create their own communities outside established structures, at least so long as they fail to gain full acceptance within them.

Whatever structural changes are stimulated by the rising number of alternative households, there is no doubt that in the near future, family changes will pose distinctive challenges to American Jewry's ethnic and religious continuity. The postponement of marriage and childbearing and increased divorce will mean that more Jews than ever before will spend significant portions of their lives outside of a conventional nuclear family. The growing hiatus between the parental home and having a spouse with a six-year old or older child – a period of diminished Jewish activity – is typically longer for American Jews today than it has ever been before. If communal institutions and patterns of Jewish ritual practice fail to adjust to this lengthening hiatus, we may anticipate fewer Jews returning to the higher levels of Jewish activity still typical of those in conventional nuclear family settings. If such a trend eventuates, then the integration of American Jews into the larger society, and, in particular, the resultant adjustment in their family behavior, would significantly diminish the expression of Jewish identity. Viewed in this manner, the urge to integrate into the larger modern society – although consistent with the last two centuries of Jewish experience – may significantly erode Jewish group identity. Perhaps nowhere has the American Jewish urge to integrate into the social mainstream been as clearly articulated as in the politics of most American Jews for the last several decades, the politics of liberalism.

7 Liberalism as the politics of group integration[1]

At least since the days of the New Deal, Jews, more than other Americans, have been disproportionately "liberal," as inexact as the term might be. An extensive literature documents substantial Jewish support over the years for liberal, generally Democratic Party candidates, even when they were opposed by politically moderate Jewish Republicans. Numerous public opinion polls and post-electoral surveys have consistently reported Jewish support for virtually all liberal positions and candidates, almost always in excess of that of other white ethnic and religious groups.[2] These include support for civil liberties, civil rights, the New Deal, the Great Society, interventionist foreign policy before the Vietnam War and restraint on the use of military force afterwards.

Starting in the late 1960s several observers began to question whether Jewish liberalism was as firm and unwavering as it had been in the past. Several sharp and bitter conflicts with blacks and other minorities, Jewish intellectuals' prominence in the neo-conservative movement, and significant Republican inroads into a once solidly Democratic Jewish electorate have all cast doubt upon the notion that Jews still stand somewhat to the left of America's political center.

Recent voting data, however, demonstrates that the Jewish masses continued to support liberal, Democratic candidates through the 1970s and they did so to an extent far greater than other white Americans (Fisher, 1979, 1981). In fact one analyst of Jewish voting in the 1980 presidential election − a writer clearly advocating a Jewish shift into

Republican voting columns – found only modest fulfillment of his aspiration. Post-election survey data indicated sustained support for liberal positions as well as a Jewish vote for conservative Ronald Reagan ten percentage points under that of other whites, a figure half that of analogous differences in previous elections (Himmelfarb, 1981). A 1981 study showed that Jews still identified as liberals much more than other whites, although both Jewish and national levels of liberalism had receded in roughly equal amounts (Yankelovich, Skelly, and White, 1981).

Apparently, then, although Jews have become more conservative in recent years, few doubt that on most political measures, Jews remain America's most liberal major religious or ethnic group. This is not to deny that certain demographically small, but politically significant elites – such as neo-conservative intellectuals, or some rabbis or organization leaders – have more frequently endorsed more conservative stances of late. Whether the larger Jewish public will follow some of its "leaders'" political shifts remains to be seen.

Explaining Jewish liberalism

Our understanding of Jewish politics in America has been plagued by conflicting data, shifting definitions, inexact interpretations, and a highly dynamic politics in the country at large and among the Jews in particular. All of these factors have fueled a lively debate – and considerable confusion – over the extent and direction of Jews' political alignments. If the current state of American Jewish politics is ambiguous, the reasons underlying the historic pattern of American Jewish leftist leanings are even less well understood.

When Jews were poor immigrants active in labor unions, their support for Socialist and liberal Democratic candidates was understandable in class terms. Having attained widespread affluence by mid-century, Jews' liberalism seemed to some more anomalous, demanding a coherent explanation.

The apparent anomaly generated several competing theories of Jewish liberalism. Political scientist Charles Liebman has been especially articulate in his criticism of several popular theories of Jewish liberalism (Liebman, 1973 : 135–59). He takes on the "religious values argument," for one, which contends that Jewish liberalism derives from a traditional religious heritage of universalism, cosmopolitanism, and concern for social justice.[3] Liebman points out that one can easily find support for "ethnic particularism, nationalism, and political conservatism" in traditional Judaism (Liebman, 1973 : 158). Moreover, contrary to what one would predict from the argument, those Jews who are most well versed in and respectful of the religious tradition usually are less liberal than more secularized Jews.

The "status-inferiority argument" focuses on the failure of American Jews to attain a high level of status commensurate with their extraordinary educational, professional, and economic achievements. According to this view, Jews seek to remake society's values so as to obtain the social prestige they feel they deserve. Liebman rejected this argument as well largely because it may explain early Jewish radicalism, but not their liberalism in contemporary America where Jews have largely won the battle for social acceptance and respectability.

The "historical argument" suggests that Jewish liberalism derives from the European Right's historic opposition to the Emancipation and its outright anti-semitism. While this perspective may explain pre-American Jewish support for the left, it leaves unanswered the question of why Jewish liberalism continues into the contemporary period. One proponent of the historical argument cites "Jews' sense of insecurity in the Gentile environment;" but as Liebman suggests, we need a more detailed consideration of the "constants in the postemancipation experiences and the perceptions of the Jews" which have sustained their liberalism (Liebman, 1973 : 147).

The opening chapters of this work argued that the key to understanding much contemporary Jewish social behavior lies in the modernization process, that is, in the transition from traditional to modern societies and in the drive to overcome centuries of stigmatization as a pariah group. Thus, Jewish liberalism − as much as modern Orthodoxy, Zionism, assimilationism, and so forth − should be seen as a reflection (if not, sometimes, a strategy) of the entry and integration of Jews into modern society. Accordingly, modernizing Jews have long held that their integration would be fostered by advancing the tolerant pluralism of middle-class liberalism or the universalist vision of the socialists, depending upon local circumstances:

Jews were enthusiastic supporters of universal humanism and cosmopolitanism. They embraced democratic nationalism, liberalism, and moderate socialism. There were variations from one region to another and one period to another. . . . Nor did all Jews respond in quite the same way. What is striking, however, is the constant search for a universalistic ethic which would cut through the differences that an older tradition had imposed, but which would permit the Jew to retain at least nominal identification as a Jew.　　　(Liebman, 1973 : 157)

The urge to adopt a universalist ethic (as well as the political and cultural ethos of the most committed universalists) provides only one level of explanation for Jews' from liberal propensities. American Jews' abiding sense of insecurity and their partial exclusion until recently from the social mainstream prompted identification with liberals in general and the Democratic Party in particular.[4] After all, these were the groups most predisposed toward intergroup tolerance.

The changing social-class character of American Jews supplies yet another level of explanation. As immigrant workers they frequently supported Socialists and their liberal Democratic fellow-travellers in the early twentieth century. Later as a rising but economically insecure middle class they supported the programs, candidates, and party of the New Deal. And, even later, as members of what some have called the "new class" – highly-educated professionals working with words and ideas – they were prominent in the development of the reform wing of the Democratic Party and a left-liberal critique of American society in the late 1960s and early 1970s. Far from undermining liberal commitments, Jews' changing class character has, in fact, harmonized with liberalism's changing style and content in recent decades.

On a third level, we should note how the interplay of minority-group insecurity and integrationist anxieties helped make liberalism the hallmark of the culturally high-brow. For many years, liberal politics within the Jewish community have connoted successful integration into the larger society, particularly its most sophisticated elements. Liberal Jews often portrayed their conservative counterparts as parochial and unassimilated. They have claimed, albeit often subtly, that their liberalism testified to their having acquired a certain level of cultural sophistication (Himmelfarb, 1973). The very term "radical chic," current in the early 1970s, itself conveys the notion that liberalism or radicalism had become matters of social prestige. Liberalism for Jews anxious about their acceptance by the larger society became a fashion, a way of signifying their successful assimilation into the most "progressive" segments of the larger society.

In sum, integrationist anxieties, class interests, and prestige politics offer three complementary explanations of why Jews in general should have adopted political views to the left of the American (or, in earlier times, the European) center, wherever that center might have been. But they also bear upon political differences within the Jewish community. If liberalism may be seen as both a strategy and consequence of integration, if it pervades the highly-educated new professional class, and if it became chic and fashionable among modernizing Jews, then certain types of Jews should be more – or less – liberal than others.

In particular, we may expect the religiously observant to restrain their liberalism for two interrelated reasons. First, they are influenced by a traditionally oriented subculture which often looks askance at many liberals' social attitudes. On issues of women's liberation, abortion, homosexuality, divorce, and marriage, for example, the articulated positions of the major Orthodox rabbinic and congregational bodies have been closer to those of the Moral Majority, to offer a graphic example, than to the American Civil Liberties Union (ACLU). Second, the observant are more likely to practice ethnic politics where the group interests of Jews take precedence over universalist concerns.

At the other extreme are very marginal Jews who manifest little religious or ethnic identification and who generally have relatively few social ties with Jewish family and friends. In so far as they are socially distant from the Jewish ethnic subcommunity they may be less subject to that community's putatively liberal political subculture.

According to this line of thinking, even if the Jewish community as a whole may be more liberal than the American mainstream, conservatizing forces should operate at either end of the ritual observance continuum. At one extreme, a traditional subculture and ethnic-group politics should restrain liberalism; and at the other extreme, ethnic assimilation should move the ritually inactive to a political mainstream somewhat more conservative than the Jewish liberal political subculture.

This discussion of American Jews and their political orientation raises several empirical questions. To start, one would want to determine the extent to which and the ways in which Jews are more liberal than other Americans. In so far as they are, how is their liberalism influenced by level of ritual observance? Is there in fact, an inverted U-shaped contour with liberalism lowest among the most secular and the most observant and highest among the many in the vast middle range of ritual practice? Moreover, how do social class and integration into American life influence Jews' politics? In particular, does Jewish liberalism follow the patterns of the rest of America? Is it more pronounced among later generations, younger people, those with higher education and those with lower incomes?

To address these questions we turn to a recently conducted (late 1981/ early 1982) national survey of American Jews. The mail-back survey contained questions on political views, Jewish practices, social and demographic matters, and other issues. It was mailed to a national sample of "probably-Jewish" households, people with distinctive Jewish names (such as Cohen, Kaplan, Levine, etc.) listed in the telephone directories of communities throughout the continental United States. The sample was constructed so as to approximate roughly the geographic distributions of American Jews as reported in the 1980 *American Jewish Yearbook*.[5] In all, approximately 1700 names were drawn from eight metropolitan areas (including both the center cities and their surrounding suburban counties) and 40 other localities (24 large, 8 medium, and 8 small Jewish communities) throughout the continental United States.[6]

How liberal?

Table 7(1) presents the data from the Jewish sample in four areas: support for 1980's presidential candidates, liberal versus conservative orientations, positions on major public issues, and political party identification. These findings appear alongside roughly comparable national data for all Americans culled from several surveys by major news and polling organizations.[7]

Even though comparisons between the Jewish and national data must be made with extreme care, we can nevertheless surmise that Jews display a nearly consistent pattern of greater liberalism in most areas. Accordingly, the Jewish respondents were 10 percentage points less likely than the general electorate to support Reagan, they were 5 percentage points less supportive of Carter, over twice as likely to favor John Anderson, and a few percentage points more likely to support minor party candidates.[8]

Jews were also considerably more likely than others to identify as liberals (by about 12 percentage points) and even less likely to adopt the conservative label (by fully 24 percentage points). These results may be compared with the July 1981 Yankelovich survey reported earlier in which Jews were also more liberal and less conservative than the rest of the country, although both Jews and others reported having moved rightward in the last few years in equal amounts. As a result, despite their shift to the right, Jews' initial excess in liberal identification relative to other Americans remained intact through the early 1980s.

Table 7(1) Distributions of responses to selected public opinion questions: comparisons of the 1981 National Survey of American Jews with data from comparable questions on recent national surveys of American adults

	1981 NSAJ[1]	other surveys[2]
presidential preference (1980 election)		
Anderson	19	7
Carter	38	41
Reagan	39	51
other	4	1[a]
	100	100
political orientation (self-described)		
liberal (and radical)	33	21
moderate	48	36
conservative (and very conservative)	19	43[b]
	100	100
liberal opinions		
defense spending – against increasing	45	(43)[c]
social spending – against decreasing	56	(28)[d]
affirmative action – favor	55	66[e]
quotas; special treatment – favor	19	10[f]
ERA – favor	72	45[g]; 52[h]
abolish death penalty	18	20[i]
homosexual school-teachers – okay	67	45[j]
busing for integration – okay	22	12[k]
government pay for abortions – okay	50	40[l]; 40[m]
toughen action against immigration – oppose	13	—
party preference		
Democratic	65	47
Republican	12	27
Independent; other	24	26[n]
	100	100
	N = 673	

Notes:

1 The wording of the questions on the 1981 National Survey of American Jews follows. Questions are presented in the order in which they are reported in *Table 7(1)*.

Whom did you vote for or favor in the last presidential election?

Anderson, Carter, Reagan, another candidate.

Which of these best describes your usual stand on political issues?

radical, liberal, moderate, conservative, very conservative.

Should the United States substantially increase defense spending? yes, no, not sure. (Response categories are the same for the next nine questions.)

Should the United States substantially cut spending on social welfare?

Should affirmative action be used to help disadvantaged groups?

Should quotas be used to help disadvantaged groups?

Should the Equal Rights Amendment (ERA) be passed?

Notes to table 7(1)—cont.

Should the death penalty be abolished?

Should declared homosexuals be allowed to teach in the public schools?

Should school-children be bused when other means of integrating schools have failed?

Should the government pay for abortions?

Should the government use stronger measures against illegal immigration?

What is your political party preference? Democratic, Republic, other party, Independent or no party preference.

2 The source and wording of questions asked on national surveys follows. Each entry is keyed to a letter-reference as indicated in *Table 7(1)* and below.

a From Fisher (1981 : 333).

b Yankelovich, Skelly, and White (1981) *Anti-Semitism in the United States, Volume II, The detailed Findings* (July) : 81. Question: "Regardless of your political affiliation – do you think of yourself as being conservative, moderate, liberal, or radical?" Percentages were recomputed to exclude the 2 per cent "no answers."

c CBS News/*New York Times* national survey, conducted 22–26 April 1981. Question: "If you had a say in making up the federal budget this year, which program would you like to see increased and which reduced? Should federal spending on *military and defense programs* be increased, be decreased, or kept about the same?" Percentage reported in the table is the sum of "decreased" (9 per cent) and "kept the same" (34 per cent) responses.

d ABC News/Louis Harris and Associates national survey, conducted 20 March–5 April 1980. Question: "I would like to read you a list of different areas of federal government spending. For each, would you tell me if you favor a major cut in spending, a minor cut, no cut at all, or would you increase spending in this area?" Percentage reported in the table refers to those who "oppose cut" in Federal welfare spending.

e ABC News/Louis Harris and Associates national survey, conducted 10–11 November 1980. Question: "All in all, do you favor or oppose affirmative action programs in industry for blacks, provided there are no rigid quotas?" Percentage reported are for whites only.

f Gallup Organization national survey of 5–8 December 1980. Question: "Some people say that to make up for past discrimination, women and members of minority groups should be given preferential treatment in getting jobs and places in college. Others say that ability, as determined by test scores should be the main determination. Which point of view comes closest to how you feel on this subject?" Percentage reported is for those favoring "preferential treatment."

g NBC News/Associated Press national survey, probably November 1980, cited in Himmelfarb, M. (1981) "Are Jews becoming Republican," *Commentary* (August) : 27–31.

h ABC News/Louis Harris and Associates national survey of 7–10 November 1980. Question: "Many of those who favor women's rights favor the Equal Rights Amendment to the Constitution. This amendment would establish that women would have rights equal to men in all areas. Opponents argue that women are different from men and need to be protected by special laws which deal with women's status. Do you favor or oppose the Equal Rights Amendment?"

i ABC News/*Washington Post* national survey of 18–20 May 1981. Question: "Turning to another subject, the death penalty: are you in favor of the death penalty for persons convicted of murder?"

j ABC News/*Washington Post*. Question: "Lesbians and homosexuals should be allowed to teach in the public schools just like anyone else." Percentage who "agreed" is reported in the table.

k CBS News/*New York Times* national survey of 22–27 June 1981. Question: "Do you favor busing of school-children for the purpose of racial integration, or do you oppose busing school-children for this purpose?" Percentage reported favoring busing in the table is for white respondents only.

cont. overleaf

Notes to Table 7(1)—cont.

l Gallup Organization national survey of 11–14 July 1980. Question: "The United States Supreme Court recently upheld a congressional ban on federally financed abortions for women on welfare except to save the life of the mother or in the cases of rape or incest. Do you favor or oppose the ban on federally financed abortions for women on welfare?" Percentage reported is for those who *oppose* the ban, and thus support government financing of abortions.

m ABC News/*Washington Post* national survey of 18–20 May 1981. Question: "Abortion is something that government should not pay for even if a woman seeking an abortion is very poor." Percentage reported is for those who *disagree* with this statement.

n Time/Yankelovich, Skelly, and White national survey of 15–17 September 1981. Question: "Are you a Democrat, Republican, or what?"

The table's last three rows demonstrate Jews' well-known penchant for the Democratic Party and their aversion to Republican identification. Jews in the survey were 18 percentage points *more* likely to be Democrats than was the national electorate, and they were 15 percentage points *less* likely to identify as Republicans.

As compared with the results on presidential preference, party, and political identification, the data on major public issues need to be interpreted with even greater care. With that advice in mind, we note that on five of these issues, Jews were much more likely to offer liberal responses than were other Americans. These questions include those on social spending, quotas (or "special treatment" in the words of the comparable general American survey question) for blacks and other disadvantaged minorities, support for the Equal Rights Amendment (ERA), tolerance for homosexual school-teachers, and favoring governmental subsidies for abortions. At the same time, Jewish support for school busing for integration exceeded that of the rest of the country by a small amount (22 per cent versus the 12 or 16 per cent reported on the national surveys), while Jews and non-Jews had fairly similar attitudes in the areas of defense spending and abolishing capital punishment. Meanwhile, despite their greater support for quotas (or special treatment) for minorities, Jews were slightly *less* likely than the rest of the country to support affirmative action generally. (Apparently respondents distinguished affirmative action – which may imply good-faith efforts to find qualified minority-group applicants – from mandatory quotas.)

The fundamental patterns in these data suggest some very broad inferences. Generally, Jews were indeed more liberal than the rest of America. Their disproportionate liberalism is clearly evident in questions pertaining to civil liberties and women's liberation. Also Jews, more than non-Jews, were prepared to endorse the most unpopular remedies for alleviating the problems of racial minorities in the United States (i.e., busing and quotas). Moreover, they remained more committed to the New Deal social programs which served them and their parents so well, and which – contrary to stereotypes of American Jews as uniformly affluent – continue to benefit thousands of poor, working-class, and elderly Jews.[9]

The departures from the pattern of disproportionate Jewish liberalism are also instructive. They hint at a selective erosion of liberalism wherever Jewish group interests are at stake. Thus, perhaps owing to anxiety about Israel's security, American Jewish support for defense spending roughly equaled that of other Americans. Elsewhere, since many Jews are both aging and urban, they are probably especially fearful of violent crime. Perhaps as a result, their views on the death penalty rather than shading toward the liberal side, paralleled those of the entire country. With respect to the issue of racial equality, Jews' historically induced suspicion of explicit recognition of group differences may pull their support for affirmative action below that of other whites. In sum, Jews were much more liberal than others in some areas, and generally no less liberal than national norms in areas pertaining to their group interests.[10]

The observant and the secular

Not only do these data substantiate that Jews were generally – although selectively – more liberal than others, they can also be used to explore how Jewish identification varied with their liberalism. For this analysis, Jewish identification was measured by an index constructed from questions on ritual observance and synagogue affiliation (*Table 7(2)*). The index yielded four distinct groups whose political views are reported in *Table 7(3)*.[11]

Almost uniformly, the "secular" (the least ritually active) and the "observant" (the most ritually active) respondents were the least liberal, or conversely, the most conservative; the ritual "minimalists" – an intermediate group – were the most liberal, while the ritual "moderates" usually scored between the "minimalists" and the "observant" in political liberalism.

The presidential vote illustrates these generalizations. Support for Reagan's candidacy may be taken as an indication of conservatism. Accordingly, Reagan support was at its zenith among the "observant" (50 per cent), second highest among the "secular" (44 per cent) and lowest among the "minimalist" group (only 30 per cent).

Figures for the Anderson and Carter supporters are also instructive.

Table 7(2)   Selected measures of Jewish identification by ritual observance scale

ritual observance:	secular	minimal	moderate	observant	all
items used to construct scale					
Passover Seder	0	79	99	98	78
Chanukah candles	0	58	85	100	66
fast Yom Kippur	0	39	72	98	54
Rosh Hashanah services	0	32	86	99	55
Sabbath candles	0	6	16	83	23
meat/dairy dishes	0	4	5	65	16
belong to a synagogue	10	15	100	100	52
other items					
Yom Kippur services	1	40	92	100	60
Sabbath services − monthly	0	1	28	48	17
Sabbath services − weekly	0	1	8	22	7
Jewish organization member	7	26	56	67	39
UJA donor	21	35	66	75	49
no Sabbath shopping	0	3	1	22	6
Jewish periodical	13	22	49	71	37
fast on Tish'ah Be-Av	1	1	2	21	5
most friends Jewish	26	63	71	77	64
self-description					
Orthodox	1	2	4	18	6
Conservative	2	27	51	60	37
Reform	21	32	33	14	27
other	76	39	12	8	30
N=	107	277	167	122	673

According to national surveys, Jews disproportionately supported John Anderson. Observers speculated that those who were unhappy with Carter's policies toward Israel turned to the independent Anderson rather than break with historic partisan and ideological predilections to vote for the conservative Republican Ronald Reagan. Accordingly, Carter support was lowest among the two most observant ("observant" and "moderate") groups. At the same time, support for Anderson was highest among these two groups (23 per cent), slightly lower among the ritually "minimalist" (18 per cent), and significantly lower among the "secular." Among this least observant group, support for Anderson just about equaled his vote in the electorate as a whole (9 per cent of the sample's "secular" Jews favored Anderson as compared with his 7 per cent national vote). In other words, the least observant Jews most clearly

Table 7(3) Public opinion questions by ritual observance scale

ritual observance:	secular	minimal	moderate	observant
presidential preference (1980 election)				
Anderson	9	18	23	23
Carter	43	47	33	24
Reagan	44	30	42	50
other	4	4	2	3
	100	100	100	100
political orientation (self-described)				
liberal (and radical)	36	40	26	25
moderate	39	48	54	48
conservative (and very				
conservative)	24	12	20	27
	100	100	100	100
liberal opinions[a]				
defense spending	42	49	40	44
social spending	54	58	56	51
affirmative action	45	59	59	49
quotas	17	23	13	21
ERA	68	80	69	62
death penalty	19	23	12	16
homosexual teachers	57	74	70	57
busing	26	26	14	22
abortions	42	60	49	41
immigration	12	16	12	8
party				
Democratic	45	70	67	69
Republican	24	7	12	12
Independent; other	31	23	21	19
N=	107	277	167	122

Note:
a See *Table 7(1)* and text for description of liberal opinion items.

departed from the Jewish subsociety's disproportionate support for Anderson, and in this respect they acted most like other Americans. That is, in so far as a vote for Anderson can be seen as a characteristic Jewish electoral response, the least observant were the least likely to vote in a "Jewish" fashion.

Self-described political orientations also follow the general patterns outlined earlier. The "observant" were the least liberal (or most conservative) of all four groups; meanwhile, "secular" Jews described themselves as conservative (24 per cent) almost as often as did the observant (27 per cent). The "minimalist" Jews were the most liberal group of all. They had the highest proportion of self-described liberals (40 per cent) and, by far, the lowest proportion of conservatives (12 per cent).

These curvilinear patterns obtain for most opinions on major public issues as well. Generally, the proportions who gave liberal responses rise with the transition from "secular" to "minimalist" respondents, and then fall, reaching their lowest levels among the "observant."

The party preference patterns are the only ones to vary somewhat from the general U-shaped contours found among other political measures. Ritually "minimalist," "moderate," and "observant" respondents are similar in that over two-thirds of these groups identified as Democrats, one-fifth as "Independents," and the rest (7 or 12 per cent) as Republicans. By way of contrast, less than half (45 per cent) of the "secular" group were Democrats, almost a third (31 per cent) were independents, and almost a quarter (24 per cent) were Republicans. Clearly, many "secular" Jews have retreated from their ethnic subculture's over-identification with the Democratic Party and have adopted party identification patterns almost identical with that of the United States generally (refer back to *Table 7(1)*).

These party preference data depart from the earlier political measures in that there is virtual consistency across the "observant," the "moderate," and the "minimalist" groups, as opposed to the variations in liberalism we found earlier. In this respect, "observant" Jews are deviant. Despite their relative conservatism in political views and presidential preference, they nevertheless identified with the Democratic Party as often as did the much more liberal "minimalist" respondents. The explanation for this anomaly may lie in the greater Jewish group consciousness of the "observant." Such a consciousness would promote continued identification with the party historically regarded as most supportive of Jewish interests, even as the relatively conservative political views of the "observant" diverge from those of liberal Democrats.

Since "observant" Jews may remain attached to the Democratic Party despite their support for conservative candidates or policies, analyses which focus on political party preference data alone may distort significant changes in Jewish politics. However the distinctive patterns pertaining to party preference do not alter the basic conclusion that most political measures — those pertaining to public opinion, self-identification, and presidential preference – repeatedly bear an inverted U-shaped relationship with ritual observance. In general, the most observant and the most secular are the least liberal.

Generation, age, and social class

Since ritual observance is associated with age and education we would do well to control for these and other major demographic variables to determine whether the inverted U-shaped contour holds up under controls. In addition, by examining the effects of generation, age, education, and income upon Jewish liberalism, we can also appreciate the extent to which various dimensions of Jewish integration into the modern society influence their political views.

Table 7(4) reports scores on both a liberalism summary index and support for Reagan.[12] The unadjusted columns report the impact of each independent variable (separately) on either political measure without controls for the other variables. Adjusted scores represent the impact of each variable taking the others into account simultaneously.

The results pertaining to the liberalism index conform pretty much to what one would anticipate. Liberalism increases with generation, but this relationship is due entirely to generations' association with other independent variables. While the third generation scored high on liberalism 21 percentage points more often (51 per cent versus 30 per cent for the first generation in the unadjusted column), that difference reduces to virtually nothing after adjustment for other variables, particularly age and education. In other words, later-generation Jews are more liberal because they were born later and because they received higher education more often than earlier generations.

In addition, younger people were more liberal than their elders. Each decrease in age was associated with an increase in liberalism; the latter rose from as little as 33 per cent among the over-65 respondents to as much as 58 per cent among those under 35. These differences were only modestly reduced by controls for generation, education, income, and ritual observance. Apparently, like other Americans, each succeeding birth cohort of Jews has been politically socialized into increasingly liberal milieus.

Education and income had opposite influences upon liberalism, as would be expected. Better-educated respondents scored higher on liberalism, while the more affluent were generally more conservative.

Although controls for generation, age, education, and income slightly

Table 7(4)   Liberalism and support for Reagan by generation, age, education, income, and ritual observance (Multiple Classification Analysis)

	Liberalism[a]		Support for Reagan[b]		
	unadjusted	adjusted	unadjusted	adjusted	N
generation					
first	30	42	33	31	30
second	38	41	38	35	234
third	51	45	39	42	230
young foreign born	—	—	—	—	20
age					
under 35	58	48	37	43	138
35–44	47	44	36	35	61
45–54	41	44	45	40	88
55–64	38	42	41	38	110
65+	33	36	37	36	113
n.a.	—	—	—	—	4
education					
high school or less	31	31	44	54	101
some College	31	30	47	48	110
BA	45	44	40	36	123
MA or more	58	59	30	25	170
n.a.	—	—	—	—	10
income					
under $15,000	45	52	22	18	76
$15,000–$24,999	44	46	30	27	101
$25,000–$39,999	36	34	46	48	113
$40,000–$74,999	36	35	46	50	116
$75,000 or more	50	48	34	37	44
n.a.	50	58	51	50	64
ritual observance					
secular	38	38	43	45	78
minimal	51	49	30	30	205
moderate	39	40	42	43	134
observant	36	39	50	47	97

Notes:

a Liberalism = 1 if 5 or more "liberal" responses to political orientation and 9 of 10 public-opinion items (all except "quotas" as listed in *Table 7(1)*); 0 otherwise.

b Support for Reagan = 1 if favored Ronald Reagan in 1980 presidential election; 0, if favored other candidate; includes voters and non-voters.

reduced differences in liberalism between the various categories of ritual observance, the same pattern of relationship between liberalism and ritual observance uncovered earlier remained intact. Liberalism was lowest at both ends of the ritual observance continuum; and it was highest among the 40 per cent or so who comprise the "minimalist" group.

The findings for Reagan support largely, although not entirely, replicated those found for the liberalism index. Accordingly, contrary to our findings for liberalism, the third generation was somewhat more prone to support Reagan; meanwhile the impact of age on Reaganism was varying and ambiguous. These anomalies aside, we again find the expected relationships with education, income, and religious observance. Adjusting for the other variables, support for Reagan declined precipitously with educational increases.[13] Meanwhile, excepting the small number of respondents earning over $75,000, wealthier Jews were substantially more likely to support Ronald Reagan.[14]

The association of Reagan support with ritual observance conforms with earlier findings for liberal political views. The "minimalists" were once again the most liberal (i.e., the most anti-Reagan). Their (adjusted) support for Reagan was only 30 per cent while comparable figures for the "observant" and "secular" categories reached 47 per cent and 45 per cent respectively. In short, the inverted U-shaped contour in the relationship between a measure of liberalism (Reagan support) and ritual observance re-emerges and is sustained despite controls for other factors.

Presidential preference: a two-step decision

The presidential preference data can be analyzed further to illustrate more graphically the peculiar relationship between Jewish identification and political tendencies this analysis has uncovered. *Table 7(5)* reports percentages supporting Reagan for president by two important factors: political orientation and ritual observance. Much as one would expect, support for Reagan declined precipitously with increasing liberalism, moving from 63 per cent among all Jewish "conservatives" (see the table's last row) to 32 per cent among the moderates, to a mere 4 per cent among the liberals. Thus, by reading across the rows, we learn that the vote for Reagan was unmistakably connected with one's overall political world-view.

By reading down the columns we can discern the impact of Jewish identification. We find that among liberals and moderates (second and

Table 7(5)   Support for Reagan by liberalism and ritual observance

	conservatives	moderates	liberals
ritual observance			
secular	68	30	—
	(38)	(23)	(17)
minimal	49	32	5
	(71)	(72)	(62)
moderate	64	35	0
	(61)	(52)	(21)
observant	76	29	—
	(51)	(34)	(12)
all	63	32	4
	(221)	(181)	(112)

third columns), Jewish identification had ambiguous relationships with support for Reagan. But among the conservatives (first column), the familiar U-shaped pattern emerges once again. Support for Reagan peaked at the two end-points: "observant" conservatives and "secular" conservatives (with rates of 76 per cent and 68 per cent respectively) was a little lower among ritually "moderate" political conservatives (64 per cent) and was by far the lowest among the "minimalist" conservatives (49 per cent).

These results demonstrate a two-step electoral decision process. Clearly, political ideology took precedence over Jewish identification in influencing support for Reagan. Liberal and moderate Jews could give the Republican conservative candidate very little support while politically conservative Jews were relatively enthusiastic Reaganites. However, once a conservative orientation opened the door to a vote for Reagan, the familiar U-shaped influence of Jewish identification came to the fore. Once again, the most "observant" and the most "secular" respondents – even among political conservatives – lent the Reagan candidacy the greatest support.

Discussion and conclusions

These findings suggest that when Jews integrate into the larger American society they – like their nineteenth-century European predecessors – integrate into a somewhat left-of-center political milieu. But the results also suggest ways in which Jews' overall liberalism has been restrained if not eroded. Jews overall are less liberal on those issues – such as defense or affirmative action – which pertain to their group interests or to their historic consciousness. Also, certain Jews are less liberal if they belong to the 15 to 25 per cent most ritually observant and synagogue-affiliated or, at the other extreme, to the 5 to 15 per cent who are least observant.

These findings, then, suggest three sorts of constraints on Jewish political liberalism:

1 A *traditional subculture*, which is most influential among the most observant and which frowns upon liberal approaches to many social issues.

2 Concern for Jewish *group-interests* politics which influences many observant and even somewhat less observant Jews, and which militates against a universalist outlook in political affairs.

3 *Assimilation* which characterizes many of the least observant and which brings them into an American social mainstream more politically conservative than the fairly liberal Jewish subculture.

If this reasoning is correct, we may predict that certain foreseeable trends will sustain Jewish liberalism while others will probably erode it. In so far as Jewish liberalism is a response to alienation from the social mainstream, we may expect sustained Jewish liberalism so long as, and in so far as, Jews continue to feel socially insecure. However, in part because America has become more hospitable to interest-group politics, Jews may now act more forcefully in expressing their parochial political concerns (Silberman, forthcoming) and thereby act in a politically more conservative fashion.

In the urban political arena, Jews may express their group political consciousness in ongoing conflicts with blacks, Hispanics, and other groups over jobs, neighborhoods, schools, and political power in classic battles of ethnic succession. In the national arena, Jewish organizations will no doubt continue to press for aid to Israel and to oppressed Jewish communities in the Soviet Union and elsewhere. In light of this political agenda, Jewish communal thinkers and leaders will continue to debate whether the left or right holds out the best opportunity for realizing Jewish group interests. The pursuit of group interests, then, may well take those Jews who care about such things into a variety of political directions since both allies and opponents of those interests will continue to reside in many political camps; and these directions are difficult to predict, owing to the vicissitudes of American politics and short-term

Jewish group interests. Advancing assimilation may well generate contradictory political consequences. We have seen that Jewish liberalism increases with declines in ritual observance up to the point dividing the most secularized 15 per cent or so of American Jews from their more observant counterparts. Thus, any declines in ritual observance through assimilation should generally advance Jewish liberalism. Since the most observant are among the least liberal, their potential shrinkage combined with the growth of moderately or minimally observant Jews may well mean an overall shift to the left.

However, further down the observance continuum, declines in observance may figuratively transfer Jews from the "minimally" observant to a more assimilated "secular" camp. The analysis demonstrated that the former are the most liberal Jews, while the latter are among the most conservative. Thus, declines in observance may simultaneously promote conservatism as well as liberalism, depending on which Jews integrate, secularize, or assimilate.

These inferences depend upon a premise of stability in the inverted U-shaped relationship between liberalism and ritual observance (i.e., Jewish identification broadly conceived). But that contour may also change as American liberals and conservatives change their orientations toward ethnicity, religiosity, and particular Jewish interests. For example, if liberals become more receptive to religious community or to ethnic interests – as many of them have become in the last decade – they would reduce strains between the practice of religiosity and leftist politics. The alignment of conservative forces with a Christian fundamentalist resurgence, or with corporate interests antipathetic to Israel, would alienate survivalist Jews from the political right; at the same time, liberals' anti-interventionism might cause those Jews who advocate American military support for Israel to look elsewhere for allies. In short, one cannot accurately predict the near-term future of Jews' political orientations on the basis of these findings.

The larger issues addressed by these data entail the impact of modernity and how it has thrust Jews into the larger society engendering both political responsibilities and political opportunities. The distinctive character of Jewish political responses to modernity, to participation in a generally tolerant society, has been influenced by the various factors this chapter has identified. These factors are directly linked with Jews' entry and integration into the larger society. In no special order they include: perceptions (accurate or not) by Jews of a greater tolerance by the more universalistic, cosmopolitan, and hence liberal-left elements in the larger society; the influence of Jews' class position, be it working-class, middle-class entrepreneurial, or highly-educated professional status; the fashionable symbolic association of liberalism with successful integration into the sophisticated, cultural, high-brow segments of the larger society; the influence of traditionalist Jewish social values restraining some dimensions of liberalism; the increasingly legitimated expression of group politics in local and national arenas; and the adoption of mainstream political values by virtue of some Jews' assimilation into the mainstream society. The interplay of these six factors alone – notwithstanding other considerations – suggests that the analysis of American Jewish political behavior at any reasonable level of complexity is extraordinarily difficult. The only thing we can say with confidence is that integration into the modern society is a crucial determinant of contemporary Jewish politics.

Modernity has undoubtedly provided the opportunity for not one, but several distinctively modern Jewish forms of political expression. In traditional societies the responsibility for operating within the larger political environment lay largely in the hands of a few communal leaders; but today's Jewish politics can be, and is, practiced by the masses. Modernity, then, can be credited with establishing Jewish politics – be it the politics of integration (liberalism) or of group survival (pro-Israelism) – as new forms of group identification.

8 Pro-Israelism as the politics of ethnic survival[1]

Integration and survival too

In the first third of the twentieth century, Zionists constituted only a minority movement within American Jewry. Zionism's opponents saw it as endangering successful integration into the larger society. They believed that if Jews would act as Zionists, that is, if they were to behave as a separate national entity, their allegiance to the United States would be made suspect.

The founding of the State of Israel in 1948, the emergence of a more assertive Jewish leadership, and the recurrent, increasingly vociferous responses by American Jews to threats to the State, all helped terminate the initial controversy over Zionism's propriety. Norman Podhoretz, then, as now, editor of *Commentary* magazine, could write shortly after the 1973 Yom Kippur war that concern for America's support for an "Israel in mortal danger . . . of losing its life . . . has turned almost every Jew in America into a Zionist" (Podhoretz, 1974 : 44). Pro-Israelism (American Jewish support for Israel) had become a mass-based movement supplanting liberalism as the centerpiece of activity for most major Jewish organizations. Hundreds of thousands of American Jews annually supported Israel both financially and politically. During the 1970s, the proportion of adult Jews who had visited Israel more than doubled, growing from 16 per cent in 1970–71 to 38 per cent in 1981 (Cohen, 1982b).

The last chapter advanced the view that Jewish liberalism may be seen as the politics of integration. As liberal activists, Jews could participate in a broad-based coalition with other Americans in pressing for inter-group tolerance, civil liberties, and social justice. Not only did liberalism provide the practical opportunity for integration, its goals attracted integration-anxious Jews. A genuinely pluralist society which adhered to its constitutional guarantees and preserved domestic tranquility by tend-ing to the legitimate needs of poor minorities, would not attack its Jews in a fit of anti-semitism as Europeans had in both traditional and recent modern times.

But most Jews' integrationist anxieties fell far short of a readiness to dissipate totally; rather, their integrationist yearnings coexisted with a survivalist impulse to preserve their group identity. Liberalism and pro-Israelism − American Jews' principal political movements − express the long-standing twin social goals of integration and survival. Thus, if liberalism is the politics of integration, then pro-Israelism can be seen as the politics of ethnic survival.

Modernity and Zionism

Although traditional Jews supported Jewish settlements in Palestine for centuries, contemporary pro-Israel activity (like other forms of Jewish politics) is in many ways an invention of the modern era. We may recall that the business of conducting Jewish politics in traditional times was usually confined to a small elite. *Shtadlanim*, wealthy Jewish leaders, would represent the community to the local authorities in such matters as taxes, residence permits, and occupation licenses. A few Jews worked as tax-collectors or administrators for local rulers, and on rare occasions, some rose to positions of genuine influence. But the common folk (Chris-tians as well as Jews) were excluded from the political life of the tra-ditional societies in which they dwelled.

The advent of the democratic nation-state in the modern era meant that the active polity would comprise most, if not all, adult citizens. Politics became more a mass phenomenon, since the principles of the Emancipation and the Enlightenment demanded that Jews participate freely in the countries' political life. Zionism (or, in America, pro-Israelism) and Jewish liberalism were two of the principal ways in which masses of modern Jews availed themselves of the new opportunities for political participation.

With the decline of traditional religious practice in the nineteenth century, early Zionists believed their movement would replace what they saw as a rapidly decaying tradition. Often highly secularized, they conflicted frequently with the European and Palestinian rabbinate (Salmon, 1978). Moreover, there were relatively few observant Zionists (e.g., the *Mizrachi*) among migrants to Palestine in the first third of the twentieth century (see, for example, Friedman, 1977; Reinharz, 1975).

In light of the secular roots of Zionism and its broad appeal to the modernizing masses, one might speculate that support for Israel today would be strongest among the ritually non-observant American Jews, who, in effect, may supplant God with country. But, such an inference would fly in the face of a good deal of evidence clearly visible to even the most casual observer of American Jewry. Today's pro-Israel activity obviously draws considerable strength from the most highly observant segments of the Jewish population (absent a few Orthodox and Hassidic sects who are hostile to Israel's existence for a variety of theological and historic reasons). Nevertheless, the actual extent to which the less ritually observant substitute concern for Israel for the traditional religious practices they or their immediate forebears abandoned remains to be assessed. In other words, we shall want to explore how much pro-Israelism varies by ritual observance as well as by such factors as age, education, and income.

In examining how concern for Israel or pro-Israelism varies, we should take into account its multi-dimensional character. Earlier chapters have examined some factors influencing philanthropic activity and there is no way to extend the analysis of available data to isolate the Israel-oriented motivations for giving to Jewish charities. Since no contemporary available data adequately examine concrete political support for Israel, this chapter's analysis of pro-Israel activity *per se* will be confined to travel to the Jewish State. In addition, lacking data on pro-Israel political activities, we shall analyze several attitudinal components of support for Israel of which we can distinguish at least three broad areas: orientation to the tenets of classical Zionism, concern for Israel, and support for her government's international policies.

Classical Zionism and Pro-Israelism

Most classical Zionists (and many contemporary Israelis too) contended that Jewish life outside of Israel is inherently unhealthy, fragile, and tenuous as well as less historically significant than Jewish life in Israel (see, most recently, Halkin, 1977). According to this view, all Jews genuinely concerned about Jewish survival, all sincere Zionists, are obliged to settle in Israel, or at least make an earnest attempt to do so.

Previous research documents that American Jews largely reject these aspects of classical Zionism, but they strongly endorse pro-Israelism (e.g., Sklare and Greenblum, 1979). The latter tendency departs from classical Zionism in its legitimation of Diaspora (especially American) Jewish life and its rejection of Zionism's overt and unabashed nationalist formulation of Jewish identity and community. Pro-Israelism also commends Jews to care deeply about Israel and to support her efforts to achieve military security and economic prosperity.

Until recently, concern for Israel was virtually synonymous with support for her leaders' policies, particularly in matters of security (Liebman, 1977). Since the mid-1970s, these two sentiments – concern and policy support – may have diverged. Today, not a few prominent Jews who profess concern for Israel disagree sharply with her government's policies (e.g. Hertzberg, 1982; Cohen, 1980d). (Most who have criticized Israeli policies have done so from a "dovish" or liberal vantage point, charging Israel with undue harshness in its dealings with indigenous Arabs and with insufficient flexibility in the diplomatic arena; however, criticism has also emerged from "hawkish" or conservative American Jewish quarters where Israel has been seen as too willing to yield to diplomatic and political pressures.) In this context, an analytical consideration of pro-Israelism in the current period should distinguish between concern for Israel and support for the political stance of her government. By examining the various dimensions and manifestations of pro-Israelism – their incidence and how they vary within American Jewry – we can learn how pro-Israelism functions as a significant dimension of Jewish identity in modern America.

The basic contours of American Pro-Israelism

The 1981–82 National Survey of American Jews asked a variety of questions pertaining to classical Zionism, concern for Israel, support for her policies, and other related matters. *Table 8(1)* reports the distribution of responses to selected questions in those areas.

As social historians, sociologists and others have often noted, the norm of settling in Israel ("making *aliyah*") – classical Zionism's chief imperative – receives little support among American Jews. Accordingly only 12 per cent of the national sample agreed with the statement, "Each American Jew should give serious thought to settling in Israel."

Table 8(1)   Distribution of responses to Pro-Israel questions and related items

	%
Classical Zionism	
Each American Jew should give serious thought to settling in Israel (agree)	12
There is a bright future for Jewish life in America (disagree)	13
Concern or caring for Israel	
If Israel were destroyed, I would feel as if I had suffered one of the greatest personal tragedies in my life (agree)	83
Jews should not vote for candidates who are unfriendly to Israel (agree)	78
I often talk about Israel with friends and relatives (agree)	67
How important is each of the following issues or problems confronting American Jews? ("very important")	
security of Israel	69
anti-semitism in America	66
assimilation	41
In general, how would you characterize your feelings about Israel?	
very pro-Israel	43
pro-Israel	50
neutral or anti-Israel	7
Support for Israel's policies	
Israel is right not to agree to sit down with the Palestine Liberation Organization (PLO), because the PLO is a terrorist organization that wants to destroy Israel (agree)	74
If the West Bank became an independent Palestinian state, it would probably be used as a launching pad to endanger Israel (agree)	64
If the alternatives are permanent Israeli annexation of the West Bank or an independent Palestinian state, then an independent Palestinian state is preferable (disagree)	41
If Israel could be assured of peace and secure borders, she should be willing to return to Arab control most of the territories she has occupied since 1967 (disagree)	40
In general Israel's policies in its disputes with the Arabs have been:	
too "hawkish"	24
about right	73
too "dovish"	3

Table 8(1)—cont.

	%
Israel and America	
US support for Israel is in America's interest (agree)	93
There are times when my devotion to Israel comes in conflict with my devotion to America (disagree)	71
Most Americans think US support for Israel is in America's interest (agree)	45
American Jews should not criticize Israel's policies publicly (agree)	39
N=	(673)

Source: 1981 National Survey of American Jews.

In addition to urging *aliyah*, classical Zionists have contended that Jewish life outside of Israel is inherently insecure owing to the twin threats of assimilation and anti-semitism. American Jews have long held a contrary, more optimistic view: Jews may be threatened elsewhere, but America is different. The table's second row demonstrates that American Jews continue to reject classical Zionism's pessimistic forecast for Diaspora Jewry. Only 13 per cent disagreed with the proposition that "there is a bright future for Jewish life in America."

Clearly, most American Jews reject classical Zionism's denial of the prospect for successful integration into American society. Nevertheless, they do care deeply about Israel and her future. Roughly four-fifths said the destruction of Israel would be "one of the greatest personal tragedies of my life" and a similar number agreed that "Jews should not vote for candidates unfriendly to Israel." About two-thirds reported talking often "about Israel with friends and relatives" and a similar number regarded the "security of Israel" as a "very important" problem "confronting American Jews," ranking it higher than all others. The vast majority (over 90 per cent) described themselves as pro-Israel, with roughly half of these "very pro-Israel" and the other half simply "pro-Israel."

While American Jews see themselves as very concerned about Israel, their support for many of her policies in the international sphere is somewhat more tenuous. The third panel in *Table 8(1)* reports the sample's views toward four fundamental contentions of Israeli foreign policy in 1981. Around two-thirds agreed with the Israeli government that the PLO and the Palestinians are seeking to destroy Israel. Nearly three-quarters supported Israeli refusal to talk with the PLO and a little less than two-thirds agreed that a Palestinian state on the West Bank "would probably be used as a launching pad to endanger Israel."

Despite perceiving Palestinians as a threat, American Jews are divided over whether to trade territory for peace. Only two-fifths of the sample joined with the then Israeli government in rejecting the proposition that a Palestinian state was preferable to annexation of the West Bank. A similar minority stood with the government in abjuring the position that Israel should "return to Arab control most of the territories she has occupied since 1967" in return for assurance of "peace and secure borders."

A useful summary measure of American Jews' evaluations of Israeli foreign policy is at the bottom of the table's third panel. Roughly one-quarter said that "Israel's policies in its disputes with the Arabs have been too 'hawkish'." Very few thought they were "too 'dovish'" and nearly three-quarters thought these policies were "about right." In these data, then, we see that only a substantial minority of American Jews supported the relatively hard-line philosophy of the Likud Party (in power in 1981). The rest were either unsure about or rejected this line of thinking. In that, they may be said to correspond to elements of the Israeli Labor Alignment (in opposition in 1981) who indicated a greater willingness to relinquish control of the administered territories, and even contemplated the establishment of a Palestinian state in those areas if peace and security for Israel could be reasonably guaranteed.

While American Jews are divided over specific questions of Israeli policy, they are nearly unanimous in denying any contradiction between their pro-Israelism and their American identities. The vast majority (over 90 per cent) concurred that "US support for Israel is in America's interest" and more than two-thirds rejected the statement, "There are times when my devotion to Israel comes into conflict with my devotion to America." This perceived consonance of support for Israel with "Americanness" parallels the protestations of early American Zionist leaders such as Justice Louis Brandeis who averred that support for Israel implies neither disloyalty to the United States nor being "un-American."

However, respondents were much less sanguine about the rest of the country seeing things that way. Less than half of the sample agreed that "most Americans think US support for Israel is in America's interest," a figure only half as large as the vast proportion who thought that American interests and support for Israel coincided. The sample was also very divided over whether Jews should "criticize Israel's policies publicly," with the majority favoring dissent. The two-fifths minority who opposed public criticism were generally older, less educated, less liberal on American political issues generally, and more supportive of Israeli policies (data not shown). In sum, the sample overwhelmingly expressed concern for Israel, generally lent support to her policies, and indicated uneasiness over the solidity of American support for Israel, even as they rejected the most fundamental tenets of classical Zionism.

Accounting for Pro-Israelism

American Jews' deep concern for Israel and general support for her government's policies are by no means uniform throughout all segments of the American Jewish population. These sentiments are influenced by several major demographic variables and, not least, by overall Jewish identification.

The following analysis of these two dimensions of pro-Israelism (concern and policy support) utilizes two indices constructed from many of the questions listed in the second and third panels of *Table 8(1)*. Accordingly, respondents received one point on the five-question "concern for Israel" index when they agreed with each of the three statements on the destruction of Israel, on not voting for candidates unfriendly to Israel, and on talking about Israel with friends and family. They also received a point for characterizing the security of Israel as a "very important" problem confronting American Jews and another for describing themselves as "very pro-Israel."

Five questions also comprised the "support for Israel's policies" index. Respondents were awarded one point each time they agreed with the statements on rejecting talks with the PLO, and the likelihood of a West Bank Palestinian state endangering Israel; they received a point for preferring annexation to an independent Palestinian state, another for endorsing keeping the territories even if Israel were "assured of peace and secure borders," and one point if they characterized Israeli policies generally toward the Arabs as either too "dovish" or "about right." Those who scored a majority of the possible points on each scale (at least three out of five) were judged "high" on "concern for Israel" or on "support for Israel's policies." (These are very arbitrary cutting points; one should not compare overall levels of "concern" or "support" on the basis of these two indices.)

Table 8(2) reports how age and education influence the two dimensions

Table 8(2) Concern for Israel and support for Israeli policies by age, education, income, ritual observance, and liberalism[a]

	concern for Israel		support for policies		
	un-adjusted[b]	adjusted	un-adjusted	adjusted	N
age					
18–39	32	37	52	57	214
40–59	46	45	66	63	185
60+	53	47	73	70	184
education					
high school or less	59	55	74	70	103
some college	49	47	71	68	124
BA	37	38	65	68	149
MA or more	34	37	49	51	137
n.a.	—	—	—	—	10
income					
under $15,000	46	42	64	61	80
$15,000–$24,999	40	40	57	56	119
$25,000–$39,999	41	44	65	68	129
$40,000–$74,999	38	39	61	63	129
$75,000+	35	39	66	70	52
n.a.	62	57	69	64	74
ritual observance					
secular	16	17	46	46	78
minimal	40	41	61	64	244
moderate	50	51	67	65	209
observant	58	56	75	71	133
liberalism					
conservative-moderate	46	44	70	68	241
liberal	43	41	66	65	209
left-liberal	38	45	45	50	133

Source: 1981 National Survey of American Jews.

Notes:

a See Chapter 7 for descriptions of ritual observance and liberalism indices. The concern for Israel index consists of five items relating to (1) reactions to the hypothesized destruction of Israel; (2) not voting for anti-Israel candidates; (3) talking about Israel with friends; (4) being "very pro-Israel"; (5) regarding the security of Israel as "very important". The support for policies index is also built with five items: (1) policies are not "too hawkish"; (2) no talks with the PLO; (3) Palestinian state would be a danger; (4) annexation is preferable to a Palestinian state; (5) lands should not be returned for assurances of peace. See text (this chapter and *Table 8(1)*) for more precise details.

b Unadjusted figures refer to simple bivariate relationships between either pro-Israel index and each of the five independent variables. Adjusted columns contain figures adjusted by Multiple Classification Analysis where the effects of each variable is reported controlling (adjusting) for the other four.

of pro-Israelism. Both education and age not only signify integration into modern society, they also serve as harbingers of the American Jewish future. Younger people are chronologically more distant from the traditional heritage of their forebears, and inevitably will replace their elders as both age. Similarly, since younger American Jews have acquired more education, the better educated will come to represent a larger portion of the Jewish population. Significantly, both age and education display parallel and complementary relationships with both pro-Israel dimensions. That is, both the older people and the less educated are more pro-Israel − measured either in terms of "concern" or "support" − than younger and better-educated respondents.

While age and education bear clear though modest relationships with the two measures of pro-Israelism, income's impact on the pro-Israel indices is both inconsistent and insignificant. With or without controls for other variables, upper-, middle-, and lower-income respondents hardly differed from one another with respect to their orientations toward Israel.

These results strikingly resemble those reported for traditional ritual behavior in earlier chapters. We saw that education and youth dampened ritual observance, while income's effects were much more subdued. Consistent with this observation, the lower middle portion of *Table 8(2)* reports that both pro-Israelism indices are closely related to ritual observance. "Observant" respondents are at least 25 percentage points more likely to score high on a "pro-Israel" index than are "secular" respondents, even after controlling for demographic differences. In particular the "secular" are the least pro-Israel, they are the most sharply differentiated from the other ritual groups in terms of their concern for Israel or support of Israeli policies. Thereafter, smaller increases in pro-Israel feelings are recorded for each advance up the ritual observance scale, indicating that pro-Israelism is almost a matter of consensus among all but the most assimilated.

Much as one would expect, then, pro-Israelism is a function of Jewish identification; more observant Jews say they care more about Israel and are more likely to express support for her government's foreign policy positions. Moreover, young people and the better educated are less pro-Israel not only because they are less ritually observant (or, perhaps, more politically liberal) but for intrinsic reasons connected with age and education. The lower levels of pro-Israel attitudes among young people (even after controlling for their lower levels of religious observance) probably derive from the birth-cohort effect observed earlier with respect to Jewish identification in general. The chronological distance between Jews in the United States and their forebears' traditional heritage has had an erosive impact upon all forms of Jewish identification including, apparently, pro-Israelism.

The impact of education should not be ascribed merely to an experience of attending college or graduate school. True, higher education exerts a liberalizing and cosmopolitanizing impact upon its students; but education also reflects the prior acquisition of certain values and social networks. In other words, we are unable to separate the element of self-selection from the *bona fide* effects of higher education *per se*. While we cannot satisfactorily explain why and how education is associated with diminished concern or support for Israel, the inverse association between education and pro-Israelism is undeniable.

Liberalism versus Pro-Israelism?

The last chapter demonstrated that younger, better-educated respondents were more likely to score high on the index of political liberalism. Since the same types of respondents also score somewhat lower on the pro-Israelism measures, one might well imagine that high liberalism and low-Israelism would go hand-in-hand.

There are, of course, more substantive reasons to suspect that liberals would evince more restrained support for Israel. Political commentators and communal thinkers in the last decade have advanced the proposition that support for Israel and advocacy of the liberal political agenda are fundamentally incompatible. Interestingly, both political conservatives and liberals have propounded this point of view.

Pro-Israel neo-conservatives, particularly those centered around the American Jewish Committee's *Commentary* magazine, regard the liberal community as inherently hostile to Israel and to Jewish domestic interests. In their view adequate support for Israel demands a strong American military posture:

> In a world full of ambiguities and puzzlements, one thing is absolutely easy both to define and locate: that is the Jewish interest. The continued security and, in those happy places where the word applies – well being of Jews, worldwide, rests with a strong, vital, prosperous, self-confident United States. (Decter, 1980 : 31)

Interestingly, leftist commentators also share this view, suggesting that erstwhile Jewish liberalism has been eroded by such parochial concerns as Israel and the domestic debate over affirmative action and quotas. Christopher Hitchens, writing in *The Nation*, interprets the perspective of pro-Israel political activists:

> Those who put Israel first, therefore, must mute their criticisms of the arms trade and the Rapid Deployment Force. They must also sub-contract their consciences when it comes to Israel's own arms trade – with Somoza before he was overthrown, with Duarte, with Botha and even with the anti-Semitic *caudillos* of Argentina.
>
> (Hitchens, 1981 : 608, 610)

Not only should Israel's supporters advocate a strong American military posture, according to Hitchens, but they should also adopt a cold-war view of the Soviet Union:

> Because the Soviet Union supports the Arab cause, and because it shamefully persecutes its Jews, it becomes harder to resist the con-clusion that the "main enemy" is the USSR. This has opened a whole flank in the liberal community to doubts about detente and rearma-ment.
>
> (Hitchens, 1981 : 610)

Finally, Hitchens makes the contrast between support for Israeli govern-ment policies and American liberalism in the starkest possible terms: "If it comes to a choice between Israeli policy and liberalism, which will American liberals choose? . . . A small but significant part of the spec-trum has chosen the first option and, thereby, consciously abandoned liberalism altogether" (Hitchens, 1981 : 611).

Hitchens is not alone on the left in suggesting that concerns for Israel's security have undermined historic American Jewish support for liberal-ism, especially in the international sphere. Legal scholar Tom J. Farer, trying to explain the rise of "Reaganism" in the *New York Review of Books* (21 January 1982), cites the Jews as one of the key groups to abandon the old-line liberal coalition. He ascribes their motives to racial tensions and to security concerns for Israel:

> Jewish businessmen, organizations, and intellectuals had played a prominent part in the struggle for reform of capitalism and race relations. . . . But growing friction between the black and Jewish communities helped to produce an overall shift of Jewish votes to the right. . . . The evidence of Arab unity within OPEC and the West's deferential response sharpened fears among American Jews about the tenacity of U.S. support for Israel. The stronger their doubts about

America's long-term commitment in the face of Arab demands, the more powerful the temptation to embrace the cold war conception of U.S.-Soviet relations never abandoned by the right wing of the Republican Party.   (Farer, 1982 : 42)

Hence, from two points on the political spectrum, we find observers arguing that simultaneous support for liberalism and Israeli security cannot long endure. Pro-Israel neo-conservatives urge fellow supporters of Israel to abandon policies which they believe have resulted in a weak America incapable of providing the Jewish State with adequate military and diplomatic backing. Left-liberals like Christopher Hitchens argue that the neo-conservatives have obtained wide support among pro-Israel Jews.

If the liberalism versus pro-Israelism contention is valid, then American Jewish liberals should lend Israel less support than conservatives. That is, either some Israel supporters may abandon their former liberal positions, or some liberals may back off from their commitment to Israel.

The bottom section of *Table 8(2)* reports the relationship between liberalism (as measured by the 10-item index described in Chapter 7, see p. 148) and both measurs of pro-Israelism. The unadjusted figures for concern for Israel show a modest decline with increasing liberalism. Thus, while 46 per cent of the conservative-to-moderate Jews scored high on concern for Israel, only 38 per cent of their left-liberal counterparts did so. However, the adjusted figures show that this initial relationship is totally due to age, education, income, and Jewish identification. Controlling for these factors, liberalism bore little relationship with concern for Israel; in fact, the adjusted column shows the highest concern for Israel among the most liberal group.

While liberalism bore little relationship with concern for Israel, quite a different picture emerges when we examine the results for the other dimension of pro-Israelism, support for Israel's policies. As the unadjusted figures in the third column of *Table 8(2)* indicate, left-liberals were considerably less supportive of Israeli policies than others; only 45 per cent scored high on the index as compared with 66 per cent of the liberals and 70 per cent of the conservative-to-moderates. This pattern remained essentially unaltered when controls for other variables were introduced.

In simple terms, then, liberals were no less caring about or concerned for Israel than conservative or moderate Jews; however, they were much less prepared to endorse essentially "hawkish" formulations of Israeli international policies. Perhaps the most cogent explanation for this finding is that liberals within the American political arena extend their general approach to international hostilities to the Middle East. Liberals in this survey generally opposed increases in US military spending, and they were more sympathetic to affirmative action and busing for integration. As a rule, then, liberals tend to prefer conciliatory solutions to international problems, and endorse diplomatic over military means for resolving those problems. Accordingly, they criticize Israel for failing to negotiate with the PLO, and urge her to make significant territorial concessions for assurances of peace and secure borders; some also deny that Palestinians or the PLO constitute an implacable and unalterable mortal danger to Israel. (These four positions constitute the heart of the support of Israeli policies index.) Some liberals apparently readily differentiate their concern for Israel from support for her government's policies.

The two dimensions of pro-Israelism we have been investigating, then, are empirically related but conceptually distinct from one another. Concern for Israel is more closely related to Jewish identification (as measured by ritual observance) than is support for Israeli policies. Moreover, concern declined in conjunction with youth (later birth cohort) and higher education, while it bore little relationship with income and political liberalism.

Support for Israeli policies was also associated with age, education, and ritual observance and it too bore an ambiguous association with income. However, while liberalism exerts little influence upon concern for Israel, it does erode support for Israeli policies. Political support for Israel, especially at times when Israeli policies diverge from the usual perceptives of American public opinion, do not necessarily reflect support for Israel generally. Obviously some report deep concerns for the Jewish State but nevertheless differ from her government's political postures; similarly, some support Israel's policies, but nevertheless fail to evince much concern for her future or security.

These results suggest impending declines in pro-Israelism among American Jews overall as younger, more educated, and less ritually observant Jews replace their elders and predecessors. While prediction is perilous, certainly the direction of American Jewish social and demographic trends point toward shrinking numbers of individuals passionately concerned about Israel and prepared to advocate her government's point of view.

Travel to Israel

Travel to Israel is obviously a partial outgrowth of pro-Israel sentiment. The several thousands who travel to Israel on UJA (United Jewish Appeal) missions, for example, testify to the inter-connectedness of travel, philanthropy, and concern for Israel, all aspects of the general concept of pro-Israelism. One wonders whether age, education, income, and ritual observance bear relationships with travel similar to their associations with the other pro-Israel measures. For example, we would expect greater proportions of older people to have traveled to Israel than youngsters. The former simply have had more time to have done so, they are more Jewishly identified, and they earn higher incomes.

Less clear is how to anticipate the relationship between travel and education in advance of our findings. On the one hand, Chapter 4 reported that the better educated performed fewer religious rituals, but up to the BA they more often participated in institutional activities. On the other hand, the preceding section (drawing upon *Table 8(2)*) demonstrated that of those with advanced degrees, relatively fewer said they cared deeply about Israel or professed support for her policies.

All things being equal, we would expect those with higher incomes and greater ritual observance to travel to Israel more often. The affluent simply have the requisite resources to spend, and the observant are more likely to possess the religious or ethnic motivation to make the trip to the Jewish State.

Table 8(3) displays the relationships between travel to Israel (that is, the percentage of respondents who reported having been to Israel at least once) with five variables of interest: age, education, income, ritual observance, and liberalism. In so doing, it reports both anticipated and unanticipated results.

As we would expect, increases in age, income, and ritual observance were associated with increase in travel to Israel. Of the three, the association of travel with ritual observance was the most powerful. While only 21 per cent of "secular" respondents claimed to have been to Israel, nearly three-fifths (58 per cent) of the "observant" Jews reported having traveled there. (Overall, some 38 per cent of the sample replied they had been to Israel, a figure equal to that reported in other American Jewish population surveys in 1981.) More of the highly-educated respondents had travelled to Israel, even after controlling for income and other variables. Last, political views had little effect upon traveling to Israel.

The unambiguous positive relationships of travel with income,

Table 8(3) Travel to Israel by age, education, income, ritual observance, and liberalism

	unadjusted	adjusted
age		
18–39	33	31
40–59	38	33
60+	47	54
education		
high school or less	27	21
some college	38	33
BA	42	45
MA or more	45	47
n.a.	—	—
income		
Under $15,000	24	31
$15,000–$24,999	36	38
$25,000–$39,999	40	40
$40,000–$74,999	42	38
$75,000+	50	50
n.a.	75	42
ritual observance		
secular	21	19
minimal	32	32
moderate	46	46
observant	58	59
liberalism		
conservative-moderate	37	38
liberal	40	38
left-liberal	40	43
N=	(673)	

Source: 1981–82 National Survey of American Jews.

education, and ritual observance indicate that travel to Israel bears some conceptual affinity with such institutional activities as belonging to a synagogue or Jewish organization, or contributing to the central philanthropic drive. The likelihood of participating in all these activities – joining, giving, and traveling – is enhanced by the financial resources afforded by higher incomes. The better educated are more likely to belong to a subculture which emphasizes participation in voluntary organizations, or, alternatively, in spending money on foreign travel.

The ritually observant are more motivated to express their strong group commitments in a variety of Jewish communal activities.

Concluding discussion

If we compare results across all three pro-Israel measures – concern for Israel, support for her policies, and travel – we find both similarities and differences. In all instances, younger people were less pro-Israel than their elders; in all instances the more ritually observant were more pro-Israel. While the better educated had lower levels of pro-Israel attitudes, and income had little effect upon them, increases in both were associated with increased travel to Israel. Last, liberalism bore no relationship with either concern for Israel or travel there, but did diminish support for some hardline Israeli government policies.

In conclusion, the bulk of American Jewry can indeed be characterized as pro-Israel. Although they are not prepared to endorse those classical Zionist positions which they think would inhibit their integration into American society, American Jews are prepared to go a long way in supporting Israel. The vast majority profess to care deeply about Israel, a considerable majority agree with most of her government's policies, and a sizable minority have expressed their commitment to Israel by having spent some time there.

Pro-Israelism is indeed a distinctive dimension of Jewish identity; but contrary to the dreams of some classical Zionists or the fears of some rabbinical leaders, it generally serves to supplement conventional forms of Jewish expression rather than to supplant them.

Epilogue
In the aftermath of modernity: diverse consequences for Jewish identity

The overarching aim of this book has been to assess the prospects for American Jewish group survival within the conceptual context of modernization, that is, the transition of Western Jews from traditional to modern societies. The opening chapters advanced the proposition that American Jews have followed paths akin to those followed by predecessor Western Jewries who emerged out of traditional, pariah-group pasts to refashion their communities and group identities in relatively open, modern societies.

Modernity invariably meant new opportunities for participation in the larger polity and economy, as well as in the social mainstream. As a result, Jews quickly assumed new demographic configurations, in particular, new generational, residential, socio-economic, and family characteristics. These in turn not only helped constitute the distinctive ways in which individual Jews integrated into the larger society; they also influenced the nature and character of modern Jewish community and identity.

Certainly, in many ways, particular socio-demographic changes among American Jews have resembled parallel trends among other major white immigrant groups. Still, Jews have exhibited distinctive patterns of evolution in each sphere of change. Moreover, differences among Jews – in terms of generation, residence, social status, and family type – even among those living at the same point in time, often correspond with certain historical realities. That is, they tend to capture successive stages of modernization; and, more significantly for our concerns, they are linked with changing patterns of ritual observance, communal affiliation, in-group segregation, and political involvement. This work has attempted to elucidate those linkages between particular key dimensions of Jewish demographic change and certain aspects of Jewish identity. In doing so, it has tried to refine our understanding of the ways in which Jews have sought both to integrate into the open society (as reflected in the major demographic dimensions) and, at the same time, to survive as a distinctive religious and ethnic group (as reflected in several concrete religious and ethnic activities).

The major findings

Certainly the findings indicate that generalizing about Jews' accommodation to the modern world is difficult, but useful nonetheless. In the analysis, we found that each dimension of demographic change bore peculiar, although interpretable, associations with various spheres of Jewish activity. Alternatively, each sphere of Jewish identity bore distinctive relationships with several dimensions of integration into modern, American society. We may review and summarize the main substantive conclusions from each of the empirical chapters as follows:

(1) Generation has diverse and, at times, offsetting and non-linear relationships with various dimensions of Jewish identity (Chapter 3). Thus, the advance of generation brought both the erosion of certain "traditional" ritual practices and the stabilization in the practice of more "modern" observances (here the terms "traditional" and "modern" may constitute *post hoc* modifiers). At the same time, generational transitions also corresponded with initial increases followed by subsequent declines in institutional affiliation. Apparently, third- and fourth-generation Jews have been less motivated by integrationist concerns than were their elders and they have been less likely to participate in the institutions – large synagogues, defense agencies, philanthropic drives – which the second generation had established, enlarged, and enhanced. In addition, later-generation Jews have fewer Jewish close friends and spouses, although they persist in having family and friendship circles consisting primarily of fellow Jews.

(2) Much of what is distinctively ethnic about many American immigrant groups has been tied to working-class subculture. If such were the case for Jewish ethnicity, Jewish group life would have been virtually decimated by the rapid social mobility of American Jews in the last

century (Chapter 4). Thus, in a fashion similar to other groups, extraordinary education achievement among Jews seems to have had especially deleterious consequences for the observance of their more traditional religious practices (e.g. kashrut, Sabbath observance). At the same time, though, education through the college degree (but not beyond) heightens institutional involvement by way of enhancing both income and adoption of America's highly affiliatory middle-class subculture. The crucial distinction among occupational groups centers on the division between self-employed entrepreneurs (whether professional or not) and salaried employees or professionals. The former are noticeably more institutionally active than are the salaried. Professional status in the aggregate exerts little observable impact upon levels of Jewish activity; but, incumbency in certain professions either elevates or diminishes institutional affiliation rates. Finally, higher income enhances institutional activity, particularly, and not surprisingly, those types which require significant disposable income.

(3) American Jews continue to move rapidly, often leaving areas where they have historically concentrated. This frequent migration temporarily disrupts formal affiliations, especially localistic ones like those to synagogues; it also brings many migrating Jews to areas with under-developed communal infrastructures (Chapter 5). But the association of geographic mobility with lower affiliation rates is not primarily a function of temporary disruption or of destination effects; in fact, it is largely accounted for by the youthfulness of the movers. In other words, it is young people who do most of the moving and they have low affiliation rates even if they remain residentially stable. The speed with which Jews establish synagogues, schools, and other institutions in new areas of settlement suggests that, in time, they tend to address the problems of immature institutionalization inherent in new Jewish communities.

(4) The American Jewish family has been changing both in line with trends in the larger American family and in line with the influence exerted by a historical dynamic peculiar to Western Jews (Chapter 6). Thus, Jews' average age at marriage has increased and continues to slightly exceed that of the national population; Jewish fertility has fallen so as to remain somewhat below that of comparably aged Americans; Jewish divorce rates have grown, but they have held at less than half the levels of white Protestants; and Jewish intermarriage has increased, but it remains below the much higher exogamy rates of all other major white American ethnic groups. These trends mean increases in Jewish singles, childless, intermarried, and divorcees (or "alternative" households).

The larger numbers of alternative families in turn have contributed heavily to the decline in Jewish ritual practice and communal affiliation in recent years. Not only are alternatives classically low participators in Jewish ritual and public life, but in recent years they have become even more remote from Jewish identity as compared with conventional Jewish households. The twin effects of alternative households – that is, their growing numbers and their diminished attachment to Jewish identity – probably pose the greatest challenge to Jewish continuity of all the demographic consequences of modern integration.

(5) Liberalism has constituted American Jews' principal political response to the opportunity to integrate into the larger society (Chapter 7). At one pole of the Jewish identity spectrum, the more segregated, more traditionally oriented Jews tend to report lower levels of political liberalism. At the other end of the continuum, Jews who are thoroughly secularized and virtually assimilated have, as a group, distributions of political inclinations very similar to those of the nation as a whole. Hence, the "middle," that is, those who affirmatively but marginally identify as Jews, are the ones who score highest on several measures of political liberalism. This inverted U-shaped contour concurs with the propositions that (a) Jews assimilate to the culturally as well as politically "progressive" elements of modern society; and (b) complete assimilation erodes Jewish political and cultural distinctiveness.

(6) Pro-Israelism – a term more adequate than "Zionism" as a characterization of American Jews' relationship with Israel – constitutes the main political expression of modern Jews' commitment to survive as a distinct polity and community, even as they integrate into the open society (Chapter 8). In recent years, active political and financial support for Israel has come to complement, if not supplement, liberalism as Jews' principal form of distinctive political involvement in the United States. In light of the last two decades' growth in Israel-oriented travel, philanthropy, political activity, and media attentiveness, one could easily contend that pro-Israelism has come to constitute a ritual surrogate for some of the religious practices observed by many American Jews' traditional ancestors. This contention would not contradict the finding that pro-Israel sympathies and activities are modestly correlated with ritual practice and other forms of Jewish commitment. The success of pro-Israelism would simply suggest that relative to their predecessors in earlier decades, today's Jewishly committed Americans have developed new forms of group expression to supplement many historic forms which have fallen into relative disuse.

Assessing modernity

The balance sheet, then, on the impact of modernity upon Jewish identification points neither in the direction of rapid assimilation, nor toward sustained and assured group continuity. Several pieces of evidence do, in fact, lend credence to the perspective of assimilationists, observers who discern signs of group disintegration and see them as most significant. Among those indicators are the many empirical connections, documented in the foregoing chapters, between two sorts of phenomena: the demographic trends which flow out of Jewish modernization – particularly, generational advancement, social mobility, and conventional family "breakdown" – and the accompanying diminution of various types of Jewish activity, particularly traditional ritual practices, but often including communal affiliation measures as well. In other words, if Jews keep changing as they have in recent decades, the "trend lines" point to diminished public and private Jewish activity.

However, several pieces of evidence also support the arguments of survivalists, those who think signs of Jewish persistence are most significant. First, despite rapid social, residential, and family mobility, Jews still retain several elements of demographic distinctiveness, even to the present day. Their social status and location in the economy, their migratory behavior and residential distribution, and their family patterns testify in some important areas to continued distinctiveness about being Jewish in America. Moreover, taken together they constitute a structural foundation for sustained group identity. Multifaceted social differentiation often gives rise to particular group political and economic interests, to distinctive cultural predilections, to social propinquity (if not virtual segregation), and ultimately, to group consciousness and solidarity. Thus, by virtue of their socio-demographic distinctiveness, today's Jews are likely to respond in similar fashions to political or economic stimuli; they are likely to share neighborhoods, social circles, and occupational groupings; and, as a result of all this, they may well maintain sentiments of common history and group destiny.

Aside from some continuity in demographic distinctiveness and social segregation, survivalist observers can point to other findings in this, if not other studies. In particular, American Jews have done tolerably well in sustaining reasonably high levels of ritual practice and institutional affiliation. They have done so by *reducing* but not abandoning certain historical forms of identification, and they have *innovated* new myths, symbols, rituals, and institutions (see, for example, Neusner, 1981).

They have done so by settling on a select group of activities, norms, and values − derived from the traditional past and reshaped by the modern present − as the bare essentials of contemporary Jewish identification. These are demonstrated in the widespread observance in at least a perfunctory manner of Passover, Chanukah, and the high holidays; in the majority of families with school-age children joining synagogues; in the near-universal celebration of key life-cycle events (birth, *bar/bat mitzvah*, marriage, and funerals); and in the near-consensual commitment to Jewish (and Israeli) survival and group defense. American Jews have supplemented ancient forms of identification with an ever-changing array of new practices, forms of communal organizations, myths, and symbols.

One of the most significant arenas for innovative activity has been the political realm. Entry into the political and social mainstream compelled Jews to address two important questions: how would (or should) modern society adjust to Jewish entry and how were Jews to reshape their identities and communities so as to integrate into the newly opened society? One response to these issues was widespread Jewish participation in left-of-center social and political movements to such an extent that left politics became synonymous with being Jewish and Jewishness often became identified with liberalism or socialism. In more recent times, the principal political preoccupations of the organized Jewish community have shifted to such increasingly particularistic concerns as Israel, Soviet Jewry, and the overt, unabashed defense of Jewish group interests in local and national politics. A highly elaborate institutional infrastructure has provided the vehicles through which American Jews express their political group identification. It consists of national intergroup relations agencies, philanthropic campaigns, social service agencies, synagogues, schools, and periodicals. Although participation in these institutions may have declined in recent years, they nevertheless remain, on the whole, quite viable. In the aggregate they represent the successful adaptation of the traditional Jewish penchant for community organization to the demands of life in modern society. Even more significantly, Jews have continued to innovate new organizational constructs. They have duplicated models found in the larger society (Political Actions Committees − funds for electoral candidates deemed sympathetic to Jewish interests − are one example), and they have responded to social movements or major cultural influences (Jewish feminist institutions (Lerner, 1976; Cohen, 1980a), and the *havurah* movement of small, self-motivated prayers-and-worship communities offer illustrations).

But the focus on the masses, rather than elites, is indeed a crucial feature of this work. The impact of modernity upon contemporary Jewish identity is clearly complex and does not submit to sweeping generalization. Further exploration of the phenomenon needs to go beyond the available quantitative data, beyond the measures of Jewish sentiment and activity commonly found in recent survey instruments. The kind of information one can obtain in a closed-ended questionnaire administered to hundreds of randomly chosen Jewish respondents is necessarily limited. However, even within the limitations of survey techniques, the indicators of new forms of Jewish commitment and identification have yet to be devised. The evidence of declines in Jewish identification tied to ongoing socio-demographic trends may "merely" signify transformation in how Jews identify; or as the analysis has largely suggested, they may reflect genuine decline in Jewish identification, however one may reasonably conceive it. This ambiguity arises from the fallibility of the available measures: they may portray respondents either as "more Jewish" or "less Jewish" than they "really" are. Some professional colleagues have criticized the measures used in this study, saying they understate Jewishness as they understand it. If valid, these criticisms suggest a rosier prognosis for the future of American Jewry, for they bespeak spheres of Jewish identity which lie outside the scope of the available questionnaire items.

However, there is certainly a contrary view. Ritual practice, affiliation with conventional institutions (synagogues, philanthropic campaigns, formal organizations), social segregation (marrying and making friends with other Jews) appear to embrace a lot of what many people mean by being distinctively Jewish. If so, then the declining trend lines in these indicators reflect a true, objective, and genuine decline in overall American Jews' ethnic and religious vitality, conceived in mass terms.

The distinction between mass and elite behavior points up another critical limitation to quickly drawing negative prognostications from this investigation. The calculus by which one evaluates historical significance is highly complex, and ultimately, subjectively determined. Historians have only recently supplemented their traditional focus on political and cultural elites with attention to the lives of ordinary people, the masses. In Jewish history, many of the most noteworthy, most admired, and eventually most influential achievements were the products of culturally or politically elite individuals living in numerically insignificant Jewish communities. Spanish Jews' vaunted Golden Age numbered only 50,000 souls; the great scholarly communities of post-Exilic Babylonia or of culturally vital pre-modern Europe were often smaller. Similarly, we may argue that from the perspective of tomorrow's historians, the typical behaviors of most American Jews may well be less crucial than the creativity, influence, and ingenuity of some of them. The actions of the masses are often no more than indicators, or simply conditions for performance of elites; one cannot justifiably draw immediate parallels between the two. Thus, several phenomena in contemporary Jewish life – the *havurot*, Jewish Political Action Committees, new social movements, advances in Jewish learning and intellectual life, creative responses to the aftermath of the Holocaust, involvement with Israel – may be, at one and the same time, both demographically limited and culturally significant.

All of this is to say that the findings, interpretations, and conclusions drawn from this investigation or others using similar methodological approaches should be understood in perspective. This type of survey research on contemporary Jewish identity is indeed useful in several respects. It does attempt to lend broad historical and theoretical significance to our understanding of Jews' ongoing adjustment to the challenges of American modernity and the legacy of the Jewish past. It does focus attention upon the influence of major demographic dimensions upon the contours of contemporary Jewish identity. It does refine and specify our conceptualization of Jewishness by showing how different measures respond uniquely to demographic trends and historical evolution. It does sketch the linkages between various elements of demographic, religious, ethnic, and political change.

However, this type of research – given the limitations of both method and available data – raises and leaves unanswered several interesting questions, large and small, global and specific. As noted above, perhaps the most crucial questions concern the unexplored areas of Jewish expression beyond the purview of conventional measures of ritual practice, communal affiliation, politics, and social segregation. This research also refrained from investigating the mechanisms through which demographic differences (or changes) influence Jewish identification. To offer a concrete illustration, we need more understanding of the precise ways in which changes in the life cycle result in changes in affiliation or ritual practice. This question, in turn, may be subsumed under the larger issue of discerning the meaning(s) of Jewishness to most American Jews. How and to what extent does Jewish commitment intersect with and influence other important spheres of activity such as the family and workworld? What combination of ideological, developmental, and social reasons motivate people to undertake particular Jewish activities? What salience, what values, and what significance do Jews attach to the central myths, symbols, and practices of contemporary American Judaism?

Finally, this work's time-bound quality itself provokes a variety of questions about future directions. Of course, such questions can be definitively answered only by examining the processes identified in this study as they unfold over time. For example, Jews have been acquiring post-graduate education in great numbers, they have been postponing childbearing, and they continue to migrate with great rapidity. All of these changes have been associated to varying degrees with diminished levels of Jewish involvement. Does that mean that the continuation of these demographic trends necessitates declining Jewish identification? Or, commensurate with much of Jewish history, will the perpetuation of these trends eventually provoke Jewry to refashion Jewishness so that it will comport with the new demographic configurations? Reasoned arguments can be made in support of either speculative position, but only the passage of time and the attentiveness of astute observers will furnish conclusive answers to these questions.

We can say that significant changes in the societies within which Jews live inevitably alter both their demography and group identity. We can also say that modern Jews have been remarkably creative in innovating numerous approaches to public and private Jewish life and have done so with a reasonable overall level of success thus far. Inevitable changes in the larger society and in many of Jews' fundamental social characteristics will continue to test and challenge Jewish religious and ethnic ingenuity. Whether – and how many – American Jews will meet those challenges, or even care enough to try, remains to be seen.

Notes

Introduction

1 For a review of recent literature on American Jewry, see Heilman (1982); Sklare (1982) contains some very thoughtful analyses of the state of the field of contemporary Jewish research; Elazar (1976) is the best single work of American Jewish communal structure. See also Sherman (1964), Sklare (1958, 1971, 1974a, 1974b), and Waxman (1981).

2 See any recent editions of the *American Jewish Year Book* for lists of Jewish periodicals and major organizations.

3 Any of a number of studies provide documentation of the observance of Jewish ritual practices. See, for example, Fowler (1977) for marginal distributions of ritual practices from the 1975 Boston Jewish Community Survey which also furnished the data for much of the analysis below. For recent data from a national sample of American Jews using low-cost mail-back techniques, see Cohen (1983a).

4 I have drawn this inference from my reading of recent organizational literature and talks with lay leaders and staff of major organizations. To cite a few examples: the old-line Zionist organizations – with the exception of Hadassah – have, for many years, been led by the same, aging personalities; B'nai B'rith, the largest Jewish membership organization, reports serious financial difficulties and major obstacles to recruiting young people; an examination of the circulation figures

for the American Jewish Congress' principal house organ reveals declines in readership over the years, as some suggest that the bulk of the AJC's membership derives from its charter-tour business. These are by no means isolated examples.

5 Cohen and Ritterband (1981) demonstrate that Jewish and Catholic fertility desires among a national sample of American college graduates increases with increases in religious service attendance. For a contrary view, see Lazerwitz (1980).

6 Examples of cross-ethnic comparative research in American ethnicity include Lieberson (1963, 1980), Abramson (1973), Greeley (1974), Alba (1976, 1981), and Cohen (1980b). For theoretical perspectives on American ethnicity, see Gordon (1964, 1975), Newman (1973), and Yancey, Eriksen, and Juliani (1976).

Chapter 1

1 I found Berger's work (1969, 1977, and 1979) and that of Cuddihy (1974) very useful in shaping my thinking of modernity and its impact on Western Jewry.

2 Interestingly, historians simply do not concur on how best to describe Europe's economic system prior to the Industrial Revolution. Some speak of the feudal economy and others are content to speak of "pre-capitalism," describing what was in terms of what it was not.

3 The term was first used by the historian Jacob Katz (1978).

Chapter 3

1 There is a considerable literature on first-generation American Jews. Some of the more useful works include: Wirth (1928), Goren (1970), Howe (1976), Kessner (1977), Gurock (1979), and Dawidowicz (1982).

2 The phrase is the title of Deborah Dash Moore's social history of second-generation New York Jews (Moore, 1981a).

3 Interestingly the age distribution of the foreign born was distinctly bimodal; in 1975 most of them were either over 60 or under 35. The analysis treats only the older foreign-born respondents, those born before 1920, as "first generation." Their younger foreign-born counterparts, most of whom were born after 1940, were born into societies which had modernized by the time of their early childhood socialization.

4 There were insufficient numbers of young first generation (labelled "foreign born" in the table) to consider explicitly in 1965. Although they are included in 1965's "all" column, they are excluded from separate mention. But they are sufficiently numerous by 1975 to warrant separate analysis. We note their average age (31) is close to that of third-generation respondents. In fact, as we shall see repeatedly, the young foreign born are very unlike the older immigrants (the "true" first generation) and in many respects close to the third and fourth generation.

5 Of course, Jewish identification for these young adults will undoubtedly rise in the years following the 1975 survey. Family life cycle, particularly having children, noticeably increases Jewish expression, and the young people in *Table 3(3)* generally had not yet reached the peak family years for Jewish identification (see Chapter 6).

6 Respondents with "high" Jewish identification were required to meet three criteria. They needed to perform at least two out of the three home-based rituals found on both surveys (Passover Seder, Sabbath candle lighting, keeping kosher at home). They needed to attend services more often than on the high holidays. And they needed to report affiliating in at least two out of three ways we have been investigating (by joining a synagogue, belonging to a Jewish organization other than a synagogue, and by donating to Jewish causes at least $25 in 1965 or $50 in 1975). At the other extreme, those with "low" Jewish identification were those who scored low in all three areas of identification. They performed zero or one of the three rituals (probably Passover Seder participation, if any); they attended synagogue less often than on the high holidays (if at all); and they satisfied none of the criteria for institutional affiliation. In other words, they belonged neither to a synagogue, nor to any other Jewish organization, nor did they make a minimal contribution to Jewish charities in the year prior to the survey.

Chapter 4

1 See the calculation by Sowell (1981 : 12). See also Goldstein (1969, 1981).

2 For reviews of the major perspectives on ethnic identity and assimilation, see Gordon (1964) and Newman (1973).

3 See, for example, Cohen (1977).

4 An analysis of US Census data shows that Russian-born Americans

(a proxy for American Jews; see Rosenthal (1975)) derived more income per year of education than did any other national-origin group. Contrary to popular assumptions, though, not all Ashkenazic Jews in modern Western societies shared a passion for higher education. Where education did not function as a channel of vertical mobility – as in early nineteenth-century United States or Germany, or in England even until the present day – Jews were not especially prone to educationally over-achieve.

5 For a local study with similar results see Hodge and Carrol (1978); for earlier data, see Alston (1971).

6 Handicapped by small sample size, Mueller and Johnson concluded that education depresses religious participation among American Jews (Mueller and Johnson, 1975). Lazerwitz's analysis of the National Jewish Population Survey conducted in the early 1970s found small relationships between education and various forms of Jewish identification (Lazerwitz, 1978).

7 The high rates of educational attainment among Boston Jews are unrelated to the concentration of post-secondary institutions there. The high educational achievement of American Jews is well-documented. Recent national data I collected in 1981 on American Jews' political attitudes (data which I describe more fully in Chapter 7) generated a distribution of educational attainment virtually identical with that reported for Boston 1975, in *Table 4(1)*.

8 The only ritual departure from this pattern of decline is Passover Seder participation. As the analysis of generation noted, American Jews have reinterpreted the Seder so as to make it comport with the larger culture; unlike some of the other practices, it no longer generally signifies foreignness, the traditional heritage, or even religious piety and therefore does not respond to the influence of education (or generation) as do other ritual practices.

9 Some support for this interpretation may be found in the figures for non-sectarian participation, both in organizations and philanthropy. Although the differences between the post-graduates and the college-only groups on any of the non-sectarian measures are generally small, the direction of the relationship relative to Jewish participation is noteworthy. Most simply, post-graduate degree holders, while *more* active in non-sectarian organizational life, are slightly *less* or no more Jewishly active than those with only a college education.

10 In general, preliminary analysis showed that retirees were more like each other on measures of Jewish identification than they were like

those actively working in their former occupations. Apparently, whatever impact occupation has on Jewish identification fades with retirement. Thus, retirees were lumped together with the other residual category respondents.

11 Additionally, we may infer from the 1975 data that some of the 25–34 year olds classified as salaried professionals may eventually join the ranks of the self-employed. Fewer professionals aged 25–34 are self-employed as compared with those aged 35 to 64. The ratio of self-employed to salaried professionals generally grows with age in both surveys; one may therefore surmise that the transition to self-employed status takes place at some point midway in one's professional career.

12 In this area, Lazerwitz, who analyzed the 1970–71 National Jewish Population Study data, found virtually no relationship between income and ritual practice or other forms of Jewish identification (Lazerwitz, 1978).

Chapter 5

1 A slightly different version of this chapter appeared earlier (see Cohen, 1983b).

2 In this regard, Jews were no different from other American white ethnics. Once concentrated, they too dispersed with the passage of time and the acquisition of some measure of affluence. See Lieberson (1963).

3 Although the better educated moved recently slightly more often than the less well educated, the more affluent *within* education groups are more stable (or less mobile) than less-affluent respondents.

4 This circumstance of under-institutionalization has a number of historic parallels, not least significant of which concerns the development of Polish Jewry. For three hundred years German Jews migrated Eastward, into Poland, even as Polish boys were sent back to yeshivas located in Germany to obtain suitable Talmudic training. Only at the end of the fifteenth century did Polish Jewry found its first indigenous Talmudic academy of significance, marking the beginning of one of Jewish history's most creative Talmudic communities (Shulvass, 1975).

5 In Boston, Newton-Brookline/Brighton serves this function of historic concentration. "Northeast Philadelphia" with its large first- and

second-generation Jewish population is such an area; and in New York several heavily Jewish neighborhoods come to mind: Flatbush, Boro Park, Brighton Beach, Forest Hills/Rego Park, Riverdale are but a few.

6 For this investigation, I initially (and ultimately vainly) attempted to disentangle these several factors. I isolated twenty towns, neighborhoods, or collections of such entities in the Boston area, assigned measures pertaining to several locality-wide characteristics, and tried to assess the relative importance of each type of characteristic for determining a neighborhood's mean level of communal affiliation. Unfortunately, the characteristics, crudely measured at best, so often corresponded – a quality statisticians called "multicollinearity" – that no unambiguous results could be derived.

7 As can be seen from *Table 5(4)*, few if any respondents who had lived in their areas more than four years were living in high-turnover areas. Thus, in examining the impact of neighborhood turnover, we can compare "high" with "medium" turnover neighborhoods only for those with four years residential duration or less; at the same time, we may compare "medium" with "low" turnover neighborhoods for people with all levels of residential duration.

8 The right panel, presenting membership rates controlling for the several background variables, reports some narrowing of the differences between newcomers in high-turnover and their counterparts in other areas. Nevertheless, at least 10 percentage points continues to separate newcomers in high-turnover neighborhoods from the synagogue affiliation rates of recent movers into other areas.

Chapter 6

1 A slightly different version of this chapter appeared earlier (see Cohen, 1982a).

2 The data are drawn from a pooling of national surveys conducted in 1960–78 by the University of Chicago National Opinion Research Center and the University of Michigan Survey Research Center.

3 Since the national data often rely on small numbers of cases, the Boston data from 1965 and 1975 are presented for comparison purposes. The latter confirm the findings in the national data and, in fact, suggest an even more pronounced pattern of postponed marriage growing markedly by the 1970s.

4 The data are from the General Social Surveys conducted by the University of Chicago National Opinion Research Center annually, 1972–78.

Chapter 7

1 Parts of this chapter appeared earlier (see Cohen, 1983a).
2 See Fisher (1979) for an excellent review of the pertinent literature.
3 The argument was recently resurrected in Earl Shorris's ignorant volume, *Jews Without Mercy* (1982), where he claims that the Jewish tradition unequivocally militates against neo-conservative opposition to the liberal social agenda.
4 That Jews still feel anxious about their acceptance in American society is indicated by the high number of them (66 per cent) in the 1981–82 National Survey of American Jews (described below) who viewed anti-semitism in America as a "very important" problem, ranking second only to concern for the security of Israel at 69 per cent. Moreover, they are attentive to reports of anti-Jewish vandalism and other incidents (Anti-Defamation League of B'nai B'rith, 1981).
5 Thus, names were drawn from the telephone directories of the eight metropolitan regions with the largest numbers of Jews – New York, Chicago, Los Angeles, Philadelphia, Boston, Miami, Baltimore, and Washington, DC. In addition, we drew names from the telephone directories of the twenty-four cities with the next largest concentrations of Jews. Finally, we divided the remaining Jewish population centers into the eight regional divisions employed by the US Census (New England, Middle Atlantic, and so forth) and further subdivided these strata into groups of localities with Jewish populations above and under five thousand people. We randomly selected one community out of the many within each of the sixteen strata (i.e., 8 regions × 2 Jewish population-size groups). Then, an appropriate number of households were drawn from the telephone directory of each community to represent all the Jews within its boundaries or its region-size stratum.
6 This sampling method entails four possible sources of bias. First, Jews with distinctive Jewish names (DJN) might be different (possibly more Jewish identified) than those without such names. Fortunately, recent research comparing the two appropriate groups (DJN and non-DJN households) from the nearly six thousand households in the 1971 National Jewish Population Study reports few and very small differences between the two sorts of respondents (Himmelfarb and Loar, forthcoming). Second, people with listed telephones tend to be somewhat older, more affluent, less often single, more geographically stable, and more often home-owners than the non-listed. Third, many

respondents have moved since their addresses were listed in the telephone directories; nearly one-fifth (almost 300) of the 1700 questionnaires mailed were returned as a result of addressees having moved. Fourth, of those who received the questionnaire, certain types of people might be more prone to complete and return it. Specifically, the better educated and more Jewishly identified might respond more often, while the infirm aged might be less apt to return the survey.

Despite these, and undoubtedly other, sources of bias, the 673 respondents who returned the questionnaire have characteristics which nearly duplicate those of more carefully drawn samples of Jews. In terms of age, Jewish identification, education, and income (adjusted for inflation) the sample closely resembles the 1971 National Jewish Population Study and the 1975 Boston Jewish Community Survey. To a small extent, the sample under-represents the very elderly and those with little Jewish identification. However, in other key respects, this sample reasonably represents the Jews of the continental United States. Moreover, comparisons of distributions of political measures of this sample with those on electoral and other surveys of American Jews demonstrate a fairly close correspondence. Levels of support for the Equal Rights Amendment, the Ronald Reagan candidacy, and the Democratic Party, for example, are virtually identical in these data to those for Jews in post-election surveys by major polling organizations in 1980.

7 Readers are cautioned that small changes in question wording often result in large changes in response frequencies. In no instance are the national and Jewish data drawn from questions with precisely the same wording. Where the American data with the closest wording available was significantly different from the comparable question on the Jewish survey, parentheses were placed around the appropriate figures reported for the American data.

8 The results of the Jewish sample depart slightly from those of most national electoral surveys of Jewish voters where a few more percentage points registered support for Carter, and about three fewer percentage points favored Anderson and minor candidates.

9 About one-sixth of the 1981–82 sample earned under $15,000 in family income and almost another quarter earned $15,000 to $25,000.

10 Note that limited Jewish support for affirmative action does not contradict their excess of support for the more extreme policy of

quotas. The former is a bell-wether attitude roughly dividing the population in half; the latter is less popular and demarcates "super-liberals" in racial matters, those with more extreme views.

11 I devised the index from the responses to six practices: attending a Passover Seder, lighting Chanukah candles, fasting on Yom Kippur, attending Rosh Hashanah services, lighting Sabbath candles, and having separate dishes for meat and dairy products. Respondents were arrayed on a continuum ranging from zero to six rituals, then classified into four groups (0, 1–2, 3–4, 5–6 rituals). The small number in the latter two groups (scoring three or more rituals) who were not synagogue members had political views similar to those scoring 1–2 on the ritual scale; hence, non-synagogue members observing three or more rituals reclassified with these less observant respondents.

12 Political sociologists and pollsters have held that one can discern several dimensions of liberalism, distinguishing, for example, between economic or welfare liberalism, social issues (such as women's rights), civil liberties, and international affairs. These data do not permit such a refined conceptualization. At most, only a few questions were asked in each domain of liberalism. We can, therefore, speak of a loosely defined concept of liberalism – operationally defined by the available items – for these American Jewish respondents. That there is some validity to this measure of liberalism derived from responses to several issue questions is supported by the correspondence, although not identity, of the issue-based index with the respondents' own definition of their political views.

All public-opinion items were correlated with one another with the exception of the question on quotas for disadvantaged groups. These nine intercorrelated issue questions and the political self-description question were combined into a summary index of political liberalism. Individuals received one point on the index for each liberal answer. This consisted of an appropriate "yes" or "no" response to each issue question, and of describing oneself as a "liberal" or "radical" on the political identification question. The index ranged from zero to ten; those scoring five or more were defined as "liberals." Analyses of the entire index, without collapsing, yielded results substantively identical with those found using the dichotomy (i.e., 0–4 versus 5–10 points) constructed from the index.

13 The adjusted figures are 54 per cent for those with high-school

diploma or less and descend to 25 per cent for those with a post-graduate degree.

14 Adjusting for other variables, only 18 per cent of those earning under $15,000 supported the Republican candidate, while roughly half of those in the $25,000 or more bracket did so.

Chapter 8

1 Parts of this chapter were reported earlier (see Cohen, 1982b, 1983a).

Bibliography

Abramson, H. (1973) *Ethnic Diversity in Catholic America*. New York: Wiley.

Ackerman, W. (1980) Jewish Education Today. *American Jewish Year Book* **80**: 130–48.

Alba, R. (1976) Social Assimilation Among American Catholic National Origin Groups. *American Sociological Review* **41**: 1030–046.

—— (1981) The Twilight of Ethnicity Among American Catholics of European Ancestry. *The Annals* **454**: 86–97.

Alba, R. and Moore, G. (1982) Ethnicity in the American Elite. *American Sociological Review* **47**: 373–83.

Allied Jewish Federation of Denver (1982) *The Denver Jewish Population Study*.

Alston, J. P. (1971) Social Variables Associated with Church Attendance, 1965 and 1969. *Journal for the Scientific Study of Religion* **10**, 3 (Fall): 233–36.

Alston, J. P. and McIntosh, Wm. A. (1979) An Assessment of the Determinants of Religious Participation. *The Sociological Quarterly* **20** (Winter): 49–62.

Anti-Defamation League of B'nai B'rith (1981) The 1981 Audit of Anti-Semitic Incidents. New York.

Axelrod, M., Fowler, F. J., Jr, and Gurin, A. (1967) *A Community Survey for Long Range Planning: A Study of the Jewish Population of Greater Boston*. Boston: Combined Jewish Philanthropies.

Bane, M. J. (1976) *Here to Stay: American Families in the Twentieth Century*. New York: Basic Books.

Becker, H. S. and Carper, J. (1956) The Elements of Identification with an Occupation. *American Sociological Review* **21**: 341–48.

Berger, P. L. (1969) *The Sacred Canopy: Elements of a Sociological Theory of Religion*. (First edition 1967.) Garden City, New York: Doubleday.

—— (1977) *Facing up to Modernity: Excursions in Society, Politics, and Religion*. New York: Basic Books.

—— (1979) *The Heretical Imperative: Contemporary Possibilities of Religious Affirmation*. Garden City, New York: Anchor Books.

Burchinal, L. G. (1959) Some Social Status Criteria and Church Membership and Church Attendance. *Journal of Social Psychology* **49**, 1 (February): 53–64.

Caplovitz, D. and Sherrow, F. (1977) *The Religious Drop-Outs: Apostasy Among College Graduates*. Beverley Hills, CA: Sage.

Cherlin, A. (1981) *Marriage, Divorce, Remarriage*. Cambridge, MA: Harvard University Press.

Cohen, N. W. (1972) *Not Free to Desist: The American Jewish Committee, 1906–66*. Philadelphia: Jewish Publication Society of America.

Cohen, S. M. (1974) The Impact of Jewish Education on Religious Identification and Practice. *Jewish Social Studies* (October): 316–26.

—— (1977) Socioeconomic Determinants of Intraethnic Marriage and Friendship. *Social Forces* **55** (June): 997–1005.

—— (1978) Will Jews Keep Giving? Prospects for the Jewish Charitable Community. *Journal of Jewish Communal Service* **55** (Autumn): 59–71.

—— (1980a) Trends in Jewish Philanthropy. *American Jewish Year Book* **80**: 29–51.

—— (1980b) *Interethnic Marriage and Friendship*. New York: Arno.

—— (1980c) American Jewish Feminism: A Study in Conflicts and Compromises. *American Behavioral Scientist* (July): 519–59.

—— (1980d) Propagandists to Peacemakers: New Roles for American Zionists, *Response* (Summer): 25–32.

—— (1982a) The American Jewish Family Today, *American Jewish Year Book* **82**: 136–54.

—— (1982b) What American Jews Believe. *Moment* (July/August): 23–7.

—— (1983a) The 1981–1982 National Survey of American Jews. *American Jewish Year Book* **83**: 136–39.

—— (1983b) Mobility and Jewish Affiliation. The Impact of Self-Selection, Disruptions and Destination. In S. DellaPergola (ed.) *Papers in Jewish Demography, 1981*. Jerusalem: Institute for Contemporary Jewry, Hebrew University.

Cohen, S. M. and Hyman, P. E. (eds) (1983) *The Evolving Jewish Family*. New York: Holmes and Meier.

Cohen, S. M. and Ritterband, P. (1981) Why Contemporary American Jews want Small Families: An Interreligious Comparison of College Graduates. In P. Ritterband (ed.) *Modern Jewish Fertility*. Leiden, Netherlands: Brill.

Cuddihy, J. M. (1974) *The Ordeal of Civility: Freud, Marx, Levi-Strauss and the Jewish Struggle With Modernity*. New York: Basic Books.

Dahl, R. A. (1963) *Modern Political Analysis*. Englewood Cliffs, NJ: Prentice-Hall.

Dawidowicz, L. S. (1982) A Century of Jewish History 1881–1981: The View from America. *American Jewish Year Book* 82: 3–98.

Decter, M. (1980) Liberalism and the Jews: A Symposium. *Commentary* 69 (January): 31–2.

DellaPergola, S. (1980) Patterns of American Jewish Fertility. *Demography* 17 (August): 261–73.

—— (1981) Quantitative Aspects of Jewish Assimilation. In Bela, V. (ed.) *Jewish Assimilation in Modern Times*. Boulder, CO: Westview Press.

Diamond, J. (1977) A Reader in the Demography of American Jews. *American Jewish Year Book* 77: 251–319.

Dillingham, H. C. (1965) Protestant Religion and Social Status. *American Journal of Sociology* 70, 4 (January): 416–22.

—— (1967) Rejoinder to "Social Class and Church Participation." *American Journal of Sociology* 73, 1 (July): 110–14.

Elazar, D. J. (1976) *Community and Polity: The Organizational Dynamics of American Jewry*. Philadelphia: Jewish Publication Society of America.

Endelman, T. M. (1979) *The Jews of Georgian England 1714–1830: Tradition and Change in Liberal Society*. Philadelphia: Jewish Publication Society of America.

Estus, C. W. and Overington, M. A. (1970) The Meaning and End of Religiosity. *American Journal of Sociology* 75: 760–78.

Farber, B. and Gordon, L. (1982) Accounting for Jewish Intermarriage: An Assessment of National and Community Studies. *Contemporary Jewry* 6 (Spring/Summer): 47–75.

Farer, T. J. (1982) The Making of Reaganism. *The New York Review of Books* (21 January): 40–5.

Fisher, A. M. (1979) Realignment of the Jewish Vote? *Political Science Quarterly* (Spring): 97–116.

Fisher, A. (1981) Jewish Political Shift? Erosion, Yes; Conversion, No. In S. M. Lipset (ed.) *Party Coalitions in the 1980's.* New Brunswick, NJ, and London, UK: Transaction Books.

Fowler, F. F., Jr (1977) *1975 Community Survey: A Study of the Jewish Population of Greater Boston.* Boston: Combined Jewish Philanthropies of Greater Boston.

Friedman, M. (1977) *Society and Religion: The Non-Zionist Orthodox in Eretz Israel, 1918–1936.* Jerusalem: Yad Yitzchak Ben-Zvi Publications.

Gans, H. (1958) The Origins and Growth of a Jewish Community in the Suburbs: A Study of the Jews of Park Forest. In M. Sklare (ed.) *The Jews.* New York: Free Press.

Gerstl, J. E. (1961) Determinants of Occupational Community in High Status Occupations. *The Sociological Quarterly* **2** (January): 37–48.

Glanz, D. and Harrison, M. (1978) Varieties of Identity Transformation: The Case of Newly Orthodox Jews. *Jewish Journal of Sociology* **20** (December): 129–42.

Glazer, N. (1972) *American Judaism.* (Second edition.) Chicago: University of Chicago Press.

Glazer, N. and Moynihan, P. (1970) *Beyond the Melting Pot.* (Second edition.) Cambridge, MA: The MIT Press.

Goldscheider, C. (1966) Trends in Jewish Fertility. *Sociology and Social Research* **50** (January): 173–86.

—— (1967) Fertility of the Jews. *Demography* **4**: 196–209.

—— (1973) Childlessness and Religiosity: An Exploratory Analysis. In U. O. Schmelz, P. Glikson, and S. Della Pergola (eds) *Papers in Jewish Demography, 1969.* Jerusalem: Institute of Contemporary Jewry, The Hebrew University.

—— (1978) Demography and American Jewish Survival. In M. Himmelfarb and V. Baras (eds) *Zero Population Growth: For Whom?* Westport, CT: Greenwood Press.

—— (1982) The Demography of Jewish Americans: Research Findings, Issues and Challenges. In M. Sklare (ed.) *Understanding American Jewry.* New Brunswick, NJ: Transaction Books.

—— (1983) Social Change and Jewish Continuity: Family, Population, and Stratification in an American Community. Unpublished manuscript. Jerusalem: The Hebrew University.

Goldstein, S. (1969) Socioeconomic Differentials among Religious Groups in The United States. *American Journal of Sociology* (May): 612–31.

—— (1981) The Jews in the United States: Perspectives from Demography. *American Jewish Year Book* **81**: 3–59.

—— (1982) Population Movement and Redistribution Among American Jews. *The Jewish Journal of Sociology* **24** (June): 5–23.

Goldstein, S. and Goldscheider, C. (1968) *Jewish Americans: Three Generations in a Jewish Community.* Engelwood Cliffs, NJ: Prentice-Hall.

Goode, E. (1966) Social Class and Church Participation. *American Journal of Sociology* **72**: 102–11.

Goode, W. J. (1957) Community Within a Community. *American Sociological Review* **22**: 194–200.

Gordon, M. M. (1964) *Assimilation in American Life.* New York: Oxford University Press.

—— (1975) Toward a General Theory of Racial and Ethnic Group Relations. In N. Glazer and D. P. Moynihan (eds) *Ethnicity: Theory and Practice.* Cambridge, MA: Harvard University Press.

Gorelick, S. (1981) *City College and the Jewish Poor: Education in New York, 1880–1924.* New Brunswick, NJ: Rutgers University Press.

Goren, A. (1970) *New York Jews and the Quest for Community: The Kehillah Experiment, 1908–1922.* New York: Columbia University Press.

Greeley, A. M. (1971) *Why Can't They Be Like Us?* New York: Dutton.

—— (1974) *Ethnicity in the United States.* New York: Wiley.

Gurock, J. S. (1979) *When Harlem Was Jewish: 1870–1980.* New York: Columbia University Press.

Hacker, A. (1982) Farewell to the Family? *New York Review of Books* (18 March): 37–44.

Halevy, Z. (1978) Were the Jewish Immigrants to the U.S. Representative of Russian Jews? *International Migration* **16**, 2.

Halkin, H. (1977) *Letters to an American Jewish Friend: A Zionist's Polemic.* Philadelphia: Jewish Publication Society of America.

Halpern, B. (1956) *The American Jew: A Zionist Analysis.* New York: Herzl Press.

Heilman, S. C. (1976) *Synagogue Life.* Chicago: University of Chicago Press.

—— (1982) The Sociology of American Jewry: The Last Ten Years. *Annual Review of Sociology* **8**: 135–60.

Heller, C. S. (1977) *On the Edge of Destruction: Jews of Poland Between Two World Wars*. New York: Columbia University Press.

Helmreich, W. B. (1982) *The World of the Yeshiva: An Intimate Portrait of Orthodox Jewry*. New York: The Free Press.

Herberg, W. (1960) *Protestant, Catholic, Jew*. (First edition 1956.) New York: Anchor Books.

Hertzberg, A. (1968) *The French Enlightenment and the Jews*. New York: Columbia University Press.

—— (1979) *Being Jewish in America*. New York: Schocken.

—— (1982) Begin and the Jews. *New York Review of Books* (18 February): 11–12.

Himmelfarb, H. S. (1977) The Interaction Effects of Parents, Spouse, and Schooling: Comparing the Impact of Jewish and Catholic Schools. *Sociological Quarterly* **18** (Autumn): 464–77.

—— (1979) Patterns of Assimilation-Identification Among American Jews. *Ethnicity* **6** (September): 249–67.

—— (1980) The Study of American Jewish Identification: How It is Defined, Measured, Obtained, Sustained, and Lost. *Journal for the Scientific Study of Religion* **19** (March): 18–60.

—— (1982) Research on American Jewish Identity and Identification. In M. Sklare (ed.) *Understanding American Jewry*. New Brunswick, NJ: Transaction Books.

Himmelfarb, H. S. and Loar, R. M. (1979) National Trends in Jewish Ethnicity: A Test of the Polarization Hypothesis. Paper presented at a colloquium on Jewish Population Movements. Ramat-Gan, Israel: Bar-Ilan University (June).

—— (forthcoming) How Distinctive Are Jews with Distinctive Jewish Names? *Public Opinion Quarterly*.

Himmelfarb, M. (1973) *The Jews of Modernity*. New York: Basic Books.

—— (1981) Are Jews Becoming Republican? *Commentary* (August): 27–31.

Hitchens, C. (1981) Israel and the American Left. *The Nation* (5 December): 605–11.

Hodge, D. R. and Carrol, J. W. (1978) Determinants of Commitment and Participation in Suburban Protestant Churches. *Journal for the Scientific Study of Religion* **17**: 107–27.

Howe, I. (1976) *World of Our Fathers*. New York: Harcourt, Brace Jovanovich.

Hyman, H. H., Wright, C. R., and Reed, J. S. (1975) *The Enduring Effect of Education*. Chicago: University of Chicago Press.

Hyman, P. E. (1979) *From Dreyfus to Vichy: The Remaking of French Jewry, 1906–1939.* New York: Columbia University Press.

—— (forthcoming) *Emancipation and Social Change: Alsation Jewry in the Nineteenth Century.*

Issacs, S. D. (1971) *Jews and American Politics.* New York: Doubleday.

Jaret, C. (1978) The Impact of Geographic Mobility on Jewish Community Participation: Disruptive or Supportive? *Contemporary Jewry* **4** (Spring/Summer): 9–21.

Katz, J. (1971) *Tradition and Crisis: Jewish Society at the End of the Middle Ages.* (First edition 1961.) New York: Schocken.

—— (1978) *Out of the Ghetto.* (First edition 1973.) New York: Schocken.

Kessner, T. (1977) *The Golden Door: Italian and Jewish Immigrant Mobility in New York City 1880–1915.* New York: Oxford University Press.

Kobrin, F. (1976a) The Fall of Household Size and the Rise of the Primary Individual in the United States. *Demography* **13** (February): 127–38.

—— (1976b) The Primary Individual and the Family: Changes in Living Arrangements in the United States Since 1940. *Journal of Marriage and the Family* **38**: 233–40.

Larson, M. S. (1977) *The Rise of Professionalism: A Sociological Analysis.* Berkeley: University of California Press.

Laumann, E. (1970) *Bonds of Pluralism.* New York: Wiley.

Lazerwitz, B. (1961) Some Factors Associated With Variations in Church Attendance. *Social Forces* **39**, 4 (May): 301–09.

—— (1962) Membership in Voluntary Associations and Frequency of Church Attendance. *Journal for the Scientific Study of Religion* (Fall): 74–84.

—— (1978) An Estimate of a Rare Population Group: The United States Jewish Population. *Demography* **15** (August): 389–94.

—— (1979) Past and Future Trends in the Size of American Jewish Denominations. *Journal of Reform Judaism* **26** (Summer): 77–83.

—— (1980) Religiosity and Fertility: How Strong a Connection? *Contemporary Jewry* **5** (1) (Spring/Summer): 56–63.

Lazerwitz, B. and Harrison, M. (1979) American Jewish Denominations: A Social and Religious Profile. *American Sociological Review* **44** (August): 656–66.

Lenski, G. E. (1953) Social Correlates of Religious Interest. *American Sociological Review* **18** (October): 533–44.

Lerner, A. L. (1977) "Who Hast Not Made Me a Man": The Movement for Equal Rights from Women in American Jewry. *American Jewish Year Book* **77**: 3–40.

Lieberman, S. and Weinfeld, M. (1978) Demographic Trends and Jewish Survival. *Midstream* (October): 9–19.

Lieberson, S. (1963) *Ethnic Patterns in American Cities.* New York: Free Press.

—— (1980) *A Piece of the Pie.* Berkeley, CA: University of California Press.

Liebman, C. (1973) *The Ambivalent American Jew: Politics, Religion, and Family in American Jewish Life.* Philadelphia: Jewish Publication Society of America.

—— (1977) *Pressure Without Sanctions: The Influence of World Jewry in Shaping Israel's Public Policy.* Cranbury, NJ: Associated University Presses.

—— (1978) Leadership and Decision-making in a Jewish Federation: The New York Federation of Jewish Philanthropies. *American Jewish Year Book* **79**: 3–76.

—— (1979) Orthodox Judaism Today. *Midstream* **20** (August/September): 19–26.

Massarik, F. (1977) Trends in U.S. Jewish Education: National Jewish Population Study Findings. *American Jewish Year Book* **77**: 240–50.

Massarik, F. and Chenkin, A. (1973) United States National Jewish Population Survey: A First Report. *American Jewish Year Book* **73**: 264–306.

Mayer, E. (1979) *From Suburb to Shtetl: The Jews of Boro Park.* Philadelphia: Temple University Press.

Mayer, E. and Waxman, C. I. (1977) Modern Jewish Orthodoxy in America: Toward the Year 2000. *Tradition* **16** (Spring): 98–111.

Meyer, M. A. (1967) *The Origins of the Modern Jew: Jewish Identity and European Culture in Germany, 1749–1824.* Detroit: Wayne State University Press.

Michael, R. T. (1978) The Rise in Divorce Rates, 1960–1974: Age Specific Components. *Demography* (May): 177–82.

Michael, R. T., Fuchs, V. R., and Scott, S. (1980) Changes in the Propensity to Live Alone: 1950–1976. *Demography* (February): 39–56.

Moore, D. D. (1981a) *At Home in America: Second Generation New York Jews.* New York: Columbia University Press.

—— (1981b) *B'nai B'rith and the Challenge of Ethnic Leadership.* New York: CUNY Press.

Mueller, C. W. and Johnson, W. T. (1975) Socioeconomic Status and Religious Participation. *American Sociological Review* **40** (December): 785–800.

Nash, D. (1968) A Little Child Shall Lead Them: A Statistical Test of an Hypothesis that Children Were the Source of the American Religious Revival. *Journal for the Scientific Study of Religion* (Fall): 238–40.

Nash, D. and Berger, P. (1962) The Child, the Family, and the Religious Revival in the Suburbs. *Journal for the Scientific Study of Religion* (October): 85–93.

Neusner, J. (ed.) (1972) *Contemporary Judaic Fellowship in Theory and in Practice.* New York: Ktav.

—— (1981) *Stranger at Home: "The Holocaust," Zionism, and American Judaism.* Chicago: University of Chicago Press.

Newman, W. (1973) *American Pluralism: A Study of Minority Groups and Social Theory.* New York: Harper and Row.

Newman, W. and Halvorson, P. (1979) American Jews: Patterns of Geographic Distribution and Change, 1952–1971. *Journal for the Scientific Study of Religion* **18** (June): 183–93.

Parenti, M. (1967) Ethnic Politics and the Persistence of Ethnic Identification. *American Political Science Review* **61** (September): 717–26.

Podhoretz, N. (1974) Now Instant Zionism. *New York Times Magazine* (3 February): 11ff.

Reinharz, J. (1975) *Fatherland or Promised Land: The Dilemma of the German Jew 1893–1914.* Ann Arbor: University of Michigan Press.

Reisman, B. (1977) *The Havurah: A Contemporary Jewish Experience.* New York: Union of American Hebrew Congregations.

Ritterband, P. and Cohen, S. M. (1982) The Social Characteristics of the New York Area Jewish Community. New York: Federation of Jewish Philanthropies.

Roof, W. C. (1974) Religious Orthodoxy and Minority Prejudice: Causal Relationship or Reflection of Localistic World View? *American Journal of Sociology* **80**, 3 (November): 643–64.

—— (1976) Traditional Religion in Contemporary Society: A Theory of Local-Cosmopolitan Plausibility. *American Sociological Review* **41** (April): 195–208.

Rosen, G. (ed.) (1978) *Jewish Life in America.* New York: Ktav.

Rosenthal, E. (1963) Studies of Jewish Intermarriage in the United States. *American Jewish Year Book* **64**: 3–53.

—— (1975) The Equivalence of United States Census Data for Persons of Russian Stock or Descent with American Jews: An Evaluation. *Demography* **12** (May): 275–90.

Salmon, Y. (1978) The Confrontation Between Hasidim and Maskilim in the Hibbat Zion in the 1880's. (In Hebrew). *Zionism* **5**: 43–77.

Sandefur, G. D. and Scott, W. J. (1981) A Dynamic Analysis of Migration: An Assessment of the Effects of Age, Family and Career Variables. *Demography* **18** (August): 355–68.

Schmelz, U. O. (1981) Jewish Survival: The Demographic Factors. *American Jewish Year Book* **81**: 61–117.

Schmelz, U. O. and DellaPergola, S. (1983) Population Trends in the U.S. Jewry and Their Demographic Consequences. *American Jewish Year Book* **83**: 141–87.

Shaffir, W. (1974) *Life in a Religious Community*. Toronto: Holt, Rinehart, and Winston.

Shapiro, Y. (1971) *Leadership of the American Zionist Organisation, 1897–1930*. Urbana: University of Illinois Press.

Sherman, C. B. (1964) *The Jew Within American Society*. (First edition 1960.) Detroit: Wayne State University Press.

Sherrow, F. S. (1971) Patterns of Religious Intermarriage. Unpublished Ph.D. dissertation, Columbia University, Department of Sociology.

Shorris, E. (1982) *Jewish Without Mercy: A Lament*. Garden City, New York: Anchor Press.

Shorter, E. (1975) *The Making of the Modern Family*. New York: Basic Books.

Shulvass, M. A. (1975) *Jewish Culture in Eastern Europe*. New York: Ktav.

Silberman, C. (1981) The Jewish Community in Change: Challenge to Professional Practice. *Journal of Jewish Communal Service* **58** (Fall): 4–11.

Sklare, M. (1958) *The Jews: Social Patterns of an American Group*. New York: Free Press.

—— (1971) *America's Jews*. New York: Random House.

—— (1972) *Conservative Judaism: An American Religious Movement*. New York: Schocken.

—— (1974a) *The Jew in American Society*. New York: Behrman House.

—— (1974b) *The Jewish Community in America*. New York: Behrman House.

—— (1978) Jewish Acculturation and American Jewish Identity. In G. Rosen (ed.) *Jewish Life in America*. New York: Ktav.

—— (ed.) (1982) *Understanding American Jewry*. New Brunswick, NJ: Transaction Books.

Sklare, M. and Greenblum, J. (1979) *Jewish Identity on the Suburban Frontier*. (Second edition.) Chicago: University of Chicago Press.

Sowell, T. (1981) *Ethnic America: A History*. New York: Basic Books.

Steinberg, S. (1980) *The Ethnic Myth*. New York: Atheneum.

Waxman, C. I. (1980) *Single Parent Families: A Challenge to the Jewish Community*. New York: American Jewish Committee.

—— (1981) The Fourth Generation Grows Up: The Contemporary Jewish Community. *Annals* **454** (March): 70–85.

—— (1982) The Family and American Jewish Community on the Threshold of the 1980's. In M. Sklare (ed.) *Understanding American Jewry*. New Brunswick, NJ: Transaction Books.

Westoff, C. (1978) Marriage and Fertility in the Developed Countries. *Scientific American* (December): 51–7.

Westoff, C. and Jones, E. (1979) The End of "Catholic" Fertility. *Demography* **16** (May): 209–17.

White, R. (1968) Toward a Theory of Religious Influence. *Pacific Sociological Review* (Spring): 23–8.

Wilensky, H. L. and Ladinsky, J. (1967) From Religious Community to Occupational Group: Structural Assimilation Among Professors, Lawyers, and Engineers. *American Sociological Review* **32** (4) (August): 541–61.

Wirth, L. (1928) *The Ghetto*. Chicago: University of Chicago Press.

Wolf, C. P. (1970) The Durkheim Thesis: "Occupational Groups and Moral Integration." *Journal for the Scientific Study of Religion* **9** (Spring): 17–32.

Woocher, J. (1980) The Judaism of the Emerging Leadership. Jerusalem and Philadelphia: Center for Jewish Community Studies (May).

—— (1981a) The 1980 United Jewish Appeal Young Leadership Cabinet: A Profile. *Forum* **42/43** (Winter): 57–67.

—— (1981b) "Jewish Survivalism" as Communal Ideology: An Empirical Assessment. *Journal of Jewish Communal Service* **57** (Summer): 291–303.

—— (1982) The "Civil Judaism" of Communal Leaders. In M. Himmelfarb and D. Singer (eds) *American Jewish Year Book* **81**: 149–69.

Wuthnow, R. (1976) Recent Patterns of Secularization: A Problem of Generations? *American Sociological Review* **41** (October): 850–67.

Wuthnow, R. and Christiano, K. (1979) The Effects of Residential

Migration on Church Attendance in the United States. In R. Wuthnow (ed.) *The Religious Dimension: New Directions in Quantitative Research*. New York: Academic Press.

Yancey, W. L., Eriksen, E. P., and Juliani, R. N. (1976) Emergent Ethnicity: A Review and Reformulation. *American Sociological Review* **41** (June): 391–402.

Yankelovich, Skelly, and White (1981) Anti-Semitism in the United States. Prepared for the American Jewish Committee, mimeo.

Zimmer, B. G. (1955) Participation of Migrants in Urban Structures. *American Sociological Review* **20**: 218–24.

Zimmer, B. G. and Hawley, A. H. (1959) Suburbanization and Church Participation. *Social Forces* **37** (May): 348–54.

Name index

Subject index